D0220274

People Skills

Also by Neil Thompson:

Anti-Discriminatory Practice (fifth edition)*

The Critically Reflective Practitioner (with Sue Thompson)*

Effective Communication (second edition)*

Grief and its Challenges*

Loss and Grief: A Guide for Human Services Practitioners* (ed.)

Loss, Grief and Trauma in the Workplace

People Management*

The People Solutions Sourcebook (second edition)*

Practising Social Work: Meeting the Professional Challenge*

Promoting Equality: Working with Diversity and Difference (third edition)*

Promoting Workplace Learning

Power and Empowerment

The Social Work Companion (with Sue Thompson)*

Theory and Practice in Human Services (second edition)

Understanding Social Work: Preparing for Practice (fourth edition)*

* Also published by Palgrave Macmillan

People Skills

4th edition

NEIL THOMPSON

© Neil Thompson 1996, 2002, 2009, 2015

All rights reserved. No reproduction, copy or transmission of this publication may be made without written permission.

No portion of this publication may be reproduced, copied or transmitted save with written permission or in accordance with the provisions of the Copyright, Designs and Patents Act 1988, or under the terms of any licence permitting limited copying issued by the Copyright Licensing Agency, Saffron House, 6–10 Kirby Street, London EC1N 8TS.

Any person who does any unauthorized act in relation to this publication may be liable to criminal prosecution and civil claims for damages.

The author has asserted his right to be identified as the author of this work in accordance with the Copyright, Designs and Patents Act 1988.

First edition 1996
Second edition 2002
Third edition 2009
Fourth edition 2015

Published by PALGRAVE

Palgrave in the UK is an imprint of Macmillan Publishers Limited, registered in England, company number 785998, of 4 Crinan Street, London N1 9XW.

Palgrave Macmillan in the US is a division of St Martin's Press LLC, 175 Fifth Avenue, New York, NY 10010.

Palgrave is a global imprint of the above companies and is represented throughout the world.

Palgrave® and Macmillan® are registered trademarks in the United States, the United Kingdom, Europe and other countries.

ISBN 978-1-137-46755-3

This book is printed on paper suitable for recycling and made from fully managed and sustained forest sources. Logging, pulping and manufacturing processes are expected to conform to the environmental regulations of the country of origin.

A catalogue record for this book is available from the British Library.

A catalog record for this book is available from the Library of Congress.

Printed and bound in the UK by The Lavenham Press Ltd, Suffolk.

MIX
Paper from
responsible sources
FSC® C010693

For Sheree

Contents

List of figures

Preface to the fourth edition

For a very wide range of people, success in their work depends so much on their ability to work effectively with other people, to influence them in a positive direction, to interact successfully with them, find areas of mutual benefit and address issues that get in the way of progress. Superficially this may sound simple and straightforward as we are interacting with people much of the time and have been doing so for many years. However, the reality is far more complex than this for two main reasons:

1 We can easily become so used to interacting routinely with people that we do not necessarily notice important processes that are going on, whether these are constructive processes that we could capitalize on or destructive ones that we could prevent from doing harm.
2 We learn how to relate to others from an early age as part of our upbringing. This gives us the basic skills, but in a professional context we are often called upon to exercise people skills at a far more advanced level (to be expert rather than just competent).

This book was written to provide a foundation for helping you to: (i) develop a heightened awareness of what is happening when we engage with other people; and (ii) become better equipped to make a positive difference by taking your existing skills to a more advanced (professional) level.

As with the previous three incarnations, this new edition will be of value to a wide range of people whose success in their work depends on effective people skills. This includes the helping professions broadly defined – that is, those concerned with the health, well-being, protection and/or development either of specific groups of people or of the population as a whole (social work and social care; medicine and health care/professions allied to medicine; community and youth work; probation and youth justice work; police work; counselling and psychotherapy; advice work; pastoral guidance; advocacy; and teaching), but we can also add managers, leaders, supervisors and human resource professionals across all sectors, as all these roles involve the need to engage effectively with others. For example, managers who have excellent technical skills, but lack people skills, are likely to be highly ineffective in their role.

These people skills are precisely the constituency of this book: the various skills that are needed by 'people professionals'. The book lays the foundation for developing a broad range of skills that are very important, indeed essential, for making sure that our dealings with other people, whether as practitioners or managers, are as effective as possible.

This is the fourth edition of the book. The first edition was very well received and was acclaimed for presenting a clear and helpful guide to such important skills as those that underpin working with people and their problems in a variety of settings. The second edition built on that initial success and also added four new chapters, thereby expanding the range of skills covered in the book. The third edition built on the success of the earlier editions, and added further extra chapters, two in each of the three parts of the book, bringing the total number of chapters to 30. This new edition now seeks to continue the tradition of offering a solid foundation for understanding various aspects of the people skills needed for effective practice in addressing people's needs and problems and maximizing their potential.

Since the publication of the third edition, two related books of mine have appeared. *The People Solutions Sourcebook* (Thompson, 2012a) contains an extended essay on the subject of problem-solving skills in working with people plus an account of 88 problem-solving methods or tools, a mixture of long-established ones and some important new approaches. It is not essential to read *The People Solutions Sourcebook* to gain the benefits of what is offered here in this book, but you may find that, as the two books complement each other so well, there is much to be gained by reading both of them. Also, managers, aspiring managers and human resource professionals should find *People Management* (Thompson, 2013) an invaluable resource. It follows the pattern of this book in offering 30 chapters, divided into three parts, on key aspects of effective people management.

But, whatever your background, if people issues are an important dimension of your work, this new edition of *People Skills* will provide you with an excellent foundation of understanding to enable you to take your abilities to new levels as you progress through your career.

NEIL THOMPSON

Acknowledgements

Across the four editions of the book I have had considerable help and support from a wide range of people and I want to reiterate my thanks to them. My appreciation of the valuable role they have played at one time or another is of significant proportions. I therefore want to express my gratitude to: Colin Richardson, Fellow of Keele University; Bob Maclaren, formerly of Wrexham County Borough Council; Andy Whitgreave and Clive Curtis, formerly of Cheshire County Council; Wendy Bates, formerly of Glyndŵr University; Irene Thompson and Graham Thompson, formerly of Bangor University; Dr John Bates, formerly of Liverpool Hope University; Bernard Moss, of Staffordshire University; and Denise Bevan, of The Hospice of the Good Shepherd, Chester.

I am once again greatly indebted to Dr Susan Thompson for the crucial role she plays in supporting all of my work. Catherine Gray at the publishers was once again very helpful and a pleasure to work with. Jo Campling, former colleague, mentor and friend, played a crucial part in the first two editions. That she is no longer with us and has therefore not played a part in this fourth edition does not alter the fact that this book owes a lot to her.

About the author

Neil Thompson is an independent writer, educator and adviser. He has held full or honorary professorships at four UK universities and has over 200 publications to his name, including a number of bestselling textbooks. He has also produced a wide range of learning resources: e-books, DVDs, training manuals and e-learning courses. He developed and manages the Avenue Professional Development Programme, an innovative online learning community based on principles of reflective practice and self-directed learning. Subscribers to the Programme become members of his online tutorial group (www.apdp.org.uk). This is one of the many ways in which Neil helps individuals and organizations to maximize their learning.

Neil has over 37 years' experience as a practitioner, manager, educator, consultant and expert witness in the human services. He is very well respected for his ability to communicate complex ideas in an accessible way without oversimplifying them.

He has been a speaker at seminars and conferences in the UK, Ireland, Greece, the Netherlands, Norway, the Czech Republic, Spain, Italy, Hong Kong, Turkey, India, Canada, the United States and Australia, and has qualifications in social work, management (MBA), training and development, mediation and dispute resolution, as well as a first-class honours degree in Social Sciences, a doctorate (PhD) and a higher doctorate (DLitt).

Neil is a Fellow of the Chartered Institute of Personnel and Development, the Royal Society of Arts (elected to the latter on the basis of his contribution to workplace learning), and the Higher Education Academy, and is a Life Fellow of the Institute of Welsh Affairs. In addition, he is a member of the International Work Group on Death, Dying and Bereavement.

He is a sought-after conference speaker, consultant and workshop facilitator. His personal website and blog are at www.neilthompson.info.

Introduction

If we accept the maxim that 'a little knowledge is a dangerous thing', then this is a dangerous book! In covering such a wide range of skills and issues, it is inevitable that an in-depth analysis is not going to be possible. It is therefore important that we recognize, right from the start, that this is an introductory text. That is, it offers the beginnings of a thorough understanding of people skills but will not provide all the answers. This book will not make you an expert in people skills, but it will help to equip you to move in that direction. It will provide you with a brief and accessible introduction to the key aspects of working with people, 30 in total. These 30 areas are divided into three main categories: personal effectiveness, interaction skills and intervention skills.

Personal effectiveness skills, such as assertiveness and stress management, have an important part to play, in so far as they help to ensure that we make the most of the personal resources available to us. Interaction skills, such as interviewing and managing conflict, are also central, in so far as they help us to handle our dealings with other people as constructively as possible. Intervention skills, such as assessment and planning, are a vital part of effective work with people in a variety of settings, as they help to ensure that we are clear about what we are trying to achieve and how we are going to go about it. All three sets of skills are therefore basic tools in any people worker's repertoire. To a certain extent, the categories are arbitrary. That is, there is no hard and fast rule as to which chapter should go into which section of the book. For example, assertiveness is presented here as a personal effectiveness skill, but could equally be seen as an interaction skill. The point remains, however, that all these skills are fundamental aspects of good practice.

In addressing the question of people skills, it is important that we recognize that many skills are mistakenly seen as 'qualities' or 'characteristics' – that is, relatively fixed aspects of a person's character or personality. There are two problems with this point of view:

1 *It is incorrect.* We take many of our skills for granted to the extent that we assume they are qualities – we do not realize that they are in fact skills that we have learned.
2 *It is self-defeating.* By regarding skills as qualities, we create artificial barriers to progress and development. Rather than begin the process of learning a new skill, we may sometimes find excuses for not doing so by

presenting the skill as a quality. For example, in terms of learning time management skills, some people have been heard to say: 'This isn't for me, I'm not the sort of person who's organized' and, in so doing, they create a block to their own learning.

What are commonly regarded as qualities, then, are more accurately presented as learned behaviours. This is an important point to note, as it means that we all have the potential for learning new skills, for developing the qualities that we see as valuable for people work. In view of this, it is essential that we challenge this misconception and adopt a positive attitude towards skill development. The biggest barrier to learning new skills or enhancing existing ones is our own defeatism, our own attitude of 'I can't'.

What is needed, then, to get the most out of this book, is a confident outlook, a positive attitude towards learning, and a recognition that developing new skills often involves giving up old habits. So, when we say 'I can't', perhaps what we really mean is 'I don't want to'. But this is the price we have to pay for learning and developing: we have to be prepared to change aspects of our behaviour. Certain skills come more easily to some people than to others; some people have to work very hard to develop skills that others have no difficulty in acquiring. The fact that we sometimes have to work hard to develop a particular skill should not be used as an excuse for not taking skill development very seriously.

However, the changes necessary for learning are surely a small price to pay for the benefits to be gained from developing our skills in working with people:

○ greater understanding of our work roles and tasks;
○ an increased likelihood of achieving success;
○ less likelihood of making mistakes;
○ a higher level of confidence;
○ greater opportunities for job satisfaction; and
○ opportunities for achieving an advanced level of practice.

Change is part of learning, and so we should not be too surprised to discover that a refusal to change amounts to a refusal to learn. Learning will not happen spontaneously – we have to be ready for it and commit ourselves to it. In order to understand this further, it is helpful to consider learning (and indeed work in the people professions in general) in terms of three dimensions: thinking, feeling and doing:

○ *Thinking (the cognitive dimension).* Although skill development is based on practising – in the sense that practice makes perfect – it is also important that we think about what we are doing so that we do not

Figure 0.1   Think–Feel–Do

simply work in a routine and unthinking way. Such a way of going about our business will not only make our work boring and unsatisfying, it is also dangerous, in the sense that it desensitizes us to potential problems and pitfalls (Thompson and Thompson, 2008).

○ *Feeling (the affective dimension).*   Working with people involves a wide range of feelings and these will inevitably have an effect on how we do our job. Sometimes, the emotional aspects of our work can be painful and difficult to deal with. Similarly, the feelings aroused by learning can be problematic. For example, some aspects of learning can appear to be quite threatening. Some situations we encounter in learning can trigger off painful memories of past experiences and leave us feeling very uncomfortable. It is therefore important that we recognize that the process of learning involves feelings as well as thoughts and actions.

○ *Doing (the behavioural dimension).*   How we act and interact is clearly a central part of how we work with people. It is also a crucial part of learning, in so far as much of our learning derives from doing. That is, although there is considerable advantage in gathering relevant information and developing a knowledge base, this is not enough on its own. Learning also involves putting those ideas into practice. In short, learning is about developing skills as well as knowledge.

The Think–Feel–Do framework is therefore an important part of the process of learning, and it is one to which I shall refer again from time to time throughout the book, especially as the framework is also helpful in understanding *doing* people work, as well as learning about it. It may be helpful for you to bear these three aspects of learning in mind as you work your way through the book.

Of course, there is no need for you to work through the book, step by step. You can, if you prefer, 'dip into' it here and there, just choosing the chapters that appeal to you. At one level, there is nothing wrong in using the book in this way, but there are benefits to be gained from working through it, chapter by chapter. For example, there are recurring themes which can add to your learning as you build up your knowledge. A step-by-step approach is therefore advised.

In each of the chapters, there is a practical exercise to help you get to grips with the issues raised. The temptation to 'skip' the exercises is one to be resisted, so that your opportunities for learning can be maximized.

In covering such a wide range of issues within one book, I have sought to keep a balance in terms of breadth of coverage and depth of analysis – the outcome is inevitably a compromise between the two. However, another balance that has been important to pursue is that between what are often seen (albeit simplistically) as characteristic masculine and feminine approaches to practice. I have attempted to combine the disciplined approach of a systematic practice with a clear focus on objectives (typically seen as a masculine approach) with the sensitivity and flexibility of a practice that takes account of human emotions, uncertainty and unpredictability (typically seen as a feminine approach). It is my view that good practice is based not on being *either* systematic *or* flexible – it is necessary to combine both, to get the best of both worlds, if we are to maximize the chances of our practice being effective.

It is important to note that skill development does not occur in a vacuum – there are also knowledge and values issues to be taken into consideration. A key task for this book is to provide the core of the underpinning knowledge that provides a basic platform for much of the skill development involved in people work. In short, skills need to be built on a firm foundation of knowledge.

The question of values is a more complicated one, as some of the discussions in this book will show. In working with people, we are inevitably facing the challenge of dealing with value issues. It would be naive in the extreme to regard people work as a value-free undertaking. Many of the issues discussed in this book are contested and open to different interpretations according to one's perspective. Many of the issues have their roots in political issues of power, life chances and ideology – they are therefore inherently value based. A willingness to be open about values and address them explicitly is therefore a key to developing expertise in the people professions. An approach that denies the significance of values will therefore be a distorted one that hampers progress.

In view of this, it is important to declare, right from the start, the value position underpinning this book. The ideas presented here are premised on a fundamental commitment to equality that recognizes the significance of discrimination and oppression in so many people's lives. People work generally involves an unequal power balance between worker and client, and so it is vitally important that such power is used to tackle inequalities, rather than widen them; to empower rather than to oppress; to be a force for positive change, rather than a vehicle for discrimination (Thompson, 2007).

A further central value is that of professionalism, not in the sense of elitism and paternalism, but in terms of a commitment to high standards of practice; an informed and sensitive approach to practice, based on clear principles and values; an open practice guided by knowledge and learning, rather than assumptions and stereotypes.

part I

Personal effectiveness

Introduction to Part I

The skills involved in maximizing personal effectiveness can be seen to be very important because they underpin all the other skills involved in working with people. That is, if we are not able to manage ourselves, we will be in a much weaker position in terms of managing situations involving other people. For example, if I do not manage my time very well, then I will be left with less time and energy to work effectively with clients and colleagues. Good people skills therefore have their roots in personal effectiveness.

Part I of the book focuses on ten particular aspects of personal effectiveness. The first is that of self-awareness. If we are not aware of what impact we have on other people, how can we make the best use of our interactions with them? This is followed by a discussion of time management, and then stress management – two fundamental aspects of self-management. After this we explore what is involved in information management – making sure that we neither drown in paper nor lose that crucial piece of information. Assertiveness comes next, with a focus on finding the balance between submissiveness and aggression. The related topic of dealing with bullying behaviour follows. Here the emphasis is on avoiding the stress that bullying and harassment can cause. Then comes using supervision, a consideration of how to make sure you get the best support possible from your line manager. 'Being creative' is our next topic. This offers guidance on how to avoid getting stuck in a rut and allowing our practice to be governed by little more than habit. Next we look at the idea of 'continuous professional development' – making sure that we continue to learn and develop, and do not get into a rut or 'go stale'. And this is a vitally important issue, for what is the point of learning if we are going to allow that learning to fade away, rather than use it as the basis of future learning and practice enhancement? Finally in Part I, we explore the challenges involved in being realistic and resilient. Realism, in the sense I am using it here, involves being able to balance positives and negatives – not allowing ourselves to become unduly pessimistic and defeatist, but not being naively overoptimistic either. Resilience, closely allied to realism, is the ability to bounce back from adversity – an important ability when it comes to responding to some of the challenges of working with people and their problems.

chapter **1**

Self-awareness

Introduction

Burnard (1992) defines self-awareness as: 'the process of getting to know your feelings, attitudes and values. It is also learning about the effect you have on others' (p. 126). In view of this, self-awareness can be seen to have a major part to play in developing people skills.

Self-awareness involves understanding our characteristic responses to situations so that we can build on our positive qualities and be wary of any negative ones that may get in the way of effective practice. Developing self-awareness is not a simple or straightforward matter and cannot be achieved quickly – although major steps forward can be made once the process is under way.

But, before looking more closely at what this entails, it is important to consider why self-awareness is necessary and what problems can occur if it is lacking.

The need for self-awareness

A commonly used phrase in what can broadly be described as therapeutic or problem-solving work is 'use of self'. In working with people, our own self or personality is often used as a tool, a means by which positive change can be facilitated. This is perhaps the most obvious reason for encouraging self-awareness – using a tool without knowing what it is or how it works can hardly be seen as a wise basis for practice! However, there are also a number of other reasons that are worth considering:

○ Self-awareness brings confidence. Having a greater awareness of who we are, and what our strengths and weaknesses are, can be a tremendous source of confidence that can allow us to operate from a much stronger position.
○ Self-awareness can also inspire confidence in the people we are working with. If we give people the impression that we lack self-awareness, then it is unlikely that they will have much faith in us, or set much store by what we are trying to achieve. In this way, confidence can be seen as infectious – it is passed from one person to another.

○ The importance of the Think–Feel–Do framework has already been commented upon. The 'feel' dimension is one that is often neglected. In order to be able to become attuned to other people's feelings, we need to be 'in touch' with our own feelings, aware of how situations are affecting us emotionally (Howe, 2008).

○ Rogers (1961) introduced the term 'unconditional positive regard' to describe a non-judgemental attitude. Making judgements about people can be a barrier to effectiveness, and so it is necessary to have a positive regard for the people we work with, regardless of any possible judgements we might make of them. Unconditional positive regard requires a degree of self-control and discipline, which, in turn, rely on a degree of self-awareness.

○ In addition to recognizing the impact of our own behaviour on others, we also need to be conscious of the impact of other people's actions and attitudes on us. This is a major point and is discussed in more detail below when the importance of 'triggers' and 'blind spots' is considered.

○ Self-awareness is also relevant in terms of dealing with prejudice, discrimination and oppression. We live and work in a society characterized by diversity – that is, differences of culture, gender, age, sexuality, language use and so on make for a very diverse society. Good practice in people skills is based on recognizing this diversity and its significance, as we shall see in Chapter 11.

○ In Chapter 3 we shall consider stress management, and the issue of self-awareness will also feature there.

○ Similarly, Chapter 9 looks at the need to continue learning – continuous professional development, as it has become known. Knowing what you need to learn, and the best way or ways of learning it, depends very much on having a degree of self-awareness.

This is certainly not an exhaustive list, but should be enough to confirm that self-awareness is an important issue that we need to understand and act upon. In order to take us a step further in that direction, let us now explore in a little more detail how self-awareness (or a lack of it) can affect other people.

How we affect others

In social interactions people have an impact on one another; we influence and affect each other. In order to maximize the effectiveness of our interactions, we need to be 'tuned in' to what effect we have on others and, indeed, as I shall explain below, to what effect they have on us. Self-awareness is a major part of that 'tuning in'. I shall therefore outline some of the important ways in which we can affect other people.

Listening

An important part of social interaction is affirmation. We affirm and recognize the other person in and through our interactions and thereby give him or her a sense of security and importance. Chapter 9 will stress the importance of active listening as a people skill, but a point to be noted here is that developing good listening relies on a degree of self-awareness, a sensitivity to how we are responding to the other person or persons. Without this sensitivity, there is a very real danger that we will fail to 'connect'.

Practice focus 1.1

Tina's birth had been a complicated and difficult one. This left her parents anxious about possible ill-effects coming to light as Tina developed. They had raised their concerns about this a number of times but felt nobody was listening to them – all they received was bland reassurance. It was only when their health visitor, on realizing how anxious they were, listened carefully to what they had to say that they started to accept the reassurances they had been given. The health visitor's skill in active listening therefore made a major positive difference to this family.

Barriers

If we are not sufficiently sensitive to how people perceive us, we may 'alienate' them, or place an unnecessary distance or barriers between ourselves and the people we are working with. Body language is a good example of this. If we lack sensitivity, we may not notice that a particular mannerism is annoying, irritating or distracting an individual or group of people.

Similarly, other aspects of personal presentation may be problematic for certain people or in certain circumstances. This includes: clichés or overuse of certain words and phrases; a tendency to 'talk down' to people; a lack of manners; a reluctance to say 'sorry' or a tendency to apologize repeatedly.

Bullying

In Chapter 5, the topic of assertiveness will be explored. A central theme in the development of assertiveness is the need to avoid 'bullying' – bullying others or allowing others to bully us. Chapter 6 explores bullying and the related topic of harassment in more detail. Being sensitive to bullying or the potential for being bullied requires a degree of self-awareness. We need to understand, and practise, the skills involved in developing an assertive approach to interpersonal relations, beginning with an understanding of how we use power, and how we respond to the power of others. That is, assertiveness begins with self-awareness.

Anger

Anger is a commonly experienced emotion and often arises in response to frustration. In the more extreme cases, we are only too aware that we are angry – it can be an intense and overpowering experience. However, it can also be a more 'low-level' experience in which the anger affects us without our realizing it. It can emerge as a smouldering resentment, rather than a flaming passion. What is often referred to as being passive-aggressive (Murphy and Oberlin, 2005). As such, it can lead to irritability, impatience, poor concentration and a tendency to deal with people harshly.

Good people skills are therefore premised on the ability to recognize one's own feelings and the impact they are having on other people. Without this awareness, interactions between people can be distorted or undermined by the unacknowledged influence of feelings of anger. Indeed, this can apply even where the person we are dealing with is not the one who gave rise to the anger. That is, feelings of anger can be generalized to the point where we 'take it out' on other people. See the discussion of 'handling feelings' in Chapter 18.

Mixed messages

Sometimes we can confuse other people by giving 'mixed messages'. That is, we can give a confusing or contradictory message by failing to communicate clearly and consistently. This often arises where there is inconsistency between what is said (the verbal content) and the way in which it is communicated (the nonverbal content). For example, if I say that I am feeling relaxed, but my body posture indicates that I am very tense, it will be difficult for people to work out which is really the case, although nonverbal communication tends to be more powerful and influential than the verbal content – see Chapter 13.

This is by no means an exhaustive list, but does give some indication of the range of ways in which we can affect others unwittingly. We now need to turn our attention to how other people can have an effect on us.

How others affect us

The effects of other people's behaviour and attitudes are often obvious and undeniable. Each day we encounter situations in which what others say or do has a significant bearing on us. Indeed, this is a central part of day-to-day interactions. However, as I noted above in relation to anger, we can sometimes be affected without fully realizing that this is the case.

There are a number of ways in which this can occur, and I shall here outline some of the major ones, as these can act as significant barriers to effective practice if we are not aware of them.

Transference

This is a term which derives from Freudian theory. It refers to the process that occurs when someone we meet evokes a set of feelings, because that person reminds us in some way (appearance, mannerisms, accent or whatever) of another person we have known and who has made an impression on us. That is, feelings about one person are 'transferred' to another. For example, if a person we meet reminds us of a key person in our life, father or mother perhaps, then our feelings towards that person will be coloured by our feelings for the other. This can apply in either a positive or negative sense. That is, if we like one person, then we may find ourselves favourably disposed towards the person who reminds us of him or her. But, if we dislike a particular person, we may find that we are prejudiced against the one who now triggers off memories of that person. Transference, then, can make a significant difference in terms of how we respond to other people and, more often than not, we are not aware that the process is going on.

Triggers

A trigger is something that causes a reaction in us. It is something which gives rise to a particular response, positive or negative, and is, in this respect, similar to transference. For example, a person who is an animal lover may respond quite strongly to a situation in which animals are involved. A worker dealing with someone who has neglected or ill-treated an animal may find it difficult to work positively and fairly with that person. Similarly, a worker who was abused as a child may have great difficulty in dealing calmly or effectively with an allegation of child abuse.

What this means, in effect, is that our values and our memories are important filters through which our everyday experiences must pass. We all have trigger points in some shape or form.

Blind spots

A blind spot is the converse of a trigger. It is something which *should* arouse a reaction but does not do so. For example, a white man may be sensitive to racism and be very committed to anti-racism while, at the same time, having little or no sensitivity to sexism. That is, he may be 'gender blind', seeing the world through a man's eyes and failing to recognize that women are likely to have a different perspective. Similarly, a person who is keen to ensure that children's rights are not overlooked or undermined may, ironically, display a very negative, patronizing or dismissive attitude towards older people. This is a point to which I shall return in Chapter 11.

Fear

Working with people involves a number of possible threats – violence, humiliation and failure, to name but three. We owe it to ourselves, therefore, to recognize that fear is a legitimate part of people work and not one we should be ashamed of. Indeed, the 'macho' attitude of fearlessness is potentially very problematic, as there is a thin line between fearlessness and complacency.

Provided that it is kept in proportion and not allowed to paralyse our efforts, fear is a healthy part of a realistic approach to working with people. Being aware of what causes us fear and developing strategies for responding positively and constructively can be seen as an important strength in people work.

Own needs

Each of us has needs. Just because we are in the business of helping to ensure that other people's needs are met, it does not mean that our own needs are unimportant. Indeed, it can be seen as positively dangerous to ignore our own needs, as this can leave us very vulnerable to stress, or even 'burnout' (Leiter, Bakker and Maslach, 2014). That is, if we do not recharge our own batteries when we need to, how can we be expected to continue to energize other people and motivate them to solve their problems or cope with their day-to-day challenges?

It is therefore very important that we are aware of what our own needs are, and take the necessary steps to ensure that they are met. A stoical approach to one's own needs is a dangerous one, as a worn-down worker could certainly do more harm than good.

Practice focus 1.2

Elaine was delighted that she had now achieved her long-standing ambition of being able to work with people with a learning disability. She committed herself fully to the work and made a 100 per cent effort. However, over a period of time she gradually became more worn down. She was plagued with a series of minor illnesses and felt unable to keep up her level of energy and commitment. It was only when a friend advised her that she needed to look after herself better that she started to regain control of her life. She began to realize that she had to take account of her own needs, otherwise she left herself too vulnerable – and therefore in no position to help meet the needs of others.

Conclusion

As time moves on we encounter new demands and new challenges. Life is characterized by change and therefore presents a need constantly to reappraise our approach, its appropriateness and effectiveness. Self-awareness, then, is not a static thing – it needs to grow, develop and adjust as circumstances change, and indeed as we ourselves change. It needs to be constantly 'on the agenda' if we are to reduce the 'hidden', 'blind' or 'unknown' areas and correspondingly increase that area which is 'open' (see Figure 1.1).

	Known to self	Not known to self
Known to others	Open area	Blind area
Not known to others	Hidden area	Unknown area

Figure 1.1 The Johari window

To conclude, then, we need to consider some of the ways in which a degree of self-awareness can be developed and maintained. I shall identify five such methods in particular:

1 A simple but effective method is to 'open our eyes', to become very self-conscious of what we do, how we react and so on. A diary or log can be particularly helpful in this respect. It should be noted, however, that this should be for a brief period only. We should not make a habit of being too self-conscious, as this can get in the way of skilled practice. Being self-*aware* can be seen as a strength, while being self-*conscious* implies being unduly concerned with oneself, and is therefore a potential weakness.

2 One problem with the above method is that it may not succeed in breaking down the defensive barriers we develop to protect ourselves. It may therefore be necessary to use certain techniques for breaking down these defences. One such technique is described in Exercise 1 below.

3 Self-disclosure can also enable us to use other people, particularly those we respect and trust, as a mirror to reflect those aspects of self that we cannot see (box 4 in the Johari window – see Figure 1.1). This can be a potentially frightening undertaking and so, as Taylor (2006) recognizes, a degree of courage may be called for: 'You need courage to look at yourself and your practice, because it takes honesty and frankness to move outside your comfort zones' (p. 49).

4 This chapter has covered a number of issues in relation to self-awareness, and so time can usefully be spent reviewing the main points and considering what they can tell us about our own level of self-awareness.

5 A key theme of this book is empowerment, the process of helping people obtain a greater degree of control over their lives. This notion of empowerment can also be a tool for developing self-awareness. By

concentrating on taking greater control over the circumstances of our lives, we can become more aware of 'what makes us tick' and what our strengths and weaknesses are. Indeed, this is a theme that will re-emerge in some of the chapters that follow.

Developing Self-Awareness

This is an exercise designed to break down barriers that stand in the way of greater self-awareness. To carry out this exercise you will need to have the use of a voice recorder and microphone, and somewhere where you will not be disturbed.

The simple task is for you to set the voice recorder to 'Record' and start talking about yourself – you can say anything you like, as long as it is about *you*. At first, social barriers are likely to inhibit you but, after a little while, these are eased and you are likely to start talking openly about yourself.

You may, if you wish, play the recording back once you have finished, but usually people find it is enough simply to talk openly without the usual social inhibitors. If you find the exercise a useful way of developing your self-awareness, as many people do, then you may want to consider repeating it from time to time.

chapter **2**

Time management

Introduction

Time management is normally a topic associated with high-flying managers and executives, and so its importance for all people workers is often not fully appreciated. Indeed, time management is associated with a number of misunderstandings and misconceptions concerning what it is, how it works, why it is important, and so on. A central aim of this chapter, therefore, is to clear up some of the confusions by presenting a clear and user-friendly introduction to time management.

What is time management?

As discussed in The People Solutions Sourcebook (Thompson, 2012a), a significant distinction commonly made is that between 'effectiveness' (doing the right things) and 'efficiency' (doing things right). While effectiveness is clearly a central concern, time management is primarily concerned with efficiency. Time is a scarce resource and therefore needs to be used to maximum effect, and certainly not wasted or channelled into efforts that get us nowhere.

In the business world, the saying 'time is money' is a well-known one and is very influential. In working with people, time can be our most precious resource. In the people professions, it is commonly recognized that our time is often the best thing we can give people – all the more reason, then, that time should not be wasted or misdirected.

However, time management is not simply about organizing our time and avoiding wasting it. An important – in fact, essential – aspect of good time management is the ability to manage energy levels, to keep motivation and commitment at optimal levels. That is, time management is concerned with not only quantity of time, but also quality of time.

The question of energy, motivation and commitment is a particularly important and relevant one for people workers. The types of problems and situations we encounter can leave us feeling drained, demoralized and, in some cases, hurt and angry. Conversely, people work can also be tedious, unstimulating and 'unstretching' at times – the paperwork, for example. The outcome of these two sets of factors is that motivation can be seen as a significant issue. It raises the vitally important question: What can we usefully do to maintain motivation and commitment in the extremes of people work?

This chapter, then, needs to address two fundamental areas: how time can be organized to best effect and how energy can be maintained at optimal levels. First, though, we need to consider, albeit briefly, how time management works, what the process actually entails.

How time management works

A common approach to time management is the 'time and motion' philosophy which involves looking in detail at how time is normally spent by an individual within the work environment. Detailed logs and time diaries are not uncommon methods, and have gained a lot of popularity over the years. While this approach does have benefits, particularly in terms of developing an overview of how one's time is used, it also has drawbacks. One particularly significant problem is that, if we focus too closely on how our time is used, the exercise can become time consuming and therefore counterproductive. Also, an emphasis on the minutiae of time use can distract attention from the significant role of energy and motivation.

The approach advocated here, then, is rather different. It is geared towards helping you to understand (and encouraging you to implement) the basic principles of time management, in terms of organizing your time and maintaining energy levels. From this point of view, time management involves becoming sensitive to the ways in which time and energy play such a central role in getting the job done (or not getting the job done, as the case may be). Studying the basic principles of time management is presented as a useful and important way of developing this sensitivity.

Also of importance in understanding how time management works are the following key points:

○ There are no right answers. What works for you may not work for other people, and vice versa. It is important to develop an approach which is well suited to your own personality, needs and circumstances.
○ You can't fit a quart into a pint pot. No matter how well developed your time management skills become, there is only so much work that can be achieved in a day. That is, while good time management can help to ensure that you do not become overburdened, it cannot guarantee that you will not be overworked.
○ Time management can be learned. At the beginning of the book, it was emphasized that skills are often mistaken for qualities. It is often

assumed that some people are 'cut out for being organized' while others are not. This is a defeatist attitude, and one which needs to be abandoned, as we all have the potential to improve our time management skills.

Organizing your time

The ability to organize one's time to best effect is an important part of working with people, as the nature of the work rarely, if ever, allows a rigid, timetabled approach. The individual worker usually has at least some degree of responsibility for deciding how to use the time available. Despite the importance of this ability, however, its significance is not often fully appreciated, and is therefore rarely given the attention it deserves. Consequently, it is not unusual to find skilled and experienced workers who struggle with the basics of time management, and therefore allow their good work to be undermined and their effectiveness to be impaired. For this reason, time spent getting to grips with the principles of organizing our time is, in itself, time well spent – indeed, this notion of investing time underpins the first principle to be considered.

Invest time to save time

Some people make the mistake of becoming 'too busy' to plan or organize their time. When this situation occurs, the person concerned has lost control, and is likely to find it very difficult to regain it. Good time management is premised on setting aside a certain amount of time to plan how the rest of the time should be spent, so that priorities can be set, problems anticipated, opportunities recognized and so on. That is, it is necessary to invest time in planning and organizing in order to save time. The person who fails to invest this time may save a little time in the short term, but is likely to waste a lot of time in the long run.

One important point to note, however, is the danger of investing too much time in planning. For some people, planning their work becomes a substitute for doing the work. Consider, for example, the tendency to make lists of tasks that need doing, without actually finding the time to do any of them. An important skill, therefore, is being able to find the balance between investing too little time and investing too much. Planning is a means to an end and not an end in itself.

Practice focus 2.1

Philip prided himself on how much work he managed to do. It gave him a great deal of satisfaction to think about how busy he had been. He enjoyed being seen as a 'busy' person – it gave him a sense of importance. However, what he was not succeeding in doing was making time to plan his work, to set priorities and retain overall control of his work. So, although he was constantly busy, he was not using his time to best effect, and therefore much of the effort he was expending was being wasted. This became apparent when Philip's line manager left and was replaced by someone who very quickly became concerned about the way in which Philip operated. Philip found it very uncomfortable to be told that he needed to develop time management skills, and it took him a long time to appreciate the importance of planning his time carefully and skilfully.

Set priorities

When we are faced with a long list of things to do, it is helpful to decide which are the most important ones and which ones need to be done first. That is, we need to set priorities.

Three things can make this difficult:

○ There are few, if any, clear criteria as to which items are more important than others.
○ There may be so many important items on the list that not all of them can be done in the time available. That is, some hard decisions may have to be made as to which important things do not get done.
○ There may be a conflict of interest. For example, you may consider a particular item on your list a high priority, while someone else who can influence you (your boss, perhaps) attaches far less significance to it.

Setting priorities, then, is not necessarily a straightforward task and can be fraught with difficulties. However, a little bit of practice in undertaking this task should help to convince you that the benefits very strongly outweigh the difficulties. One word of caution worthy of note relates to the danger of being too rigid and regimented in setting priorities. If we lose a degree of flexibility, setting priorities can become more of a hindrance than a help.

One thing that can be helpful is to consider the consequences of not completing a particular task. How serious would it be if it did not get done? This is not a hard and fast rule but can be helpful in getting us to think about the relative importance of competing priorities.

Keep a clear focus

A lot of time can be wasted when we lose track of what we are trying to achieve, when the focus of what we are doing becomes blurred and unclear. Indeed, this can become a vicious circle. Being busy can lead us to lose our focus, to become sidetracked, and this, in turn, can put us under greater time pressure, which increases the tendency to become unfocused – and so the circle goes on.

In view of this, the skill of keeping a clear focus, even at times of great pressure, can be seen to be an important basis of effective time management. The notion of keeping a clear focus is closely allied to systematic practice, and so this is an issue to which I shall return in Chapter 22.

Avoid waste

At one level, it may seem obvious that it is important not to waste time. However, despite this being self-evident, it is surprising how often basic steps to avoid wasting time are not taken. Examples would include: personal visits being made to seek information that could have been obtained by phone; two members of a team attending a meeting at which only one team member's presence was necessary; lengthy and detailed records being kept when a brief account of the salient points would have sufficed; undertaking tasks that are better suited to others, such as clerical work; continually phoning someone and failing to make contact when a brief letter would allow the task to be done.

This is not to say, for example, that all home or site visits should be replaced by telephone calls. Clearly, that would be absurd. However, there are times when a visit is not essential and is an unnecessary waste of time. What is needed, then, is the ability to identify occasions when time is likely to be wasted, and use the time more constructively. This links in with the discussion in Chapter 1 of self-awareness, in so far as a higher level of sensitivity and awareness is called for. The skill of recognizing opportunities to save time is one that can be developed through effort and experience – and one that repays the investment.

Use of diary

A diary is a basic tool of time management. It can be used as a means of planning, monitoring and co-ordinating. It is not simply a place to keep a note of appointments. For example, if an important report needs to be written, a diary can be used for allocating time to write it. In this way, the diary becomes more than a reminder for appointments; it becomes a central focus for time management.

There are skills and techniques in using a diary that can be developed. A diary gives you a greater sense of control over your own time and guards against the embarrassing problem of forgetting a particular appointment or being 'double booked'. One simple, but very effective, technique for putting a diary to good use is to draw a line down the centre of each page. You can then note down time commitments or appointments on the left and things that need doing on the right. At the beginning of each day you can look at the previous day's list and cross out those that have been done or are no longer applicable. Then, those that remain are the ones that need to be 'carried over'; that is, they need to be written on the right-hand side of today's page.

The three-minute rule

In the course of a week, a number of minor, 'bitty' tasks can so easily accumulate. Each of these may be a simple or undemanding task, but when they build up into a pile, they can present quite a headache. Wading through a number of small tasks can be very tedious, and so there is a tendency to procrastinate. Once this starts to happen, of course, the 'pile' gets bigger, and this, in turn, increases the aversion to tackling them – and so a vicious circle is set up.

A simple way to prevent this problem arising is the 'three-minute rule'. If you are presented with a task that can be completed in less than three minutes (signing a form, writing a brief reply to an email, and so on), then do it straight away. This prevents a backlog building up, and ensures that more time-consuming problems do not occur later as a result of a delay in the completion of one of these brief tasks.

Working together

Collaboration and teamwork can enable sharing of tasks and/or the most appropriate allocation of tasks (capitalizing on people's strengths, avoiding weaknesses), and can therefore make a significant contribution to effective time management. Note, however, the significant word 'can'. It is by no means certain that working together will produce better use of time. Attempts at collaboration can also lead to overlap, gaps, inconsistencies and a considerable amount of time wasted on fruitless debate, leading to indecision and poor use of available resources, including time. 'Working together' therefore needs to be more than a slogan and requires an investment of time and energy to make it work. Effective collaboration requires clear parameters and role expectations to prevent confusion and conflict halting progress. We shall return to this point in Chapter 20.

Figure 2.1   Managing time and energy

Managing energy levels

Organizing and co-ordinating time commitments and use of time clearly has an important part to play in making the best use of scarce resources. However, what we need to explore in more detail is how energy levels can be managed to best effect, how motivation can be sustained.

Timing

Some of us are 'morning people', and some of us are definitely not. That is, some people function very well first thing in the morning, whereas others may struggle at that time but come to life later, when perhaps the early birds are starting to fade. The implication of this is that it pays to know our optimum time periods so that we can plan our tasks accordingly. For example, it could well be a mistake to schedule a difficult and demanding task for a time of day when we are not at our best. This, then, is an aspect of time management that links closely with the discussion, in Chapter 1, of self-awareness. We can benefit from understanding not only our strong and weak points, but also our strong and weak times. Careful and informed planning can therefore help to match our energy peaks and troughs with the varied tasks we face in a way that uses that energy to maximum effect.

The best person for the job

Often tasks are allocated within a team or staff group, with little or no consideration of who is the best person for the job. This can be a barrier to effective time management, in so far as it misses opportunities to build on strengths. Each of us has strengths and weaknesses, as well as aspects of our job that we enjoy and aspects we do not enjoy. By focusing on what we are good at and what we enjoy, higher levels of motivation can be maintained, and more can be achieved in the time available. It is therefore worth exploring within a team or staff group what people's preferences are so that each person can, as far as possible, play to his or her strengths.

Practice focus 2.2

Pat enjoyed her job overall but there were some aspects that she did not enjoy at all – and it was often these aspects that left her feeling tired and demotivated. One day, however, she found that one task she particularly disliked (playing a part in the induction of new staff) was something that her colleague, Jean, actually found very satisfying and rewarding. This realization allowed Pat and Jean the opportunity to compare notes on their respective tasks and duties and explore possibilities for 'trading' aspects of their workloads. This proved a very successful way forward and they both felt their jobs (and their performance) had improved by collaborating in this way.

The worst-first rule

When we face tasks that we are not looking forward to, or we actively dislike doing, it pays to do them sooner rather than later. That is, by 'getting them out of the way', we can achieve a sense of satisfaction and relief – and this can have a positive effect on morale and energy. An example of this would be making a potentially difficult phone call first thing in the morning.

If, by contrast, we procrastinate and do not tackle these unpopular tasks, they can 'niggle' us, wear down our motivation and generally have a negative effect on our work performance. It therefore helps to go for the 'worst first' by identifying the tasks we are reluctant to do, and doing them first.

Take a break

The notion that 'I am too busy to take a break' is a dangerous one. It is also misinformed, in so far as it does not recognize that a refreshed worker can achieve more than a tired one. When time is tight and we have a lot to do, we can easily fall into the trap of trying to press on without taking a break. But we need to recognize that this is a false economy. For example, a person who works for an hour and a half, then takes a 15-minute break and then works for a further hour and a quarter is likely to achieve more (and probably of a higher standard) than someone who works straight through for three hours without a break. Working on without a break will leave you feeling tired and jaded, more prone to errors and generally functioning at a less than full capacity.

The expanding workload

If we are not careful, work can expand to fill the time available. If we are not sufficiently time conscious, tasks can take longer to complete than they need to. This is important in terms of motivation. If motivation is low, tasks can take more than their fair share of time and this, in turn, can sap motivation.

By making the effort to complete work tasks in a reasonable time, we can obtain a sense of achievement, greater control and confidence. In this way, the effort to avoid the 'expanding workload' problem can be repaid by increased motivation, rather than the drain on motivation associated with it.

Be positive

Energy levels and motivation can be maintained and enhanced by a positive attitude. A negative outlook, by contrast, contributes to low morale and less job satisfaction. This can become a vicious circle in which negativity and low morale reinforce each other and, over a period of time, make each other worse.

Being positive, on the other hand, can produce a 'virtuous circle' in which a positive outlook leads to a higher level of job satisfaction and morale, and these, in turn, contribute to a positive outlook. The importance of not losing sight of positives is a point we shall explore in more detail in Chapter 10.

Working together

Just as working together can be of benefit in terms of organizing our time, so too can it be of help in terms of energy and motivation. Teamwork, collaboration and mutual support can pay dividends with regard to generating positive feelings of:

○ security and confidence (safety in numbers);
○ commitment to supporting others;
○ camaraderie, group identity and a sense of belonging; and
○ enhanced pride and pleasure in joint successes.

Conclusion

Being well organized in terms of the use of time is not, as we have seen, a fixed quality. It is a set of skills that can be learned and developed through practice and experience. The suggestions given here can take you some way towards improving your time management skills. However, they can only work if you are committed to them – going through the motions as if they will help you without your believing in them will be of little value.

The essential ingredient, then, is confidence – in two senses. First, we need confidence in ourselves that we can learn, that we can develop new skills. Second, we need confidence in the techniques that we are using. If this confidence can be mustered, then the scope for improved personal effectiveness is immense.

Exercise 2

Getting Organized

This chapter has offered a number of pointers for improving your time management skills. Now, in order to help you begin to put them into practice, this exercise has been designed as a first step in the right direction.

First, take a sheet of A4 paper and keep this by you as you review the whole chapter. Note down on the paper the particular practical guidelines that you feel could be put to good use in your own work situation (the 'worst-first rule', for example). Once you have completed this, you will have an action list, and you can now go about planning how you are going to implement your new time management strategy.

chapter **3**

Stress management

Introduction

All jobs involve a degree of pressure and the risk of stress to a certain extent, but working with people can leave us particularly prone to stress. This chapter explores three key aspects of stress management:

- *Stressors.* The common sources of pressure that can lead to our experiencing stress.
- *Coping methods.* The ways in which we try to deal with our pressures.
- *Support.* The ways in which we can be helped to cope.

Having looked at these three sets of issues, we will then be in a position to consider the skills and strategies we need for keeping our pressures under control and making sure stress does not cause us any harm.

Pressure and stress

To begin with, it is important that we are clear what we mean by stress. Arroba and James (1992) define stress as a person's response to an inappropriate level of pressure. There are two particularly important words in this definition – 'response' and 'inappropriate':

1   The word 'response' emphasizes that stress arises as a result of how *we react* to pressures – and this alerts us to the fact that some stress management skills are about controlling our reactions, as well as controlling our pressures. I shall return to this point later.
2   The word 'inappropriate' emphasizes that stress is not just a matter of *too much* pressure, but can also arise as a result of *too little* pressure – that is, when we are bored or understimulated.

From these interrelationships (see Figure 3.1), we can see the difference between *pressure*, which can be positive (a source of stimulation and motivation)

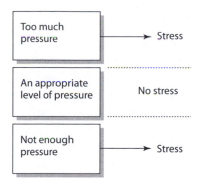

Figure 3.1 Levels of pressure

or negative (a source of worry and tension), depending on the circumstances, and *stress*, which is always negative and harmful. So, we can see that:

○ Stress is not the same as pressure – pressures are inevitable, but stress can be avoided.
○ Stress is more likely to occur when there is too much or too little pressure.
○ Stress depends not just on the level of pressure we experience, but also on how we respond to those pressures.

It is important that we are clear about this distinction so, if you are not quite sure about the difference between the two, it is worth rereading the explanation above before going on to the next section.

The effects of stress

Stress can do a lot of harm in a number of ways, including the following:

○ *Stress-related illnesses.* Stress is believed to be a major contributor to heart disease, ulcerative colitis and so on.
○ *Vulnerability to disease.* Stress lowers our resistance to illness in general.
○ *Low motivation.* We become less enthusiastic and experience low morale.
○ *Reduced job satisfaction.* We can tend to focus on the negatives and lose sight of the positives.
○ *Tension and irritability.* This can lead to disagreements and conflict.
○ *Proneness to error.* We are likely to make more mistakes and, in working with people, this can be very costly.

This is not an exhaustive list, but is enough to make it clear that time and effort spent preventing or combating stress can be seen as a worthwhile investment.

> **Practice focus 3.1**
>
> A team of five staff were coping reasonably well with their workload and not experiencing major problems. However, one day, Peter, one of the staff, was threatened with violence in carrying out his duties. The incident was not taken seriously by his managers and they tried to laugh it off as 'one of those things'. Peter, however, felt vulnerable, unsupported and undervalued. A few days later, a medical certificate was submitted to confirm that he was to be on sick leave for two weeks as a result of 'nervous exhaustion'. During that time, the remaining staff had an average additional 25 per cent workload in order to keep the service running. This placed them under a great deal of strain, but they managed to cope. However, at the end of the fortnight, a further certificate was received from Peter, this time for four weeks. The staff team began to feel despondent and wondered whether Peter would ever return. Consequently, Pam, who had been experiencing marital difficulties recently, reached the point where she could not cope any further. She too went on sick leave, thereby leaving three staff to cope with the work of five – a total workload increase of 40 per cent. The three remaining staff now felt under immense pressure and began to doubt whether they would ever see light at the end of the tunnel. The whole situation had become very fraught and dangerously close to breaking down altogether.

Understanding your own potential for stress

Because stress depends on *your* response to pressure, stress is a very personal matter and will vary from person to person. It is therefore important that you understand how pressure and stress have an impact on *your* life. Exercise 3 at the end of this chapter is designed to help you develop a picture of your own circumstances with regard to stress management.

Having a picture of what pressures you are subject to, what coping resources and support you have, is an important part of stress management. Without this picture, you are working in the dark. However, it is not enough on its own – understanding stress is one part of stress management, but it is not the whole story. We also need to develop our stress management skills and strategies, and it is to these that we now turn.

Skills and strategies

As was emphasized above, the experience of stress is very variable and linked to personal circumstances. However, this is not to say that there are no overall patterns or general guidance that can be given. On the contrary, there are a number of general principles and guidelines that can be identified, as the examples given here demonstrate:

1 *Know yourself.* This may sound like a cliché, but it is none the less important to have a good level of self-awareness so that you know your own strengths and weaknesses – the strengths you can draw upon when you need to, and the weaknesses that may leave you vulnerable. As we noted in Chapter 1, self-awareness is an essential part of good practice in working with people. It is also an essential part of good stress management. Without a certain level of self-awareness, stress management could prove to be far more demanding than it needs to.

2 *Set objectives.* It is usually helpful to set objectives, to have clear targets to aim for. This helps to avoid uncomfortable feelings of drift and aimlessness. It also helps to motivate us and help us gain job satisfaction when objectives are achieved. As the saying goes, 'If we don't know where we are going, any road will take us there.' Setting targets and being clear about what we need to do to achieve them will therefore help us to know which road we are going down. It will help to fend off the feeling of being lost and confused which is so often part of the experience of stress. The question of setting objectives is a very important one and it is a topic to which we shall return in Chapters 21 and 22.

3 *Change your attitude.* Changing our attitude towards something can change the way it affects us. For example, if you set yourself the target of being the greatest people worker the world has ever known, you may find this puts you under an unhealthy amount of pressure! What may be necessary, then, to prevent you from suffering an undue amount of stress, is for you to change your attitude. You may have to settle for aiming for something a bit more modest. Aiming for excellence, for example, may prove to be a source of motivation and stimulation (positive pressure), whilst aiming to be the best may actually go beyond this and put you in stress territory. Stress is your response to an inappropriate level of pressure, so changing your response to life circumstances can be an important and effective way of managing pressures. This is a technique known as 'cognitive restructuring'.

4 *Be assertive.* Chapter 5 addresses issues of assertiveness, and so I shall not pre-empt what is to be said there. However, it is worth emphasizing that being assertive (finding the comfortable balance between being submissive and being aggressive) is a significant part of stress management. This is because assertiveness helps to stop other people getting what they want at your expense, and also helps to avoid conflict, or at least minimize its harmful effects. This should become clearer when we reach Chapter 5.

5 *Keep control.* This is not simply a message about 'Do not panic!' – although that is appropriate advice! When we are under pressure, it can be quite easy for us to lose control, to lose our grip on what we are doing. For example, an important study of child abuse once showed that child protection workers often made mistakes as a result of the pressures they

were experiencing – they allowed their judgement to become clouded, and costly errors resulted (DoH, 1991). Staying calm and keeping on top of the situations you deal with is therefore wise advice. This does not mean that you have to take control and become an authoritarian dictator – it means not losing your grip on what is going on around you, not allowing yourself to become a passive victim of circumstance. There are many things over which we have little or no control, and we have to accept that (see the discussion of the CIA framework in *The People Solutions Sourcebook*). However, some people can be very defeatist and underestimate how much control we do have (consider the example of time management given in Chapter 2).

6 *Set boundaries.*   Life can be confusing at the best of times but, when we are under pressure, it can become extremely confused and confusing. And this is why it is important to develop the skills involved in setting boundaries. This involves, in particular, recognizing boundaries of responsibility – you have to be clear what is your responsibility and what is not. This is for two reasons: (i) if you are responsible for something but do not realize that you are, you could find yourself in serious difficulty if things go wrong; (ii) if you take upon yourself the weight of things for which you are not responsible (for example, other people's duties), you are giving yourself an additional unnecessary burden – one which could cause you considerable harm. An important stress management skill, therefore, is the ability to recognize the boundaries of responsibility (Thompson, 2015a).

7 *Time management.*   As we noted in Chapter 2, effective time management is an essential part of a successful approach to working with people. It involves managing not only our time but also our energy – through motivation and commitment. This principle applies also to stress management – maintaining energy and motivation so that resources for coping with pressure are not overwhelmed by those very pressures. Making a good job of managing your time is also a significant contribution to keeping control (see point 5 above) and thereby helping to keep stress at bay. Wasting time and allowing energy levels to flag is therefore poor preparation for dealing with the rigours of people work.

8 *Use support.*   Some people try to cope stoically with their pressures without any help from anyone else. They see asking for help or support as a sign of weakness, and therefore something to be avoided. This is a dangerous strategy, in so far as it sets us apart from a network of support which, at times, can make all the difference between coping and not coping. To avoid this danger, it is therefore necessary to reject this 'be tough' attitude of not needing support (Cranwell-Ward Abbey, 2005). A major step in this direction is to recognize that asking for support is a sign of strength, not weakness – a sign that we are adopting a sensible and realistic approach to stress management.

> **Practice focus 3.2**
>
> Sandra had realized that her new job would be a demanding one, but she had not appreciated just how difficult it was going to turn out. She felt very overloaded and unsupported. At first, she decided to be stoical about it and to get by as best she could. She tried to put her own needs to one side and 'get on with the job' without raising any concerns about how she felt. However, one day she made a mistake that could have had very serious consequences. From this she was able to see the dangers of trying to brush workload issues under the carpet. She began to talk to people about how difficult she had been finding her work. She was then totally amazed at the supportive response she received to this. Her colleagues expressed considerable willingness to help and support her. One colleague made a very telling comment that helped Sandra realize her mistake in not asking for support earlier: 'We'd got the impression that you were the sort of person who wanted to keep herself to herself and didn't want to be part of a team.'

9 *Avoid unhelpful coping methods.* Some coping methods are helpful, positive and constructive. However, others can be destructive and harmful – more trouble than they are worth. For example, if we attempt to cope by heavy drinking, responding with violence, or trying to deny there is a problem, the net result is likely to be even greater pressure or even worse problems – the medicine can be worse than the illness. There is therefore much to be gained by avoiding such destructive responses and developing more positive ones. In particular, it can pay dividends to focus on active coping (tackling the pressures or problems we face), and not to rely too heavily on passive coping (trying to escape from our pressures or problems).

10 *Be kind to yourself.* One of the common characteristics of stress is that people can tend to be very hard on themselves. They can set themselves unrealistic targets (see point 3 above), undervalue their achievements and generally make life difficult for themselves. It is often the case that the more we encounter stress, the greater is our tendency to do this. Consequently, a basic part of stress management is to be kind to yourself, to keep your strengths and weaknesses in perspective, and not adopt an unduly harsh or negative attitude towards yourself. An important step towards this is to acknowledge that this tendency exists and, when it begins to take hold, take steps to talk to someone we trust to help get things in perspective.

Conclusion

These, then, are some of the basic building blocks of stress management. Following the guidelines here will not guarantee success, but should take you in the right direction towards maximizing your ability to deal with pressure and minimize the risk of stress causing you harm. It is to be hoped that the ideas and suggestions here will encourage you to carry on learning and developing your stress management skills. Stress is potentially a very destructive problem, as it can:

- lead to ill-health;
- reduce effectiveness;
- undermine, or even destroy, relationships; and
- create a pressurized atmosphere for colleagues, and so on.

It goes without saying, then, that stress management is a set of skills to be taken very seriously.

To end this chapter on a positive note, we should recognize that many of the other skills discussed in this book can also make a positive contribution towards stress management. These include time management, assertiveness, beating the bully, being creative, effective communication, influencing, being systematic, and ending. The skills base being developed, then, can be seen as one in which different elements become mutually supportive, and add a further dimension to the learning and development that are taking place.

Exercise 3

Stress, Coping and Support

For this exercise, you will need to take a sheet of paper and divide it into three columns, with the following three headings: Stressors; Coping Methods; Sources of Support. Under each of the headings list as many examples as you can. That is, under 'Stressors', list as many potential sources of stress for you as you can. Under 'Coping Methods', list the different ways in which you try to cope with your pressures. Under 'Support', write down the sources of support you can draw on.

This exercise can help you gain an overview of the stress issues that you face, and can therefore help you plan how you deal with them. For example, it may help you realize that you need to develop your support networks, or it may give you confidence in realizing that you are well supported. It is not a test, so feel free to consult colleagues or friends to help you if you run out of ideas.

chapter **4**

Information management

Introduction

One of the challenges we face in living in the 'information age' is to avoid drowning in paper and other sources of information. Just as important is to be able to avoid missing one or more key pieces of information because it gets lost in the welter of forms, memos, letters, reports, emails and so on that keep coming at us from all angles. This chapter, then, is concerned with looking at how we can manage the flow of information to make sure that we retain the important bits without getting overwhelmed by the sheer weight of information that modern working practices tend to produce. Information overload is a very real danger, and can have serious consequences, and so it is important that we take seriously the demands of information management.

First we shall look at the various sources of information, the channels through which the various items of information come to us. We shall then move on to explore how such information can be stored, retrieved when required and/or disposed of, before summarizing some of the principles of handling information effectively.

Receiving information

One of the reasons we need to think carefully about information management is that the potential or actual sources of such information are so varied that it is relatively easy to lose track of the welter of items that can assail us. As technology develops, it seems that we are prone to receiving more and more information – whether we like it or not! What, then, are the various sources of information that we need to be aware of? The following are some of the main ones, although this is by no means an exhaustive list.

Correspondence

There are two main types of correspondence, external and internal. It is usually the case that external correspondence is in the form of letters (and, increasingly email), while internal correspondence is largely by email. In some organizations there can be a constant flow of emails to add to the influx of letters from outside the organization.

Many of these are of limited importance, but others may be crucial in terms of notifying you of a change of policy or procedure that may have a direct effect on your work. We therefore have to make sure that we do not lose the important ones in a mass of paper. An essential skill, therefore, is to be able to identify which items are of significance and which are not, without spending a great deal of time poring over them all.

Forms

Many office systems generate a considerable amount of paperwork through various forms. Many of these forms are of a standard or routine nature and can be processed in a fairly straightforward way. However, others demand more attention and an individualized response. Sadly, many problems in organizations tend to arise from staff failing to make this distinction and consequently dealing with exceptional circumstances as if they were straightforward – this is a well-recognized failing associated with bureaucratic systems. Effective administration systems are those that deal with routine matters routinely and exceptional matters exceptionally, and do not lose sight of the boundaries between the two.

Another important distinction to make is between those forms that are for information only and those that require some sort of action or response. Clearly much can go wrong if we fail to make this distinction. Forms should be helpful tools, but they can easily become sources of problems if not handled properly.

Reports

Reports are written for various purposes, either directly related to specific individuals, families or groups that we are working with or more generally geared towards policies, management procedures and working practices. Whatever type of report they may be, they are all likely to have some importance for us and therefore have to be taken into consideration in managing information. Report writing and related matters are discussed in more detail in Chapter 14.

Telephone calls

For some people workers in particular, the telephone is a basic essential working tool. For such workers, the average working week may consist of several hours on the phone. Whether and how we keep records of such telephone conversations is a matter for professional judgement and/or policy guidance in each case, but what does have to be borne in mind is the significant danger of failing to make a record of an important telephone conversation, and the absence of such a record leading to major problems further down the line (for example, in the event of a complaint, inquiry or investigation). Of course, for most people it would be unworkable to keep a record of every telephone conversation, and so again it is a case of having to be able to distinguish between what needs to be recorded and what does not.

In this age of mobile communication we also have to consider issues relating not only to landlines but also to mobile phones. Who should have your mobile number and in what circumstances should they use it? Should you have a separate mobile phone for work purposes or are you happy to use your personal one? If the latter, is that compatible with your organization's policy? And how do you stop people ringing you on that number outside of office hours? These are all important questions that need to be considered.

Similarly, it is important to be clear about in what circumstances it is appropriate to use text messages (the practice of some organizations notifying staff that they have lost their job is a sad but perfect example of why these issues need to be considered).

Emails

Emails are, of course, a relatively recent source of information and can cause major problems. It is not unusual for some people to take a period of leave, only to return to work and find literally hundreds of email messages waiting for them. This is not a good way to settle back into work after a period of absence! Clearly a coherent and workable strategy for dealing with emails is called for. We shall return to this point below.

Practice focus 4.1

Kate was pleased to know that, in her new post, she would have access to email, as she was keen to make the most of the technology available in the company. However, she soon found herself in difficulties. This was because she received a large number of emails and tried very hard to respond more or less immediately to them all. This put her under immense pressure and she was starting to feel very stressed. It was only after a helpful supervision session with her line manager that she managed to find a way of coping. She was taught that she had to treat emails like any other aspect of her work and therefore had to prioritize, leaving some emails for a while before replying (and often finding that things resolved themselves in the meantime anyway) and not replying to others at all (it came as a relief to her to realize that not all emails necessarily need a reply).

Trade journals and newsletters

Many workers receive a number of trade journals and newsletters about various aspects of their work. If we are not careful we can end up at either one destructive extreme or the other. On the one hand, we may find that important information is missed because these periodicals remain in a stack, unopened.

On the other hand, staff can feel overwhelmed and may even experience stress as a result of the information overload involved. An important response to such sources of information, then, is that it is generally essential to prioritize and decide which periodicals (or which parts of periodicals) we are going to concentrate on and which we will not bother with.

Circulars and discussion papers

Most organizations produce a steady stream of circulars about policy, procedures and practice as well as discussion and consultation papers. Again there is a limit to how much information we can absorb. One possible response is to deal with such matters on a team basis. That is, for team members to share responsibility for dealing with such matters and providing brief summaries for their colleagues. It is not necessary for everybody to read everything.

Information storage, retrieval and disposal

Given the wide range of sources of information around us, what can we do to deal with those items that we want to keep for future reference? How can we file them in such a way that we can gain easy access to them in future? And how should we dispose of items we no longer need? These are the questions we now address.

Storage and retrieval

The more information we have available to us, the more storage space we need, whether that is physical space – for example, in a filing cabinet – or space on a computer hard disk or other such electronic medium. Clearly, such space is not infinite, and so the question of how to make the best use of the storage space available is an important one to address. However, before we look at that question, there is another one we need to consider, namely: how do we decide what information needs to be kept and what can be disposed of? There is no simple, general answer to this question, as the situation will differ from setting to setting. However, as a general rule, we would need to establish what information we have to keep:

○ for legal reasons (statutory requirements);
○ as a basis for future work;
○ for historical or archive purposes; and
○ for reference purposes.

We also have to be clear about where and how we intend to store the information. An important deciding factor is the question of how we would want to retrieve the information. There is little point in storing information if we are not able to retrieve it when we need it. What is needed, then, is a system of retrieving information quickly, reliably and efficiently.

There is no easy answer to the question of how we should store the information available to us. Various systems and subsystems exist and different people feel comfortable with different ways of working. None the less, whatever system we choose to use, we should make sure it meets the following guidelines:

- Information that needs to be accessed frequently should be more easily accessible than information that will need to be drawn upon less often.
- Indexing systems for retrieval need to be clear and effective – there is little point having masses of very important information if you do not have a simple and effective system for finding what you want.
- Confidential information will need to be stored in such a way as to ensure it remains confidential (for example, in a locked filing cabinet or in a password-protected computer file or folder).
- Computer-based information should be backed up regularly – a computer system that 'crashes' or otherwise loses stored information can cause enormous heartache and extra work if there is no backup file available.

In whatever way we decide to handle the masses of information that come our way, it is important that we decide upon how we are going to do it sooner rather than later, as having a backlog of information to sort out, catalogue and store can be an immensely time-consuming task to deal with – and can also be a drain on morale and motivation. It is therefore important that we devote time to establishing a clear and effective system at a fairly early stage so that we are ready to manage the flow of information without allowing it to become a flood.

Practice focus 4.2

Lee and Steve had been good friends for many years before they both started their degree course. On day one of the programme they were advised to set up a filing system to store information relating to the various modules they would be studying, their placement work and so on. They both thought this was a good idea. Lee went home that evening and made a start on developing a filing system. Steve said he would leave it until the weekend and then make a start. By halfway through the first semester, Lee was pleased that his system was working really well and, when it came to preparing for his assignment, he knew exactly where to find the information he needed. Steve, by contrast, never did get round to setting up that filing system and had various miscellaneous piles of paper dotted around his house and any attempt to find the information he needed was likely to be a difficult, time-consuming and frustrating experience. So, while Lee was feeling reasonably confident about tackling the assignment, Steve was feeling the pressure quite a lot and was very much regretting not having set up a system in the first place.

Disposal

If there is too much information for us to store it all, then clearly we need to have the means of disposing of what we no longer require. Of course, it is not just a matter of dumping it all in the bin – it is not that simple for two reasons. First, what is not worth keeping for you may be of great importance to someone else. Information management systems involve a network of people and not just you as an individual. You may therefore need to look at how you can pass on information you no longer need to others who may find it of great use. Second, confidential information has to be disposed of appropriately – for example, by being shredded.

Principles of effective information management

What, then, does an effective information management situation consist of? The following pointers should help us to summarize our answer to that question:

- It is important to be selective. It is unrealistic to expect to be able to read all the information that comes our way, let alone store it. It is therefore important that we learn how to 'let go' and to accept that we cannot deal with all the possible sources of information.
- Once we have decided which information we will deal with, we then need to 'process' it appropriately, dividing it up into categories: to be acted upon in the short term (action list); to be acted upon in the medium to long term (pending list); and to be kept for possible future use (reference), and storing it accordingly.
- We need to 'keep on top' of information management – the information keeps flowing so, if we do not deal with it effectively, it can overwhelm us, leading to lower morale and perhaps a higher rate of errors and misunderstandings.
- Different people manage information in different ways, but there is much to be gained by learning from the good practice of others, so do not be afraid to ask for advice or 'tips'. There is no single 'right' answer.
- Don't be afraid to use the various tools of information management – diaries, notebooks, computers, files and folders and so on. It is surprising how many people attempt to manage information without learning how to use the basic tools.
- Be aware of the range of sources of information and avoid duplication. For example, there is little point taking up a lot of time and space storing information that is readily accessible from another source (a library or from the Internet, for example).

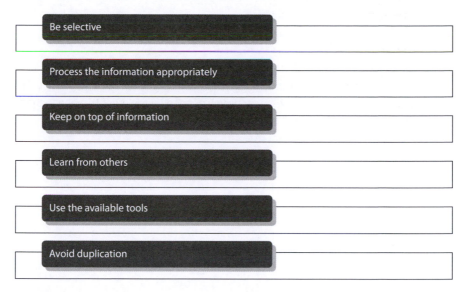

Be selective

Process the information appropriately

Keep on top of information

Learn from others

Use the available tools

Avoid duplication

Figure 4.1   Principles of information management

Conclusion

The idea that the development of the computer age would lead to a 'paperless office' has, of course, been shown to be a complete fallacy. What we have now is a deluge of computer-based information *as well as* the traditional forms of paper-based information, rather than *instead* of them. The challenges of managing the flow of information have therefore grown over the years, and so we need to be sure that we are sufficiently well equipped to handle those challenges.

Perhaps the single most important lesson that can be learned about information management is that we need to develop and maintain a system that meets our needs in terms of the various sources of information, the various purposes for which we wish to process and store information, and the different levels of priority we assign to the mass of information we need to wrestle with on a day-to-day basis.

What is very clear is that we do have to learn the skills of information management. Simply hoping that all this information will somehow sort itself out is clearly a strategy doomed to failure. The question, then, is not *whether* such a strategy will lead to difficulties, but rather *when*. It is to be hoped, then, that this chapter will have laid the foundations for getting to grips with the challenge of managing the immense flow of information that we all face.

Exercise 4

Information Audit

This exercise involves undertaking an 'information audit'. In order to do this, you will need to list all the different sources of information that you face in your day-to-day work. For each one, identify what steps you need to take in order to manage the flow of information as effectively as possible.

chapter 5

Assertiveness

Introduction

Personal effectiveness depends, to a large degree, on the extent to which we are able to assert ourselves. If we are too shy or retiring, people may take advantage of us or have little faith in us. At the other end of the spectrum, if we are too pushy or overbearing, we run the risk of alienating people who may prefer to keep their distance from us. In this respect, personal effectiveness can be seen to hinge on success in achieving a healthy balance between the two extremes.

This is the basis of assertiveness, finding a constructive balance between the two extremes of being submissive and being aggressive. This involves a number of skills that can be developed through practice in general and the use of certain techniques in particular. This chapter, then, is geared towards helping to lay the foundations for developing or enhancing these skills.

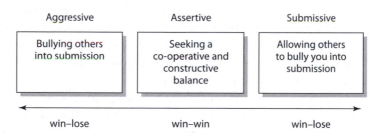

Figure 5.1   The assertive balance

Being non-assertive in our dealings with other people means:

○ not expressing our own needs;
○ allowing others to have their own way at our expense; and
○ saying yes when we mean no.

By contrast, being aggressive means:

○ disregarding the needs of others;

○ having our own way at the expense of others;
○ generating a great deal of resentment and ill-feeling.

In both cases the situations can be described as 'win–lose' scenarios. That is, while one person may gain from the situation, there will inevitably be a loser, someone who ends up worse off than was previously the case. In fact, we could go a step further in arguing that these are actually 'lose–lose' scenarios, in the sense that both parties lose out either directly or indirectly. For example, the aggressive person may benefit in the short term by winning the day, but may lose out in the longer term as a result of the trouble his or her actions have stored up for the future.

The aim of assertiveness, then, is to produce 'win–win' scenarios, situations from which all parties emerge positively, with no one losing out. This is a central feature of effective people skills as it makes a significant difference to the outcomes of interpersonal relations. It is therefore important to explore ways in which such positive outcomes can be promoted.

Becoming assertive

In a classic text, Jakubowski (1977) proposed eight 'Tenets of an Assertive Philosophy'. I shall discuss the significance of each of these in turn.

1 By standing up for ourselves and letting ourselves be known to others, we gain self-respect and respect from other people.

Being a 'shrinking violet' does little to earn the respect of others, nor does it provide a very firm foundation on which to build self-respect. This raises significant questions about self-esteem. If, due to low self-esteem, we do not stand up for ourselves, we will not earn respect, and will not, therefore, have opportunities to boost our self-esteem. In this way we can become trapped in a vicious circle of low self-esteem.

It is therefore important that, in working with people, we are able to act assertively by standing up for ourselves. If we are not able to represent our own interests, how will we be able to represent the interests of others?

2 By trying to live our lives in such a way that we never cause anyone to feel hurt under any circumstances, we end up hurting ourselves – and other people.

It is ironic that, in trying not to hurt the feelings of others, we can produce a situation in which a great deal of hurt is caused. That is, if we do not face up to difficult situations, for fear of hurting someone's feelings, then issues will not be resolved, and greater harm may be caused in the long run. Consider, for example, the case of a male colleague who is not undertaking his work properly. He is skimping on important aspects of the job, but you know that it will hurt his feelings if you bring the matter to his attention. However, if you do not bring it to his attention, then the poor quality of his work may produce a very damaging outcome for all concerned. The desire to avoid hurting people's feelings is, of course, a positive part of people work but, as this example illustrates, it needs to be balanced against other considerations.

Sometimes it is necessary to risk hurting people's feelings, and a reluctance to take this risk can prove very problematic indeed. Being assertive involves not being frightened of hurting someone's feelings if this is necessary for the greater good. This can be done tactfully, gently and constructively – it does not have to involve an aggressive response.

3 *When we stand up for ourselves and express our honest feelings and thoughts in a direct way, everyone usually benefits in the long run. Likewise, when we demean other people, we also demean ourselves, and everyone involved usually loses in the process.*

Direct expression of feelings makes a positive contribution to assertiveness, while masking one's feelings can stand in the way of making progress. In particular, hinting can cause resentment and act as an obstacle to effective communication.

Direct expression of feelings tends to be far more effective than indirect expression in terms of making constructive progress. For example, stating simply and clearly: 'I feel annoyed that...' sets the scene for a more constructive outcome than would a more indirect expression of one's annoyance.

The question of demeaning other people is also important in terms of constructive outcomes. This is closely linked to Carl Rogers's (1961) concept of 'unconditional positive regard' discussed earlier – the need to do our best by the people we work with, regardless of how positive or negative our feelings towards them may be.

Practice focus 5.1

Ruth had worked with teenagers for a long time, but she had had very little experience of child protection work. When she met Terri's father, who had previously been convicted of abusing her, she found it very difficult to swallow her feelings of revulsion for him. However, Ruth recognized that, because he still played an important part in Terri's life, it was important for her to relate to him in order to support Terri. She therefore had to use her assertiveness skills in being able to relate to him in a way that neither rejected him nor overcompensated for her negative feelings towards him. She realized that finding this balance would be difficult but also recognized that it was important to establish a positive relationship.

The emphasis, then, must be on creating an atmosphere of openness and positive regard, with no hidden agendas.

4 *By sacrificing our integrity and denying our personal feelings, relationships are usually damaged or prevented from developing. Likewise, personal relationships are damaged when we try to control others through hostility, intimidation or guilt.*

A relationship premised on a lack of integrity or denial of feelings is a relationship that has very unsound foundations, and is therefore very vulnerable in a number of ways – for example, in terms of unresolved tensions that are not addressed and therefore 'fester' beneath the surface. It can also place a great deal of strain on those concerned.

Similarly, attempting to control others through some form of coercion can prove stressful for those on the receiving end, and, especially if it backfires, for the person doing the coercing. Coercion does not have to involve physical threat. It can be much more subtle in bullying people into following a course of action or accepting a point of view. Making people feel guilty is a clear example of this more subtle form of coercion. It is important, then, that we do not allow our eagerness to help people overspill into coercing them into a particular form of behaviour. Indeed, this is a central theme of assertiveness.

5 *Personal relationships become more authentic and satisfying when we share our true reactions with other people and do not block others sharing their reactions with us.*

Once again this refers to the need to avoid hidden agendas, to put matters 'on the table', rather than deal with them underneath it. Achieving this openness can be particularly difficult when emotional issues are to the fore. For example, in dealing with matters of loss and bereavement, it may be very painful to share feelings and reactions. The person concerned may feel too vulnerable to talk openly and, indeed, the worker may feel very reluctant to discuss such sensitive issues, even though such discussion may be an important part of the processes involved in grieving (Thompson, 2012b).

Even in less extreme circumstances, feelings of threat and vulnerability can hamper open expression of feelings and effective communication. Working towards creating an atmosphere in which people feel safe to express their feelings and reactions openly is therefore an important aim to pursue.

6 *Not letting others know what we think and feel is just as inconsiderate as not listening to other people's thoughts and feelings.*

Successful interpersonal relations depend, to a large extent, on each party being sensitive to the thoughts and feelings of the other. Indeed, this reflects a basic premise of assertiveness – the need to find a positive balance between the interests of the respective parties so that the rights and needs of each are not unnecessarily compromised. However, other people may find it difficult to be sensitive to what we are thinking or feeling if we are holding back on what our thoughts or feelings are. Thus we may block the development of assertiveness by preventing others from entering into the spirit of openness and sensitivity that characterizes assertiveness.

7 *When we frequently sacrifice our rights, we teach other people to take advantage of us.*

This is a very telling comment. Assertiveness involves developing a partnership of mutual respect. If we do not demonstrate self-respect by standing up for our rights, then we make it difficult for other people to respect us. For example, if we allow some people to treat us badly without raising any objection, then we give other people the message that we do not mind being treated in this way – or even that we expect to be treated in this way.

Clearly, then, giving up on our rights not only abandons our own assertiveness, but also encourages others to abandon their assertiveness by taking advantage of us.

8 *By acting assertively and telling other people how their behaviour affects us, we are giving them an opportunity to change their behaviour, and we are showing respect for their right to know where they stand with us.*

This again emphasizes the mutuality inherent in the concept of assertiveness. By being assertive in our own actions and interactions, we lay the foundations and set the scene for others to act assertively. Indeed, this is a great strength of assertiveness, in so far as an assertive approach on our part makes it more difficult for people to act aggressively towards us, and encourages non-assertive people to enter into a more equal partnership with us.

Being assertive therefore creates a positive atmosphere in which constructive change can take place. It helps people to know where they stand and to understand the likely outcomes, positive and negative, of their actions.

Assertiveness involves having a certain degree of confidence in yourself (to make sure that your needs and interests are not submerged in other people's), having a positive attitude towards all people (including yourself) based on honesty and integrity (Moss, 2007).

A common thread running through these views of assertiveness is that of lifestyle or personal philosophy. That is, assertiveness is seen not simply as a technique (or set of techniques) for improved interpersonal relations, but rather as a way of life, in so far as it implies a value position – a stance which values the individual and his or her rights. In this respect, it chimes well with the ethos of the people professions, and so it is not surprising that it is a popular approach to people work. However, as such an approach, it is not without its limitations and drawbacks. It is therefore important to comment on what some of these are before leaving the topic.

The limitations of assertiveness

A common criticism of assertiveness is that it is too narrow a concept, in so far as it does not take adequate account of such important issues as gender, culture and class. Let us consider each of these in turn.

Gender

There are different social rules for men and women, and this reflects the way society is structured and organized (see Chapter 11). This is an important issue with regard to assertiveness, as there is a tendency to interpret women's and men's behaviours differently. Consider, for example, the situation as depicted in Figure 5.2.

	Men	Women
Non-assertive response	Unmanly not a real man	Feminine
Assertive response	Manly a real man	Strident

Figure 5.2 Assertiveness and gender

It is therefore important, in relation to issues of assertiveness, to be sensitive to the gender dimension, as this is clearly an important aspect of interpersonal relations. It is no coincidence that assertiveness is closely associated with the Women's Movement.

Practice focus 5.2

David and Beth were training officers in the same organization. They had been invited to attend a meeting to discuss multidisciplinary collaboration across agencies. Beth made a number of points in the meeting that were not taken up. However, when her colleague, David, sought to support her by reiterating the points she had made, they were taken far more seriously.

Beth was pleased that David had supported her, but was very angry that, once again, there was a tendency for a woman's views not to be heard unless articulated by a man.

Culture

Assertiveness, as it is usually presented, can be criticized for being 'ethnocentric'. That is, it is based on dominant white cultural norms, with little or no attention paid to cultural differences. The fact that some cultures have different sets of expectations with regard to what constitutes acceptable interpersonal interactions is not taken into account. For example, social etiquette concerning showing deference may, for some eastern cultures, clash with the principles and expectations of assertiveness.

In view of this, it is important that cultural sensitivity be brought to bear, so that people's values, background and identity are not disregarded or overlooked. This is an under-researched and poorly developed area, and so there is a need for caution in assuming that the principles of assertiveness apply to all ethnic groups in all circumstances – there are no simple guidelines to follow. As I shall argue in Chapter 11, there is no substitute for ethnically sensitive practice.

Class

Critics have also pointed out that assertiveness rests upon a set of middle-class norms and is not as applicable or effective in working-class communities. Whether this is actually the case remains to be established by research. However, students learning about assertiveness do often make the point that, for some working-class people, the notion of equality inherent in assertiveness would be seen as a sign of weakness. That is, some forms of working-class culture rely on proving oneself in what, from an assertiveness point of view, would be seen as an aggressive way.

A further limitation of assertiveness is that it implies that everything is negotiable, that all conflicts can be resolved rationally. This is a naive point of view that fails to recognize the significance of power. It fails to acknowledge that some things are not negotiable, that there is not always scope for compromise. For example, where unsuccessful attempts have been made to persuade a colleague to cease using racist language, it may be necessary to institute disciplinary proceedings.

These criticisms of assertiveness are not intended to undermine the value of assertiveness, but rather to identify its limitations, to sketch out the boundaries of its applicability and appropriateness. The concept of assertiveness has a great deal to offer as one of the basic strands of personal effectiveness. However, it needs to be seen in perspective, so that its usefulness is not overextended, so that it is not stretched beyond the limits of its value.

Conclusion

Assertiveness is something that we are all capable of, to a certain extent at least. However, in view of its valuable role as an aspect of self-management, it is a set of skills that repays the investment of time and energy required to develop and enhance them. Each day we have opportunities to act assertively, to avoid the unhelpful extremes of aggression and non-assertion. The challenge, then, is to capitalize on those opportunities to maximize our personal effectiveness by making our interpersonal interactions as positive as possible.

Assertiveness is also important as a set of skills to be used within organizations, groups and networks. Many aspects of people work involve the need to influence others within the context of a group, an organization or some other form of network (see Chapter 6). The skills of assertiveness therefore have a much broader applicability and bring a considerable range of potential benefits.

Exercise 5

Developing Assertiveness

This is an exercise based on observation. Your task is to watch the interactions of others and identify examples of:

- non-assertive behaviour;
- assertiveness; and
- aggressive behaviour.

What are the differences among the three? How can you tell? Make some notes about your responses to these questions.

chapter **6**

Beating the bully

Introduction

In Chapter 2 we looked at the important area of managing stress. It has long been recognized that one of the most significant contemporary sources of stress is bullying and harassment in the workplace (Field, 1996). Unfortunately, it has also been recognized that bullying is not uncommon in the modern workplace (see, for example, Stephens and Hallas, 2006). Being able to withstand or avoid the problems associated with bullying and harassment is therefore an important aspect of personal effectiveness for many people in many organizations, as it is clearly the case that being bullied is likely to have a significantly detrimental effect on an individual's ability to perform to the best of their ability. Being able to 'beat the bully', if or when we encounter one, is therefore an essential part of personal effectiveness.

In addressing this important issue we begin by clarifying the nature and basis of bullying and harassment before moving on to consider what can be done to deal with the problems at the levels of the individual, the team and the organization.

What is the problem?

Bullying in the workplace for adults is very much like bullying in the playground for children, in so far as it involves one or more people 'throwing their weight about' in a cruel and destructive way. This can have a hugely detrimental effect on the people so affected. As I have argued previously, the list of negative effects of bullying and harassment is a very long one:

> People who fall prey to bullies can experience any combination of the following as a result of how they are being treated:
>
> ○ stress;
> ○ tension and anxiety;
> ○ feelings of humiliation and a loss of dignity;
> ○ depression;
> ○ health problems or an exacerbation of existing health problems;

- a fall in work output and/or quality;
- sickness absence;
- strained relationships;
- irrational feelings of guilt;
- a lack of confidence;
- a negative and defeatist attitude;
- lower productivity and therefore, for many people, lower earning power;
- a lack of career advancement;
- the need to resign or move to another job

(Thompson, 2015b)

Bullying, then, refers to a person in a position of power using that power in such a way that it unfairly causes problems and distress for others. As managers tend to have more power in organizations than staff, this tends to refer more to managers, but this is not always the case – staff can be bullies too. Bullying is closely related to harassment, which refers to the persistent undermining or intimidation of an individual or group of people, usually because they are members of a particular social grouping (for example, sexual harassment primarily targeted at women and racial harassment primarily targeted at black people).

The problems can arise because power is deliberately abused. That is, the person in the position of power knowingly uses that power in an inappropriate way (for example, a male boss trying to use his power over a female employee to pressurize her into a sexual relationship with him). However, it is important to note that power can also be misused unwittingly. That is, a person may be so naive or insensitive that they fail to realize the impact of their actions (see Practice Focus 6.1). Of course, the fact that someone is causing problems unintentionally does not make such behaviour acceptable.

Practice focus 6.1

Margaret was the head of a large division, with a large number of staff to supervise. She was a firm believer in participative management and went to great lengths to consult with staff and invite their views. However, Lyn, the only disabled member of staff, was clearly treated differently. Her views were either not sought or, when they were, they were generally dismissed, sometimes rather harshly with laughter or ridicule, often referring to her disability as if this somehow invalidated her point of view or the positive contribution she could make. Lyn felt that she was being discriminated against and was very distressed by Margaret's persistently negative attitude towards her. She felt that her systematic exclusion from consultation was a form of harassment and made a complaint against Margaret. Margaret was genuinely quite horrified by this complaint, as she had no idea that this was what she had been doing. Her deep-seated prejudices against disabled people had been emerging without her being able to recognize what was happening. (From Thompson, 2015b)

Bullying can take many forms. These include, but are not limited to, the following:

○ intimidation, threats and victimization;
○ humiliating, demeaning and/or ridiculing;
○ unfair sanctions or 'oversupervision' (supervising somebody far more closely than is necessary);
○ spreading malicious rumours;
○ undermining – for example, through excessive criticism; and
○ offensive language or jokes.

In addition to these general problems there are the more specific factors involved in harassment. For example, sexual harassment consists of a range of behaviours that involve inappropriate sexual touching or comments, often geared towards attempting to establish a sexual relationship. Similarly, racial harassment consists of actions that undermine and disadvantage ethnic minority staff as a result of racial stereotypes and other forms of discrimination.

Bullying refers to a person in a position of power using that power in such a way that it unfairly causes problems and distress for others.

Figure 6.1   Bullying

How do we deal with it?

There are four levels at which we can deal with bullying and harassment. We shall look at each of these in turn.

Individual responses

Chapter 5 presented the benefits of assertiveness in dealing with actual or potential conflicts. The skills of assertiveness can therefore be brought to bear in responding to bullying behaviours. This involves not allowing people to intimidate us or put us in positions where we feel unduly compromised. However, as bullying and harassment generally involve unequal power relations, it is important that we do not leave ourselves open to further problems.

Our own personal response to someone who is acting inappropriately towards us may involve not only assertiveness skills, but also interpersonal skills more broadly. For example, if someone is causing us difficulties without realizing that they are doing so, it may take a very skilled form of communication to get this message across to them.

It is also important that we (i) enlist the support of others wherever and whenever we can (see below); and (ii) keep records of what is going on. Records are important for two main reasons. First, it may become necessary at a later stage to rely on formal procedures to halt bullying and harassment (disciplinary or grievance proceedings, for example), and so your records may be needed as evidence if the problem is to be resolved through the use of such procedures. Second, the bully may at some point attempt to use such procedures against you, and you may therefore require written records to defend yourself.

Another important aspect of an individual's response to consider is that of what has come to be known as 'whistle blowing'. As a result of the implementation of the Public Interest Disclosure Act 1998 in 1999, staff are protected from unfair dismissal or victimization for blowing the whistle on, amongst other things, bullying and harassment. Many organizations now have policies and procedures which detail how an individual employee can raise concerns without fear of a major backlash. Such 'confidential reporting procedures', as they are often known, could prove invaluable to someone who is being bullied or harassed, and so it is worth finding out whether such procedures exist within your employing organization. But, even if the organization does not have such procedures, the law on 'whistle blowing' still applies. Check with your trade union if you have any doubt.

It is very easy for someone who is being bullied to try to accept it as part and parcel of organizational life, just 'one of those things' that you have to contend with in your working life. Although this may well be an easy thing to do, it is not without its difficulties. This is for (at least) two reasons:

○ By not challenging what is going on, you may be unintentionally helping it to continue by allowing the bully to get away with it – and this may be not only to your detriment but also to the detriment of your present and future colleagues.
○ Being subjected to such bullying is likely to reduce your personal effectiveness, to make you a less effective and efficient member of staff, and so both you and the people you are seeking to help in your professional capacity are likely to suffer unnecessarily.

Team support

The point was made above that anyone being subjected to bullying and/or harassment should enlist the support of others. This is a very important point for three reasons:

- Being bullied or harassed can undermine confidence and lead to a sense of deskilling, and so having the support of others is an important antidote to this.
- It may well be that others are in a similar position but have been keeping it to themselves, and so seeking support may also *give* support to others.
- The abuse of power is a key issue in bullying and harassment, and so a collective team response can be very important in terms of altering the balance of power, given that the power of a team to tackle an issue is much greater than that of any single individual.

It should therefore be clear that there is much to be gained from teams of staff working together to tackle bullying and related problems. Indeed, bullies often survive in organizations because they have adopted a 'divide and conquer' strategy and they would be far less able to inflict damage on people if a spirit of collective support were in evidence.

A team response can take many forms. It can involve, for example, putting the matter on the agenda of a team or staff meeting, although this is likely to be seen as a confrontational approach if the bully is the team leader. It can involve a memo being sent to a suitable senior manager, signed by all the team members, expressing concern about the situation. However, in taking such action, it is important to consider carefully the normal protocols for raising concerns. For example, bypassing a particular manager in raising the issue may not only alienate that manager and thus risk losing his or her support in dealing with the bully, it may also potentially lead to disciplinary charges if established procedures are not properly followed. It is important, therefore, that such situations are handled carefully and sensitively. The problems being caused by the bullying may be very painful and difficult and may require an urgent response if further difficulties are to be avoided. However, we should not allow the pressures to tackle the problem to lead us into a situation where we run the risk of making matters worse.

Perhaps one of the most important things a team can do is to support the individual(s) concerned, helping to confirm that bullying and harassment are not acceptable and that any shame associated with these matters belongs to the perpetrator, and not to the persons on the receiving end of such inappropriate behaviours.

Practice focus 6.2

Richard had been head of section for a number of years and, although his style of management was far from supportive or sophisticated, it was not a major problem. However, when he obtained a temporary promotion he quickly found himself in a far more pressurized environment in which he needed to be on his mettle in terms of motivating and influencing his staff. Unfortunately, he seemed to lack the skills to do so and therefore started to rely on pressurizing his team into doing what he wanted them to do. The team were very unhappy with this, as they were already in a highly fraught situation and were looking to Richard for leadership, not crass insensitivity and a total lack of awareness of people's feelings. Consequently, the team made a complaint to Richard's line manager as a result of which Richard resigned his temporary promotion and returned to his head of section post before the matter was fully investigated. Many people heaved a sigh of relief when he subsequently left the organization altogether. Even he had the insight to see that, while he could bully individuals, he was not going to be able to survive if the whole team stood up against him.

Organizational responsibility

Bullying is often presented (sometimes by people who should know better) as a form of 'strong leadership', whereas, of course, it is the precise opposite – it is a sign of failed or inadequate leadership (Thompson, 2015b). A leader who has to rely on intimidation to get staff to do what is required of them is a leader who either lacks the necessary communication and influencing skills (see Chapter 16) to motivate staff appropriately or misguidedly decides not to use those skills. An organization therefore has basic preventative responsibilities in terms of ensuring that its managers not only have the necessary leadership skills, but are also actually using them (Gilbert, 2005).

It can also be argued that an employing organization should be monitoring the behaviour of its managers and staff so that, if bullying and/or harassment are taking place, this should become apparent in order that the problems can be tackled, rather than allowed to fester. Indeed, organizations can be held 'vicariously liable' for bullying and harassment – that is, they cannot plead ignorance as a defence if a case is made against them (see the 'Legal remedy' section below). To ignore the possibility that bullying and harassment are going on is therefore a very risky strategy, as an organization could be in serious trouble if it cannot show that all reasonable steps were taken to protect staff from the harm that comes from being bullied.

Where an organization does become aware that bullying and/or harassment are going on, then it has a legal responsibility, under its 'duty of care' towards its employees, to do something about the problem and to ensure that it does not continue. In these days of increased awareness of the issues, it is to be hoped that organizations will become increasingly enlightened in dealing with the issues – for example, through developing appropriate policies and procedures which make it clear to all concerned that bullying and harassment are unacceptable and will not be tolerated;

providing training and development opportunities; offering support to people who suffer at the hands of bullies; and so on.

Legal remedy

The law relating to bullying and harassment is complicated and far from straightforward. However, it should be noted that there are several potential avenues for staff affected by bullying to seek remedy or redress through the legal system, although not all sets of circumstances are covered by the law. It is advisable to seek specialist legal advice if you are considering taking a case to court, and your trade union or professional association is likely to be your best bet for your first port of call.

However, it should be remembered that taking a case to court can be extremely stressful, not least because the whole process can be very longwinded and is potentially fraught with a number of difficulties. This is not to say that you should be discouraged from doing so, but it is certainly advisable to explore all other potential avenues for seeking redress if at all possible, before taking the major step of pursuing litigation.

Conclusion

It is very sad indeed that, in the twenty-first century, we still have to contend with the problem of people being bullied and harassed in the workplace, but we have to recognize that we are still a long way from eliminating the problems. The concept of 'dignity at work' is a relatively new one that has been introduced to describe a commitment to ensuring that staff are treated with respect and dignity in the workplace. It is to be hoped that this can become more than a slogan and actually be a basic part of working life.

Beating the bully, then, is a challenge that anyone can face, as it is certainly a myth that only inadequate or incompetent people get bullied. In tackling the problem of bullying, much depends, as we have seen, on team and organizational responses and even on the courts. However, it should also be recognized that there is much each individual can do to tackle the issues. This refers to individuals who are on the receiving end of such ill-treatment but also to their colleagues who can be in a position to take a stand.

A hurried, simplistic, ill-thought-through approach to tackling the problems can make matters worse and can walk all over the sensitivities and sensibilities of complex and potentially very painful situations. There is therefore much skill to be deployed in dealing with these matters carefully and judiciously – making the most of the various people skills needed to tackle complex problems in organizations.

Exercise 6

Getting Support

If you were being subjected to bullying and/or harassment, who could you call upon for support? List below the individuals and organizations who are likely to be of help to you. In particular, consider who would be helpful in assisting you in maintaining your confidence and self-esteem, as it has been shown that these can be seriously undermined by bullying.

chapter **7**

Using supervision

Introduction

The tasks involved in people work can be extremely demanding at times. They are often complex and 'messy' with no simple or straightforward solution (Schön, 1983). They often need to be thought through very carefully, and there is much to be gained from discussing issues with a senior colleague who is not directly involved in the situation. This is a key aspect of supervision and underlines the benefits that can be drawn from effective line management. This chapter therefore explores the important role of supervision in developing and maintaining personal effectiveness.

What is supervision?

Supervision is, in principle at least, a process through which an organization seeks to meet its objectives through empowering its staff. This involves a range of tasks:

○ monitoring work tasks and workload;
○ supporting staff through difficulties;
○ promoting staff development;
○ acting as a mediator between workers and higher management, where necessary;
○ problem solving;
○ ensuring legal and organizational requirements and policies are adhered to; and
○ promoting teamwork and collaboration.

These are achieved partly through day-to-day contact, and partly through more formal meetings or 'supervision sessions'.

For people workers there is considerable variation in the use of supervision. For example, social work has a long tradition of supervision, while its use is far less well established in other professions such as nursing, although mentoring, a process closely akin to supervision, is being increasingly emphasized. The significance of supervision is none the less of major proportions, regardless of the extent to which it is commonly practised, as it can play a vital role in the success or otherwise of people work. It is therefore worth considering the benefits of supervision, and it is to these that we now turn.

The benefits of supervision

Effective supervision can often be the difference between: success and failure; stress and job satisfaction; worry and reassurance; good practice and excellent practice. Its significant role should therefore not be underestimated. In particular, we should appreciate the positive benefits that can be derived from supervision. These include:

○ an opportunity to share concerns;
○ a forum for reviewing actions and checking plans;
○ a more objective perspective on work currently being undertaken;
○ constructive feedback, both positive and negative;
○ a source of confidence and reassurance; and
○ opportunities for personal and professional development.

This is by no means an exhaustive list but should suffice to paint a clear picture of the potential benefits of supervision. Furthermore, we should also consider what may occur as a result of adequate supervisory support not being available. That is, a lack of effective supervision may not only rob workers of the support they need, but may actually act as a source of pressure in its own right (Thompson and Gilbert, 2011).

Morrison (2013) also emphasizes the importance of supervision and outlines a set of beliefs on which his view of supervision rests. These are:

○ Supervision is the worker's most essential professional relationship.
○ What goes on *under* the 'supervisory table' is often as significant as that which goes on *over* the 'supervisory table'.
○ Supervision is a complex and skilful process which can be learnt – you are not born with or without those skills.
○ Supervision is improved by analysing what we feel, think and do and by trying new things out with support for ourselves as supervisors.
○ Supervision is one of the most important managerial activities in an organization.
○ Supervision is a major organizational strategy for the protection and empowerment of minority or vulnerable groups whether they are clients or our own staff.
○ Supervision can be one of the most rewarding tasks in social care work.

These are principles that are also endorsed here and inform many of the points made in this chapter. They reinforce both the value of supervision and its complexity.

The elements of supervision

Supervision is an important basis for establishing and developing workplace well-being. As such, it can be seen to involve four main elements: managerial accountability and standard setting; staff development and learning; staff care and support; and mediation or conflict resolution. I shall outline each of these four elements in turn.

Accountability

Line managers have some degree of responsibility for the work of the staff they supervise. They will therefore need to have some oversight of the work being undertaken. This will allow a process of standard setting, which plays an important part in contributing to the overall process of quality assurance.

In this way, the supervisor can ensure that legal requirements are met and that organizational policies and procedures are followed. However, this is not simply a 'checking up' procedure. It can give workers a sense of confidence and reassurance that any mistakes that are made (and, of course, mistakes inevitably will be made) are likely to be picked up at an early stage so that any damage done can be kept to a minimum.

If this role is fulfilled sensitively and skilfully by the supervisor, it can create a strong sense of security and a feeling that there is a reliable safety net if things should start to go wrong. However, if undue emphasis is given to this element of supervision at the expense of the others, supervision can become very 'heavy handed' and can be resented and resisted by staff – a positive tool becomes a problem.

Practice focus 7.1

Linda had always worked in situations where she had been given considerable autonomy and minimal supervision. She therefore found it quite a shock when her new line manager supervised her work in some detail, with a clear focus on accountability. At first, Linda resented this, but she soon came round to valuing this aspect of supervision as it gave her a degree of confidence and security in knowing that she was not alone and unsupported in making important decisions.

However, she also recognized that her new line manager was very skilful in this role, and feared that someone who lacked the necessary skills and sensitivity could have created a very tense and unhelpful atmosphere.

Staff development

The staff of an organization are its most important resource, in the sense that the success or failure of the organization depends to a great extent on the actions and attitudes of staff. Staff are a 'human resource' and so, for them to be of maximum benefit to the organization and to the people who use its services, it is important that steps are taken to promote staff development.

This is often achieved through courses and other forms of training. However, the line manager also has a significant role to play through supervision. The supervisor can help to identify opportunities for learning and help to capitalize upon them. He or she can also play a crucial role in identifying barriers to learning and helping to break them down. This does not mean that the supervisor is expected to be an 'expert'. However, it does mean that he or she should have the skills of facilitating and promoting learning and the confidence to put these into practice.

Staff care

People work is, as we noted in Chapter 3, fraught with a number of pressures that can easily lead to stress. The role of the supervisor in helping to insulate staff from these pressures is therefore a very important one in terms of staff care.

There are many dangers in undertaking people work unsupported, not least because of the emotional demands of this type of work. Morrison (2013) includes the following in a list of important aspects of the supportive function:

○ creating a safe climate for the worker to look at her/his practice and its impact on them as a person;
○ debriefing the worker and giving them permission to talk about feelings, especially fear, anger, sadness, repulsion or helplessness;
○ helping the worker to explore emotional blocks to their work.

Mediation

The line manager is in an intermediate position between the staff he or she supervises and the senior management hierarchy. The supervisor is therefore well placed to act as a mediator between the two sets of people, and indeed has a responsibility to do so.

A key part of this is the process of negotiation (see Chapter 19). It may involve representing staff's interests to higher management or guiding staff through organizational changes imposed from above. In this respect, the mediation role reflects elements of accountability, staff development and staff care.

Figure 7.1   The four elements of supervision

The four elements are not mutually exclusive and do overlap to a certain extent. Unfortunately, a weakness that is relatively common is that of supervisors sticking too closely to their 'favourite' element, the one with which they feel most comfortable. For example, a supervisor who enjoys the role of standard setting may engage in 'snoopervision' by being too zealous and defensive in checking staff's work. Such an approach is likely to cause resentment and mistrust. Similarly, a supervisor who enjoys the staff development element may focus almost exclusively on promoting learning, and thereby neglect other significant aspects of the role. A good supervisor is therefore one who is able to balance all four elements of the role.

Problems and barriers in supervision

Supervision is a skilled activity, and some of these skills relate to being able to negotiate barriers and resolve problems that stand in the way of effective supervisory practice. These problematic areas include:

○ *Destructive processes.*   Avoidance behaviour is one such very common destructive process, and creating a dependency relationship is another. If we are not careful, supervision can become a non-productive forum for game-playing (Morrison's notion of what goes on *under* the table, as discussed earlier). It is sometimes necessary to 'name' the process, for one party to bring the process out into the open by commenting explicitly upon it – see *The People Solutions Sourcebook.*

Practice focus 7.2

Carol very much enjoyed her role as a supervisor and gained a lot of satisfaction from the role. However, there was one member of staff who caused her some difficulty. This was because he had the habit of changing the subject whenever she raised certain topics. Carol was very irritated by this and felt that this was getting in the way of progress. Finally, she reached the point where she could tolerate it no more and confronted him as to why he kept changing the subject. By 'naming the process' in this way, she was able to halt this destructive process and allow progress to be made. By confronting the issue directly, Carol created the opportunity to discuss constructively the anxieties that were leading to the tendency to avoid certain topics of discussion.

○ *Unfinished business.* This relates to previous experiences of supervision. If there have been previous problems in a supervisory relationship, these may be 'carried forward' to the current situation. There may, therefore, be a need to exorcize the ghosts of previously problematic supervision.
○ *Personality clashes.* These do occur from time to time, but the term can also be applied inappropriately on occasion. For example, the clash may have more to do with a conflict of values than personality *per se*. Similarly, there may be conflicts arising from differences of ethnic group, gender, class or age. For example, a worker may resent being supervised by a younger person.
○ *Imbalance of elements.* As mentioned above, an overemphasis on one of the elements at the expense of the others can be very problematic. This applies not only to the supervisor, but also to the worker. For example, a worker may seek to guide supervision in a particular direction and thereby make it difficult for the supervisor to maintain the necessary balance.
○ *Burnout.* Where staff have reached a point of emotional exhaustion, their commitment to supervision is likely to be very low, as they have probably given up hope of making progress in their work. Indeed, it is a characteristic of burnout that work is undertaken in a routine, emotionally sanitized way, and so supervision is likely to be a difficult process.

These are just some of the ways in which supervision can be blocked or rendered ineffective. It is primarily the supervisor's responsibility to remedy the problems encountered. However, there are steps that the supervisee can take to contribute to a successful process of supervision – making supervision work is, after all, a joint responsibility.

The worker's responsibility

The skills of personal effectiveness can be seen to include those of making the best use of the supervision opportunities available. These skills can be developed, in part at least, by following certain guidelines. Chief amongst these are the following:

○ *Avoid 'macho' attitudes.* To take advantage of the benefits supervision can offer, we have to be open to accepting help and support. A 'be tough' attitude is a significant barrier to effective use of supervision. All staff, even the most highly competent, can benefit from supervision. Being open to receiving help and support should not be seen as a sign of weakness.

○ *Do not collude.* If you have a supervisor who indulges in game playing or destructive processes, it is important that you should not collude with this. It may be very difficult to challenge your 'boss', but playing along with games can lead to even worse problems in the long run.

○ *Ensure you receive supervision.* You can play a proactive part in receiving supervision, if necessary. If a supervision session is cancelled, make sure you book an alternative time. If no one receives supervision, raise the subject at a staff meeting and try to get a system of supervision organized. If your line manager is unwilling to provide supervision, try to organize supervision from a senior colleague or develop group supervision (see Morrison, 2013).

○ *Identify your own needs.* Be clear about what you need and expect from supervision. Exercise 7 is designed to help you with this. Once you have identified what you need, make sure your supervisor becomes aware of what these needs are.

○ *Be assertive.* Chapter 5 emphasized the need to be assertive, to stand up for one's rights without infringing the rights of others. An assertive approach towards supervision can pay dividends. In particular, it can promote an open supervisory relationship in which constructive feedback works both ways. This can make a significant difference in terms of realizing the positive potential of supervision.

○ *Use time management.* Some people comment that they are 'too busy for supervision'. This is a misguided approach to the subject as it fails to recognize the need to invest time in order to save time (see Chapter 2). Effective supervision can prevent mistakes being made, increase motivation and encourage creative solutions. In this way, supervision can actually help to save a great deal of time and make the best use of the limited time resources available. It is therefore important that we are able to make time available for supervision.

○ *Prepare for supervision.* The time that can be allocated to supervision is inevitably limited. It is therefore helpful to prepare for supervision so that the time can be used to maximum effect. For example, it is a good idea to set priorities, to plan in advance what are the most important issues to be addressed. This helps to set an agenda at the beginning of the supervision session so that discussions do not become unfocused and unproductive.

A positive, proactive approach to supervision can be seen to be a very important part of personal effectiveness. Workers who neglect the significance of supervision or adopt a passive approach to it are seriously undermining their own potential for effectiveness.

Conclusion

Supervision can be seen to play a critical role in promoting good practice. If it is positive and constructive, it can be a tremendous source of confidence, learning and support. However, where it is handled badly or does not take place at all, workers can be left feeling unsupported, unappreciated and lacking guidance. The role of the supervisor is therefore a very important one.

The responsibility for providing supervision lies clearly and firmly with the line manager. However, the central point to be emphasized is that the worker too has some degree of responsibility for ensuring high-quality supervision by not colluding with the absence of supervision and by taking whatever reasonable steps he or she can to make supervision a success.

Exercise 7

Expectations of Supervision

This exercise is designed to help you be clear about what you hope to gain from supervision, what you see as the potential benefits for you personally in your current circumstances. Consider carefully what you expect from supervision, and what you see as your needs. Discuss this with a colleague or your line manager if you wish. Use the space below to make some notes.

chapter **8**

Being creative

Introduction

I am a great believer in the value and appropriateness of the adage: 'If you always do what you've always done, you'll always get what you always got.' In other words, forms of practice that are based on unthinkingly repeating actions over and over again will not produce new or better results. In effect, what will occur is that, at best, we will fail to learn and progress and, at worst, our effectiveness will diminish as we became more jaded and 'in a rut' over time.

Creativity is the precise opposite of that. Instead of simply following set patterns unthinkingly, we are called upon to be imaginative and explore a range of possible ways of addressing the situation. This process enables us to draw on a much wider range of potential solutions, and is also a much greater source of interest and job satisfaction than simply following set patterns.

This chapter is therefore concerned with exploring how we can develop our creativity as part of a process of maximizing our potential for self-management.

Understanding creativity

One important factor to recognize is the significance of habit (see the discussion of the 'Three Hs' in *The People Solutions Sourcebook*). Habit is a powerful force that tends to be a very strong influence on behaviour. If we are not thinking carefully about how best to respond to situations, then there is a very real danger that we will react by simply repeating a set of stock actions – that is, habit will take over. Habits can be very useful for dealing with simple, straightforward routine matters that require little reflection or understanding, but the danger comes when we make the mistake of overgeneralizing and adopt an habitualized response to situations that are too complex or specific in their character to warrant a simple approach based on habit. This is an important point in relation to reflective practice, which warns us against the dangers of uncritical approaches based on a lack of understanding of the complex issues involved in the situations we are trying to address (see Chapter 30 for a discussion of the important role of reflective practice as a foundation for dealing with people and their problems).

In effect, habit can be seen to numb the brain, in the sense that relying on habit bypasses our critical faculties and our ability to develop a sophisticated understanding of what we are dealing with. Adopting a creative approach therefore involves making sure that we do not allow habit to dominate our practice and seduce us into dealing mechanistically with unique, complex situations in simple, standardized ways (Isaksen, Dorval and Treffinger, 2011).

An important part of being creative involves being prepared to venture outside our comfort zone. Comfort zones have considerable value, but they also have significant limitations. Their value comes from offering a degree of security ('ontological security' is the technical term), a sense of rootedness or foundation that enables us to have a sense of who we are and how we fit into the wider world. They are a safe haven to which we can return from difficult, challenging or distressing experiences.

However, if we get *too* comfortable in our comfort zones, we will not learn, grow or broaden our horizons. In this way comfort zones can prevent us from having new experiences, trying new approaches or developing our knowledge and skills. They can also prevent us from being imaginative or creative – leaving us stuck in a rut. Being creative involves opening ourselves up to fresh ideas and new insights. This amounts to being able to get ourselves outside the tramlines of habit that can restrict us, or, as it is often put these days, it involves 'thinking outside the box'. 'Pushing the envelope' is another term that is being used increasingly these days to refer to going beyond fixed and therefore limiting patterns of thinking and acting.

Practice focus 8.1

Godwin had been in the same post for two years when his employers introduced a new appraisal scheme. He had been in post long enough to feel that he 'knew the ropes' and could do the job reasonably well, he was therefore not at all anxious about the appraisal and felt quite comfortable all round. However, he was very surprised, and quite perturbed, when the appraisal meeting resulted in criticisms of him for being too unadventurous in his approach, for staying within his comfort zone and not trying out new ideas. Although the overall standard of his work was acceptable, there was a strong view that he had not taken the opportunities to develop that had been available to him and that he had stuck too closely to what he knew best, basing his work more on habit than a commitment to achieving the highest standards of work he could. He realized that he was going to have to give the situation a lot of careful thought, as he recognized that they had a point: he had done nothing to go beyond the basics of getting the job done.

Edward de Bono is a writer closely associated with the notion of creativity through his writings on 'lateral thinking': 'Lateral thinking is specifically associated with the ability to escape from existing perceptual (and conceptual) patterns in order to draw up new ways of looking at things and doing things' (1986, p. 114). Creativity, then, involves moving away from the tramlines that lock us into routine practices and narrow perspectives.

A major barrier to developing creativity is an attitude that says: 'I can't. I'm not the sort of person who's creative.' As I commented in the Introduction to this book, this is a defeatist attitude that confuses skills with qualities. This is particularly significant with regard to creativity, as it is sometimes seen as having an almost magical quality, as if it were a 'special gift'. However, de Bono's comments on this are again helpful: 'There is a great deal of rubbish written about creativity because – like motherhood – it is automatically a good thing. My preference is to treat creativity as a logical process rather than a matter of talent or mystique' (1986, p. 114). Creativity, then, can be learned; it can be developed through deliberate effort and experience. It is a set of skills.

Another barrier that can stop us getting away from these limitations is relying on stereotypes or distorted assumptions about being creative – for example, the idea that only 'artistic' people are creative. If we look back over history, we will see that some of the most creative people have been scientists rather than artists. So, having little or no artistic skill does not debar anyone from being creative.

A further distorted assumption that stands in the way of developing creativity is the oft-voiced idea that: 'we don't have the resources to be creative'. Clearly this is a misunderstanding of creativity, as times of shortage of resources are precisely when creativity comes into its own. As the saying goes, 'Necessity is the mother of invention' – that is, it is precisely when resources are limited or even non-existent that creativity is called for and when it can have its greatest impact.

Primarily, what being creative amounts to is being able to change perspective, to see situations from different angles or points of view, so that we develop our understanding of the situation by appreciating the different elements. This enables us to explore a range of potential solutions, rather than be limited to what we normally do. That is, it gives us an opportunity to expand our repertoire. Some people find this difficult and are strongly wedded to a very limited range of tactics for dealing with the situations they are trying to influence. For example, I have had an interesting experience on a number of training courses where I have given some examples of creative approaches to problem solving, with the result that there is then a long discussion about the ideas I have presented and how these could possibly be used in practice. The great irony here is that the discussion invariably focuses on *my* ideas, the examples I have given, rather than on the process of developing *their* ideas – that is, the message I am trying to put across on the course about the value and importance of being creative by developing new approaches is not being received. When I make the point explicitly that the course is an opportunity to develop *their* ideas, rather than discuss mine, the irony is not lost on the group and they appreciate how easy it is to remain within our 'box' and not think more broadly and imaginatively. However, it seems that we have to go through this process of recognizing our tendency to rely on other people's ideas rather than develop our own, before the value of creativity is appreciated.

Developing creativity

Students training to enter the people professions are often anxious to be presented with ready-made techniques to use in practice, a toolbox of methods that can be applied in a simple or straightforward way. Such expectations, although understandable, are both unrealistic and unhelpful.

They are unrealistic because there are only a limited number of techniques that can be applied across a range of situations, and these will not be enough, in themselves, to provide an adequate repertoire for people workers. They are unhelpful because they are based on an inappropriate model of professional development. The worker should be seen not as a receptacle or storehouse to be 'stocked up' with methods and techniques, but rather as a generator of ideas and potential solutions (see my comments below about professionalism and see also the discussion of problem solving in *The People Solutions Sourcebook*).

There will be common themes across the situations encountered (and this is where theory can be of great value, as we shall see in Chapter 30), but there will also be features unique to each situation. People workers therefore have to be equipped to deal with novel situations by generating novel solutions. It is therefore worth considering, albeit briefly, how a creative approach can be developed.

The point was made earlier that we can learn how to be creative – it is not a quality that a person either has or does not have. It is a set of skills that can be developed over time. To promote this type of development, I shall present five strategies for stimulating a creative approach. These are:

○ *Changing angle.* Have you ever noticed how different a room looks if you sit in a different position from your usual one? Changing our 'angle' on a situation can give us a new perspective, with fresh insights. It can therefore pay dividends to switch position, metaphorically, so that we see the situations we are dealing with from different angles. This is also an important part of working in partnership, learning to see situations from other people's points of view so that we can more effectively work together. One way of changing angle is to ask yourself: 'In tackling this situation, how would so-and-so deal with it?' – with 'so-and-so' being a trusted and respected colleague. In this way, you can help yourself to broaden your perspective on the situation in hand.

○ *Developing a vision.* Both Chapters 17 and 22 stress the importance of having clear objectives. This is because they help to prevent drift and vagueness from standing in the way of progress. This involves developing a vision of where we want to be, the point we want to reach. This type of vision can also stimulate creativity. If we know where we are now and where we want to be in future, then we can map out the various routes for getting there, different 'modes of transport' and so on. By generating such options we are avoiding the narrow focus of seeing only one way forward.

○ *Stepping back.* Sometimes we can get so close to a situation that we 'cannot see the wood for the trees', and we therefore get bogged down or lose our sense of direction. By 'stepping back', we can put some distance between ourselves and the situation that we are tackling. Stepping back from a situation gives us a breathing space and helps us develop a fresh perspective (see the discussion of 'helicopter vision' in *The People Solutions Sourcebook*).

○ *Letting go.* The technique of brainstorming can be a very helpful one by allowing people to make lots of suggestions without having to worry about whether they are sensible, logical or workable. In this way, the straitjacket of conventional thinking can be thrown off and the potential for creative solutions is released. By 'letting go' in this way we generate a wide range of possibilities, many of which will have to be rejected as unsuitable. However, amongst these, there may well be a veritable nugget of gold. It is important to note, though, that brainstorming is not just a matter of drawing up a list of possibilities. The idea behind it is that we develop as many ideas as possible, including any bizarre or apparently unworkable ones. This can be very helpful in a number of ways:

- It can introduce ideas that initially seem outlandish, but which, on further consideration, have at least an element of workability about them.
- An unworkable idea may start off a chain of thought that leads to a workable idea emerging.
- The very process of generating a wide range of ideas, even outrageous ones, helps to free us up and get the creative juices flowing, as it were.

○ *Provocation.* This is another concept from de Bono, and he explains it in the following terms:

> A patterning system like the mind creates patterns which we then continue to use. Most of our thinking is concerned with fitting things into these patterns so that we can act usefully and effectively. But to change patterns

and to unlock those 'insight patterns' which are readily available to us (only after we have found them) we need something entirely different. Provocation is the process. With provocation we do not describe something as it is or as it could be. With provocation we look at the 'what if' and 'suppose' . . . Provocation creates an unstable idea so that we may move on from it to a new idea.

(1983, p. 200)

Practice focus 8.2

The team had been through a very difficult and demanding year due, in no small part, to a major reorganization. Consequently, they were glad of the opportunity to have an 'awayday', a day away from the office where they reviewed the previous year and planned for the forthcoming one. On this day, they used the technique of 'provocation' in order to plan and set priorities for the future. This involved looking at possible situations that could arise and speculating on how they might deal with them. This was a very creative technique similar to brainstorming. It allowed the team to look at the future from different angles and thereby break away from traditional or routine practices and perspectives.

Figure 8.1 Strategies for developing creativity

Creativity is, in large part, a set of personal skills, and each individual will have developed them to a smaller or greater extent, as the case may be. However, it would be a mistake to see creativity as purely an individual matter. There is also a social dimension to it, in so far as the support of other people can be important and the environment in which the work takes place can also be very significant, in the sense that it can either help or hinder (see the discussion of leadership in Chapter 17). One very important aspect of this social dimension is the potential for working together, creating and using opportunities for bouncing ideas off each other. Creativity does not need to be a solitary activity. Indeed, creativity can flourish in situations where people stimulate ideas in one another and support each other in developing them further. This can also help to develop a culture of creativity by helping to challenge the not uncommon idea in many workplaces that it is not 'the done thing' to consider different ways of working.

Conclusion

Developing our potential for creativity is clearly an important enterprise and one that is worth investing time and effort into. Being creative provides a foundation for both reflective practice (to be discussed in Chapter 30 in Part III) and professionalism. While bureaucracy largely involves following instructions and requires little or no creativity, professionalism is a matter of developing a picture of the situation (see the discussion of assessment in Chapter 23) and developing a plan of how best to respond to the issues involved. There is no set way of doing this. The professional is called upon to weigh up a range of possible courses of action and, in partnership with other key people involved, determine how best to proceed. This is premised on creativity and, in turn, this process of professional assessment and planning reinforces the need for, and value of, creativity.

In another work, I have referred to the 'Three Rs' of professional practice: resourcefulness, robustness and resilience (Thompson, 2009a). When it comes to being creative, it is clearly the first of these, resourcefulness, that is to the fore. Being creative means being resourceful – using the resources of our own imagination and insights to develop innovative approaches that make a positive difference and broaden our repertoire of helpful approaches.

Freeing ourselves up to be creative, open to new ideas and fresh insights, can be seen as a vitally important part of self-management. Allowing ourselves to stay within the limited bounds of habit and comfort zones amounts to missing excellent opportunities to maximize our potential to be the best we can and to do the best we can. The challenge of creativity is therefore a crucial one, and one that can be very costly to us in terms of lost potential if we do not take it seriously and rise to it as effectively as we reasonably can.

Exercise 8

Developing Creativity

Take an everyday object: a pencil, a paper clip, a shoe-lace or whatever. See how many different uses you can find for each such object. Try this with friends and colleagues to see who can be most creative. Having done this, think carefully about how this creative approach can be adapted to your work situation.

chapter 9

Continuous professional development

Introduction

Continuous professional development (CPD) is increasingly being recognized as an important part of working life. It is a concept that acknowledges the danger of getting stuck in a rut and failing to learn and develop. CPD is an essential element of modern management, based on principles of human resource management (Beardwell and Claydon, 2011), which sees the staff of an organization as its most important resource. This is closely linked to the Investors in People initiative in which employing organizations can receive accreditation for their commitment to staff development. The use of personal portfolios to chart personal and professional development is also becoming more popular. Increasingly, then, the value of CPD is being appreciated, although there sadly remain very many organizations who have yet to make a commitment to staff development. They remain oblivious to the problems that such an unenlightened approach can cause.

This chapter explores the importance of CPD, barriers to achieving it, and strategies for making the most of the learning opportunities that arise in the course of people work. I begin by asking why learning should be accorded such importance.

Why learn?

The reasons why learning is important are many and varied. The following examples serve to build up a picture of the significant role of CPD as a contributory factor to the development and maintenance of personal effectiveness:

○ *Job satisfaction.* People work can be both very demanding and very satisfying, potentially a source of considerable stress *and* considerable job satisfaction. CPD can help to tilt the balance in favour of job satisfaction, in so far as learning can be a significant source of stimulation, motivation and achievement. As well as providing a boost to confidence, learning can also bring a great deal of pleasure. Learning is not only a means to an end, it is also intrinsically motivating – a worthwhile activity in its own right.

> **Practice focus 9.1**
>
> Rashid enjoyed his training but was now feeling swamped and overloaded in his new job, with little energy left for further study or training. However, when the opportunity arose of undertaking a course of advanced level training, he was persuaded by a colleague to enrol. This proved to be a very positive decision. He gained tremendous satisfaction and stimulation from the course – and actually felt less overloaded than he had done previously, even though he now had an additional commitment. This helped him to become determined that he would never allow himself to get into a rut – he would always be seeking new opportunities for learning and development.

○ *Improved practice.*   A focus on continuous professional development helps to enhance standards of practice by enabling staff to sharpen skills, extend their knowledge base, broaden their repertoire and build confidence. High-quality practice therefore owes a great deal to CPD.

○ *Avoiding burnout.*   There is a danger that workers can become entrenched in an unproductive, routinized way of working. Ultimately, this can lead to burnout, a form of emotional exhaustion in which work is carried out in a mechanical way, with a minimum of thought and feeling. Clearly, this is a dangerous state of affairs for worker, client and organization. CPD can play a crucial role in preventing this problem from arising.

○ *Personal development.*   While professional development is clearly important, so too is *personal* development. A focus on learning provides a basis for personal growth and development by facilitating and encouraging self-awareness. It helps to promote self-esteem and a positive self-image.

○ *The adventure of theory.*   It is unfortunate that many practitioners see theory in negative terms, as something abstract and unconnected with practice. However, a more positive (and realistic) view sees theory as a source of guidance and inspiration, a world of ideas to be explored with enthusiasm, with a view to ensuring that our practice is an *informed* practice (Thompson and Thompson, 2008). CPD can play an important part in promoting the positive use of theory.

○ *It is dangerous not to.*   Schön (1983) uses the term 'overlearning' to refer to the tendency to become complacent and practise in an unthinking and uncritical way. Good practice involves being alert, sensitive and open to the significance of new experiences. CPD helps to maintain this openness and guards against the complacency that can make practice insensitive, and therefore dangerous.

It is clearly important, then, that learning should be high on the agenda for staff involved in people work. In order to facilitate this, we need to understand the basic principles underpinning the process of learning.

The learning process

A common misunderstanding about learning is that experience is the best teacher:

> It is commonly said that experience is the best teacher. However, in reality this is not actually the case. For example, consider how many people there are who have a lot of experience, but have actually learned little or nothing from it. Experience creates the potential for learning but, in itself, it teaches us nothing directly. It is what we *do with* experience that is the best teacher. The experience provides a basis for learning, but experience alone is not enough. That experience has to be 'processed' – that is, it needs to be translated into actual learning.
>
> (Thompson and Thompson, 2008, pp. 63–4)

This fits well with Kolb's (1984) theory of adult learning, which is seen as having four stages:

○ *Concrete experience.* Day-to-day experience forms the first step in a chain of learning.
○ *Reflective observation.* Reflecting on our experience helps us to begin to draw out the learning points.
○ *Abstract conceptualization.* This stage of the learning process involves forming links between the new experience and previous learning and experience. These links build up a 'mini-theory' or conceptual framework.
○ *Active experimentation.* A cycle of learning is completed when new ideas are tried out in practice.

This process is illustrated in the following example:

> Anne is a ... student on placement in a social services office. She is allocated a case in which she is asked to carry out an assessment of the needs of an elderly woman. Reading the referral and discussing the case with her practice teacher form the first concrete experience. She reads and listens carefully and forms a picture of what is expected of her. This is her reflective observation. When the supervision session is over and the case is now allocated to her, she begins to form links with the wider areas of knowledge she possesses, including course-based knowledge – the ageing process, the social construction of dependency, client self-determination and so on. This is the abstract conceptualisation and produces the strategy or set of

hypotheses which will guide and inform her active experimentation, that is, the first interview.

(Thompson, Osada and Anderson, 1994, pp. 11–12)

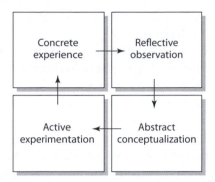

Figure 9.1   The process of learning

This model of learning raises a number of important points, including the following:

1 *Learning is an active process.* Consequently, experience will not automatically produce learning. For example, a person may have many years' experience in a particular line of work, but may have learned very little from that experience. The amount of experience is therefore not a reliable indicator of learning.
2 *The individual is responsible for his or her own learning.* While others may support, facilitate or encourage learning, ultimately it is only the individual who can make it happen. This means, as we shall see below, that the attitude of the individual towards learning is a key factor (see the discussion below of self-directed learning).

Barriers to learning

There are a variety of ways in which learning can be blocked or halted, and so it is important to be aware of what these are so that they can be avoided, or dealt with as and when they arise. The following list includes some of the most significant barriers to learning, but is not intended to be exhaustive. Indeed, a full list would be a very long one. For present purposes, I shall focus on the following key issues:

○ *Anti-intellectualism.* As mentioned earlier, many practitioners reject the value of theory and prefer to 'stick to practice'. The essential linkages between theory and practice are not appreciated (see Chapter 30), and this stands in the way of learning.

○ *Anxiety.*   A small amount of anxiety can be a spur to learning by 'keeping us on our toes'. However, where the degree of anxiety becomes excessive, learning is held back. This is because, in a situation of high anxiety, the focus moves from learning to concentrating on self-protection. That is, the threat associated with anxiety becomes all-important and leaves little or no room for learning.

○ *Lack of confidence.*   A defeatist attitude which says 'I can't do that' easily becomes a self-fulfilling prophecy. Such a negative, unconfident attitude is very counterproductive in terms of producing positive practice outcomes. Similarly, such attitudes are counterproductive in terms of positive learning outcomes. Maximizing learning therefore depends on having a confident attitude.

○ *Stress.*   When work or other pressures reach the point that they become harmful, the stress involved in this can make clear thinking difficult and make us lose sight of what is going on around us. When this occurs, learning opportunities very much take a back seat. At times of stress we tend to become preoccupied, and this has the effect of making us less open to new learning.

When pathways to learning are blocked by these or other obstacles, considerable frustration can arise, and this in turn can make the possibility of learning even more remote.

Strategies for learning

Being aware of potential barriers to learning and adopting a proactive approach towards them is, in itself, a primary strategy for promoting learning. However, there are also a number of other strategies that are worth considering in order to maximize the potential for CPD:

○ *Training courses.*   This is perhaps the most obvious strategy. However, attending a training course is only one part of a learning process and may have little effect on subsequent practice if the learning points are not applied and consolidated in the work environment (Thompson, 2006). The learning potential of a training course can be enhanced by prior preparation, a proactive approach to learning during the course and a reflective approach after the course.

○ *Supervision.*   The important role of supervision has already been emphasized in Chapter 7. Effective supervision can make a major contribution to CPD. Professional practice issues explored in supervision can extend the knowledge base, improve skills and boost confidence.

○ *Evaluation and review.*   By reviewing and/or evaluating our work, we can learn what worked and what did not (see Chapter 27). In particular, there is much to be learned from looking at *why* particular actions were successful or unsuccessful. Regularly reviewing and evaluating practice is therefore not only a sound foundation for good practice, it is also an excellent platform from which to do a great deal of learning.

○ *Feedback.*   Evaluation and review may explicitly involve feedback, as may supervision. However, feedback also tends to occur at other times, sometimes spontaneously, sometimes when specifically asked for. Such feedback provides valuable opportunities for learning, whether the feedback is critical or complimentary.

○ *Student supervision.*   As any experienced educationalist will confirm, a teaching role also involves learning. By being involved in the training of students, trainees or less experienced staff, we can derive benefits for our own professional development. Students often bring a fresh perspective, and an enthusiasm for learning that is quite refreshing, if not contagious.

○ *Secondments.*   After a period of time in one job, it can be very beneficial to spend a short time in another job on a temporary basis. This type of job switch or 'secondment' can generate a number of learning opportunities and provide fertile ground for professional development. Such secondments can be difficult to arrange, but are certainly worth pursuing whenever possibilities present themselves.

○ *Research.*   Occasionally opportunities arise to undertake, or contribute to, small-scale research. The chance to examine an aspect of people work in a systematic way, with some degree of rigour, can bring a number of benefits in terms of professional development. Not least amongst these is the motivation to enter the world of ideas and explore the linkages between theory and practice.

○ *Reading.*   People work requires a great deal of learning from actual experience, but this is not to say that such learning cannot be enhanced, extended and complemented by reading. Many books and journals are written in a style that makes it difficult to follow the arguments that are being presented. However, we should not allow this to discourage us from using the written word as an invaluable source of opportunities for learning.

○ *E-learning courses.*   There is now a growing range of e-learning courses available. They are not necessarily a direct substitute for conventional training courses, but they can make an important contribution to learning in their own right.

○ *Online learning communities.*   This is a relatively new idea. It involves being part of a supportive group of people working together online to help each other learn, with some degree of tutorial support from the programme leader plus an online library of learning resources and related facilities (such as an e-portfolio to record and consolidate learning). It is not a course as such, with a beginning a middle and an end, but rather an ongoing learning forum based on principles of reflective practice and self-directed learning.

Practice focus 9.2

When James began his training course, he was full of enthusiasm and was looking forward to studying. However, he was very soon to become disheartened. He found many of the items on the 'Recommended Reading' list were very difficult to understand. This affected his confidence, as he felt that his difficulty confirmed that he was not intelligent enough to do the course. However, after discussing his concerns with a tutor, James felt better to have discovered that many students struggle in adapting to the style of writing often adopted by academic writers. He went back to the books with a renewed confidence, and a determination not to allow academic writing styles to stand in the way of his learning.

These, then, are some of the strategies that can be used for learning within the broader framework of promoting continuous professional development. Identifying these strategies can help to get CPD on the agenda. However, no strategy will be of any value if it is not underpinned by a commitment to CPD in the first place. An important idea here is that of 'self-directed learning'. Traditional approaches to learning are characterized by a process in which the 'teacher' (tutor, trainer, course committee) defines what is to be learned and how it is to be learned. What is likely to work much more effectively, especially in a context of professional learning, is where the learner is helped to work out for him- or herself what needs to be learned and how best to learn it. An individualized approach, with the learner in the driving seat, is likely to be far more successful than a blanket approach geared towards a wide range of learners with widely different needs, preferences, priorities, approaches and circumstances.

Conclusion

Some people may see learning as a threat, as it involves being open to new ideas and experiences, and being prepared to let go of previously cherished taken-for-granted beliefs. It is also often the case that an acceptance of learning is seen as a sign of weakness, an acknowledgement that there is a deficit that needs to be made up. This negative and defensive view of learning is an unnecessary barrier to professional development, and could so easily pave the way for a form of routinized, uncritical practice.

A commitment to CPD and a willingness to take responsibility for one's own learning are important aspects of personal effectiveness in their own right. In addition, they can also be seen as important in support of the other aspects of personal effectiveness – self-awareness, stress management and so on. CPD is therefore a basic element in developing and sustaining high standards of practice.

Exercise 9

Developing Learning

A useful way of promoting your own development is to use an 'Action Plan for Learning' along the lines of the example below. In the left-hand column, list your current priorities in terms of learning. On the right-hand side, write down some possible ways of addressing these. You might find it helpful to undertake this jointly with a colleague or your line manager.

Action Plan for Learning

ISSUES TO BE ADDRESSED   STRATEGIES FOR ADDRESSING THEM

chapter 10

Being realistic and resilient

Introduction

Working with people is a demanding enterprise. There is therefore a very real danger that some workers will find the work so overwhelming that they retreat into an attitude of cynicism or defeatism. This sort of pessimistic outlook is not helpful, either for the people we are seeking to help, for ourselves, or for our employing organizations. By the same token, approaching the work with rose-tinted spectacles that see only the positives and neglect the significant challenges and dangers involved in the work is woefully inadequate. What is needed, then, is a balance between the two extremes, and this is what in this chapter I shall be referring to as 'realism'.

This chapter also focuses on resilience, the ability to bounce back from adversity. This topic is included because: (i) such an ability is a very useful basis for working effectively with people and their problems; and (ii) we will struggle to achieve a balanced realism if we are not able to recover from the negative experiences we will inevitably encounter from time to time.

I begin by looking at the benefits of positive psychology, before also identifying its limitations and the need for a more balanced approach rooted in resilience.

Positive psychology

In recent years, there has been a significant growth of interest in a form of psychology known as 'positive psychology'. It is based on a commitment to the value of optimism as an outlook on life. It has grown out of the work of Martin Seligman, an American psychologist who first wrote about learned helplessness (Seligman, 1975), but later extended his work to include a focus on optimism (Seligman, 2006).

When Seligman wrote his classic text on learned helplessness, the dominant thinking in psychology at that time was behaviourism. It emphasized the importance of understanding human behaviour as being conditioned by particular stimuli – that is, an individual's behaviour could be understood as being a learned response to a particular stimulus or set of stimuli. When Seligman's research showed that behaviour could also be strongly influenced by a person's attitude, rather than simply behavioural stimuli, this heralded the beginning of a major critique of the dominance of behaviourist thinking, because it meant that, if Seligman's research was to be believed, there was more to understanding behaviour than the presenting stimuli. To a non-specialist, this would appear to represent a minor change of focus, but in reality, Seligman's challenge to the dominant orthodoxy was very significant indeed, as it undermined the basic foundation of behaviourist psychology.

Seligman's research had introduced the notion of 'learned helplessness'. This was based on research he carried out which showed that, in circumstances where the stimuli experimental subjects were exposed to did not lead to a specific outcome, they quickly learned to give up. That is, when the experimenters arranged the circumstances in such a way that the actions of the animals involved made no difference as to whether they were rewarded or 'punished', the test subjects simply gave up trying. They abandoned any hope of being able to influence the outcome and simply became resigned to being helpless. This approach was strongly criticized by the behaviourist thinkers of the time because it undermined their basic tenet that all behaviour stems from a conditioned response to environmental stimuli. In effect, Seligman's research laid the foundations for what has come to be known as 'cognitive behavioural work'. This is because his approach showed that it is not purely environmental stimuli that produce behaviour; there are also 'cognitions' – that is, beliefs and attitudes – that shape people's behaviour.

This was the beginning of the development of cognitive behavioural therapy, with an emphasis on 'core beliefs'. A core belief is a strongly held view about oneself or an aspect of one's life. For example, whether a person has high or low self-esteem will depend on their core belief about how worthy they are. If someone has a fundamental belief that they are not worthy, then they will have low self-esteem (a low sense of self-worth) and this can be a significant factor in terms of shaping future behaviour. To take this thinking a step further, according to the cognitive behavioural way of thinking, when someone becomes depressed, this will be in large part because of core beliefs that person has about him- or herself – for example in relation to self-esteem and related matters.

Seligman was particularly interested in the significance of such factors for the problem of depression. From his work, there developed the notion of positive psychology, the idea that if people have a core belief which is fundamentally optimistic, they will have more success in life. He provides a great deal of research evidence to support his view (Seligman, 2006). He sees pessimism, by contrast, as a significant problem, particularly as it can relate to depression. He writes of the significance of 'explanatory styles', which are characteristic ways of making sense (developing a cognition) of our experiences as we encounter them. He developed the idea that where three Ps are present, there is a greater risk of depression:

○ *Permanence.* This refers to the tendency to regard difficult or negative circumstances as permanent. For example, if somebody experiences a disappointment, they may rationalize this by saying to themselves: 'I am always unlucky', rather than see this as a specific temporary example of bad luck.
○ *Pervasiveness.* While permanence refers to an overgeneralization in terms of time, pervasiveness refers to an overgeneralization in terms of space. That is, a person who has a pessimistic outlook is likely to see bad luck and difficult circumstances in a much broader perspective than is actually the case. For example, someone who shows lack of skill in a particular area may overgeneralize by saying something like: 'I'm a very unskilled person', without recognizing that they have perhaps significant skills in other areas.
○ *Personalization.* This refers to situations where people individualize the circumstances that relate to a wider group. For example, if a member of a team in a particular sporting context should experience defeat, they may explain this as an individual failing, rather than see it as a matter for the whole team: 'I let the side down.'

Where all three of these Ps are present, then the risk of depression is significantly higher than would otherwise be the case.

Practice focus 10.1

Patryk had been suffering from depression for over three years and the medication he had been prescribed had done no good whatsoever. In fact, it had made the situation worse because of the side-effects of the drugs and his resentment at having to rely on what he saw as the crutch of drug treatment. This reinforced his sense of helplessness. However, when he had a new GP, he was pleased that a referral was made for him to receive cognitive behavioural therapy (CBT). He looked it up on the internet and, although this made him aware that there were doubts about its long-term effectiveness, he was pleased to see that the research indicated that it was often very effective in the short term at least. He realized that the help it could give him might be enough for him to come off the medication, and that in itself would be a very positive step forward.

The therapeutic help CBT offered him made such a big difference by helping him realize that he had such a negative outlook, such a strong tendency to interpret events in negative ways (reflecting the three Ps). By beginning to change his outlook on these matters, he was beginning to see light at the end of the tunnel. He was intelligent enough to know it would not be a magic cure, but it gave him hope that he would be able to leave the anti-depressants behind and make a fresh start.

On this basis, Seligman argues the case for a positive psychology, one premised on optimism rather than pessimism. He and his fellow travellers do not reject the value of pessimism altogether. They do acknowledge that it has some value: 'The balance sheet seems to come out heavily on the side of optimism, but there are times and places where we need our pessimism' (Seligman, 2006, p. 113). Segerstrom, another proponent of positive psychology, explains this more fully:

> believing you're a good driver could lead you to drive faster and without a seat belt; believing you're unlikely to have a heart attack could make you think you don't need to exercise or watch what you eat; and believing you're unlikely to become an addict could lead you to experiment with potentially addictive drugs.
>
> More alarming, people are most optimistic about events that can be controlled by their own behaviour, such as getting venereal disease, diabetes or sunstroke. These problems can be averted by practising safe sex, eating a good diet, exercising and staying out of the sun. What if optimistic beliefs about the likelihood that you will have these problems make you careless? What if your feelings of invulnerability to sunstroke make you insensible to signs that you're getting overheated and dehydrated? This would lead to a rather ironic consensus of optimism: optimism makes you more likely to experience exactly the kinds of problems that you could have avoided.
>
> (2006, p. 132)

However, despite these limitations to an exclusively optimistic outlook, positive psychology none the less advocates an emphasis on optimism, rather than a balanced approach to the mix of positives and negatives that characterizes human experience.

Problems with positive psychology

As we have seen, positive psychology is premised on the significance of optimism. However, focusing on optimism is not entirely unproblematic. For one thing, optimism does not take account of the significance of scarcity – that is, optimism is based on a philosophy of plenty. One common criticism of positive psychology, therefore, is that it is a philosophy of rich western people and is not appropriate in conditions of poverty and scarcity. For example, it ignores the fact that depression is far more common amongst women and poor people than is the case for the general population. James makes important comment about this overemphasis on optimism in discussing the problems associated with an undue emphasis in our society on building up material wealth:

> This attempt to misinterpret our natural state as optimistic is attractive ... because it encourages us to be the happy clappy, consumerism-obsessed,

unquestioning dupes of corporations and politicians. It has allowed the growth of a whole industry (books, therapies, management consultancy, sports psychologists) propounding positive psychology, pathologizing all of the negativity which might lead people to question either their upbringing or their society.

(2008, p. 197)

Positive psychology can therefore be seen to be sociologically and politically naive (Ehrenreich, 2009).

An overemphasis on optimism can also be seen to be problematic, in so far as it ignores the significance of sadness as a therapeutic process – for example, the positive role of mourning after a major loss. That is, when somebody is grieving, sadness plays an important role in releasing pent-up emotions ('catharsis', to use the technical term), and so focusing on positives is not necessarily always a good thing.

Linked to this is the idea, deriving from the work of the German philosopher, Friedrich Nietzsche, that what does not kill us makes us stronger, or at least has the potential to do so (Kaufmann, 2013). This is closely linked with ideas of transformational grief and post-traumatic growth. The former refers to situations in which experiencing a major loss can be extremely painful, but can lead to positive developments in our lives. For example, we can grow and become better people as the result of the impact of a major loss. The latter refers to a similar type of situation in which a trauma may produce a very painful and difficult reaction, but the result of this situation is positive in the medium to long run in terms of bringing about profound positive changes to our life. For example, someone who was going through their life without really appreciating the positives could, as a result of a trauma, become very appreciative of what the world has to offer. Post-traumatic growth also often has the effect of helping people develop more intimate and meaningful relationships (Thompson, 2012b).

An overemphasis on optimism can also lead to the danger of denying loss and pain as significant factors in human existence. If we are not equipped for these matters because we pretend they do not exist, by 'focusing on the positive', then we are less likely to be in a strong position to cope with those challenges when they arise in our lives. There is also the related danger that we will neglect those who are in distress – for example, by dismissing such matters as morbid and not in tune with our 'optimistic' outlook, preferring instead to look on the bright side. Positive psychology, then, is an approach that has some benefits in terms of bringing understanding but also has significant limitations. James again offers helpful comment:

form as truthful and accurate an assessment as possible of yourself and your society, rather than living in a rose-tinted bubble of positive illusions.

Unless you make an unsparing diagnosis of yourself and your situation, you will be incapable of changing them for the better. Warding off depression with dishonest or fantastical assessments will not build you a solid platform from which to progress.

(2007, p. 153)

Realism

Is the glass half empty or is it half full? From what I shall refer to as a 'realist' point of view, the answer is that it is *both* half empty *and* half full. Life is a mixture of great joy and great sadness, of hope and despair. Finding the balance of realism, that is, the balance between positives and negatives, can be a very difficult one to succeed in, but it is a very worthwhile process none the less. Focusing simply on either optimism or pessimism is problematic, because it relies on an essentialist understanding. That is, it assumes that individuals have an underlying 'essence' or nature, a fixed way of being, rather than appreciating that human beings are 'in flux' – constantly changing and developing in response to personal and social circumstances. A much more sophisticated approach to such matters is called for, and it is my belief that an emphasis on realism rather than optimism is the way forward.

'Realism' is a term that is used in different ways in different contexts. I am using it here in the sense of adopting a balanced approach to the positives and negatives of life. In practical terms, being realistic means:

○ *Not being pessimistic.* By this I mean not distorting reality in a way that focuses only on the negatives. That is, not seeing negatives where they do not exist or being unduly negative about situations that are for the most part a mixture of positives and negatives.
○ *Not being naively optimistic.* This means not trying to see the world through rose-tinted spectacles, as this is also a distortion of reality. It will leave us ill-equipped for dealing with the very real challenges of human existence.
○ *Weighing up risks and opportunities.* This involves being able to capitalize on the positives of our lives while being tuned in to the dangers, so that we are in a strong position to avoid them and, where necessary, to deal with them when they do arise.
○ *Having self-belief.* This is a matter of not simply looking on the bright side of life, but having confidence in ourselves to be able to deal with whatever life throws at us, positive or negative.

> **Practice focus 10.2**
>
> Pam had always adopted an attitude of 'looking on the bright side' and would avoid anything she saw as 'morbid'. However, when her husband, Len, was killed in a car accident, her whole world was turned upside down. She became very depressed for quite a while, constantly focusing on what she had lost and on how much she loved Len. However, over time, she slowly began to come out of her depression and begin to face up to life again. She tried to go back to her happy-go-lucky former ways, but it all felt so false now. How could she 'look on the bright side'? However, what she did come to realize was that she had a new-found maturity. Having lost Len she was very aware of the blessings she still had, but she was also aware that it does not pay to be naive about the pain and suffering that are also part of people's lives. Ironically, such a devastating blow as the loss of her husband had helped her grow as a person. She felt better equipped to cope with life's challenges without trying to brush them under the carpet and realized that the whole experience – extremely painful though it was – had made her more resilient.

Figure 10.1 The balance of realism

Resilience

Being resilient is a matter of being able to bounce back from adversity, to pick ourselves up after we have been knocked down in some way. And, of course, working with people means that we will be 'knocked down', metaphorically speaking, from time to time. Some people will be harmed by such experiences, some will get right up again and get back to normal fairly quickly, but yet others will not only get back up, but also learn and grow from the experience.

In Chapter 29 we will discuss the significance of trauma. A traumatic experience is one that harms us in some way, leaves a psychological wound. Those experiences that we do not bounce back from have the potential to be traumatic and therefore potentially highly problematic. The experiences that we learn and grow from are examples of the post-traumatic growth we discussed earlier – those situations that can be extremely painful and difficult, but which can none the less provide important opportunities for benefitting in some way from coping with the challenges encountered.

Resilience can therefore be understood as picking ourselves up after a major challenge has hit us hard in some way and, where possible, going beyond that to achieve post-traumatic growth. The notion of resilience is doubly important, in so far as: (i) it is a firm foundation for our own practice; and (ii) there is much to be gained from using our people skills to help other people build up their resilience over time.

Conclusion

People workers have two main sets of challenges to deal with: dealing with our own problems and challenges (our *personal* challenges) and dealing with other people's (our *professional* challenges). Being realistic can be helpful on both counts. It can ensure that we do not try to live our lives based on a delusion – whether that be an optimistic delusion ('life is a bed of roses') or a pessimistic one ('life is nothing but pain and suffering'). It can also help us to assist others whose lives may be blighted by such delusions. It gives us the opportunity to develop over time the skills we need for achieving such a balance and helping other people do so. Realism therefore offers the benefits of a balanced approach to life, and so, as a self-management skill, being realistic should be an important part of every people worker's repertoire of skills. Realism is also an important basis for developing resilience, strengthening our ability to recover from negative experiences and regain our sense of balance.

Changing deeply ingrained habits – whether our tendency is towards an optimism that risks neglecting life's challenges or towards a pessimism that blinds us to life's joys and rewards – is not easy, but the rewards for developing realism are quite significant. A realistic approach affords a much stronger basis for tackling the very significant challenges we encounter in the people professions and for developing the resilience that will stand us in such good stead.

Exercise 10

Finding the Balance

Think about where you stand on the continuum between optimism on the one extreme and pessimism on the other. What changes might you need to make to get as close as you can to the middle ground of realism? What steps might you need to take? Who can you trust to help and support you? Which parts do you feel are likely to be the most difficult? What can you do about rising to these challenges?

To help you with this you might want to consider what benefits you would gain by being more 'realistic'. Use the space below to make some notes.

part **II**

Interaction skills

Chapters

Introduction to Part II

Working with people inevitably involves interaction, the coming together of two or more people, sometimes with common aims, sometimes with conflicting ones. These interactions can be the focal point of people work, crucial determinants of success or failure. It is therefore important that we explore the range of processes and skills that have a bearing on interpersonal interactions in the context of people work.

We begin by considering human diversity, the variety of backgrounds that people bring with them to interactions. From this we move on to consider communication skills. These are divided into three categories: verbal, nonverbal and written. Although these are covered in separate chapters, they are, of course, closely related to one another.

Communication is also a major theme in the ensuing chapter (15) where interviewing is the topic under consideration – and, indeed, communication is also very relevant in Chapter 16 where we examine the importance of influencing skills. This prepares the way for a discussion in Chapter 17 of leadership, an important topic that involves influencing not only individual people, but also team and organizational cultures that can stand in the way of progress. In Chapter 18 the focus is on the emotional dimension of people work, the ways in which feelings can affect interactions. Next, we examine issues relating to handling conflict. This includes the skills involved in negotiation and handling aggression. These are essential skills in terms of both helping others and protecting ourselves from harm. Finally, in Chapter 20 we see what is involved in working effectively across professional boundaries.

It is often through interpersonal interactions that change takes place, that problems are solved and the quality of life improved. Interactions are therefore at the heart of people work, and so the skills and knowledge involved are well worth the investment of time and effort needed to develop them. This part of the book is designed to take you in the right direction, to help you move forward in a positive and constructive way through the range of challenges that characterize work in the people professions.

chapter **11**

Valuing diversity

Introduction

When we interact with other people, we do not start from a neutral standpoint. We bring with us a whole range of values, beliefs and assumptions. These are linked to the person we are, the range of social factors that influence and shape identity (see Chapter 1). For example, the way I relate to other people will owe much to my gender, my ethnic group, my class background and so on. These factors, in turn, will interact significantly with the equivalent factors for the persons concerned. That is, the gender, class and so on of the other people involved will also be significant in influencing the outcome of the interactions.

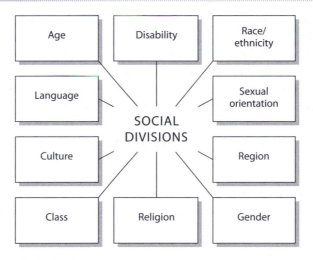

Figure 11.1   Social divisions
(Source: Thompson, Murphy and Stradling, 1994)

This presents a very complex picture in terms of the possible mix of interlinking factors. Man/woman, black/white, young/old are just some of the variables that play a part in shaping social interactions. Each individual is a member of a variety of social groups and categories (gender, class, ethnic group and so on), and these have a significant bearing on our experience. It is often on the basis of such social groups that people are subject to discrimination and oppression. There is no end to the ways in which people can be discriminated against or oppressed. You do not have to be a member of a particular social group to experience the negative effects of prejudice and discrimination. However, it would be naive not to recognize that certain groups in society are exposed to a disproportionate amount of negative attention – for example, women and black, disabled or older people.

In the interactions between individuals and groups, there is therefore an ever-present danger of certain people being disadvantaged in the process. In this way, diversity (the differences between people) is a potential source of discrimination and oppression.

Being different from the mainstream can so easily be equated with being inferior, and so there is a need to respond positively to diversity, to value differences and be sensitive to the dangers of discrimination. This chapter therefore explores some of the key issues in relation to valuing diversity.

First, we need to be clear why a sensitivity to diversity is important. Basically, the need to be sensitive to, and positive about, diversity is crucial because an approach that ignores such issues runs the risk of:

○ *Alienating people.* Making members of certain groups feel that they do not belong in society.
○ *'Invalidating' people.* Creating the feeling that one's views, perspective or experience are not valid because they differ from the mainstream.
○ *Missing key issues.* Not noticing crucial factors because we are not sensitive to how significant they are for the person(s) concerned.
○ *Becoming part of the problem.* Failing to challenge discrimination and oppression, and thereby playing a part in their continuance (Thompson, 2012c).

There are, then, strong reasons why the skills involved in dealing with diversity should be high on the agenda.

Aspects of diversity

Diversity relates to the fact that we are all unique individuals. However, diversity also relates to the fact that society is made up of various groups, to which power, influence and opportunities are unequally allocated. Equality of opportunity (or its absence) owes much to the ways in which society is structured – its social divisions. I shall therefore comment on the major social divisions and some of their implications for people work.

Class

Class is a term used to describe a person's socioeconomic position in society and is therefore closely linked to issues of income, wealth and status. Giddens explains class in the following terms:

> We can define class as a large-scale grouping of people who share common economic resources, which strongly influence the types of lifestyle they are able to lead. Ownership of wealth, together with occupation, are the chief bases of class differences.
>
> (2006, p. 300)

Unfortunately, there is a great deal of prejudice associated with class. For example, working-class people are often assumed to be less capable or intelligent than their middle-class counterparts. Such a view fails to take into account a range of social factors (the education system, for example) that stack the odds in favour of certain groups. The negative view of working-class people is therefore simplistic. It reduces a complex social issue to a simple matter of individual capabilities.

In working with people from different class backgrounds, it is important not to make assumptions based on class stereotypes. For example, it is dangerous to assume that a working-class person is likely to be less responsive to counselling and better suited to a directive approach. The aim of empowering people should not be dependent on a person's class background.

A further important issue with regard to class is the need to avoid the class differences between worker and client being emphasized by mannerisms, style of speech or body language (see Chapter 13). This does not mean that middle-class workers should pretend to be what they are not. But, it does mean that we need to be aware of those class characteristics that may act as a barrier to positive interpersonal relations.

Finally, in relation to class, a further point to be recognized is the danger of collusion. This can occur when worker and client share a common class background. For example, a middle-class health visitor may be less sensitive to the possibility of child abuse when working with middle-class families, thereby both reflecting and reinforcing the stereotypical assumption that child abuse is predominantly a working-class problem.

Race and culture

The UK shares with the majority of western societies a status as a multicultural society. That is, the overall population is composed of a wide variety of ethnic groups, representing a range of cultures, religions and languages. The common tendency to see the UK as a white homogeneous nation is a gross distortion and oversimplification of the actual situation. It is also a dangerous view, in so far as it:

○ devalues minority cultures;
○ disregards significant aspects of people's lives;
○ acts as a platform for racist attitudes and actions; and
○ stands as a barrier to good practice in people work.

Practice therefore needs to be *ethnically sensitive*. That is, it needs to address questions of cultural values, practices and needs.

However, ethnically sensitive practice is not enough on its own. Practice also needs to be *anti-racist*. This is because ethnic differences become confused with assumed biological differences on the grounds of 'race'. In particular, superficial differences such as skin colour are often misinterpreted as indicators of profound biological differences.

Practice focus 11.1

Helen had often worked with clients from ethnic minorities and recognized the importance of taking into account cultural beliefs and practices. However, it was only when she began to work with the Khan family that she began to appreciate the significance of racism as a dimension of their experience. She learned of the abuse and harassment that members of the family had been subjected to. She heard about the many examples of discrimination that had become so commonplace for the family. That particular night, after her first discussions with the family, she found it difficult to sleep – she kept thinking back to the appalling examples of racism that she had heard about that day. She realized that, in future, she would have to be far more aware of the implications of racism for black clients than she had ever been before.

Such assumed biological differences are then used to argue that some 'races' are inferior to others. That is, cultural *difference* becomes translated into biological *inferiority*, and racism is thereby introduced. Consequently, people workers have to be very mindful of the existence of racism and the ways in which the celebration of human diversity gets lost in a destructive mythology of racial inferiority. Sivanandan, in addressing a predominantly white audience, captures this well in the following passage:

> Now there is nothing wrong about learning about other cultures but it must be said that to learn about other cultures is not to learn about the racism of your own. If we are going to compare our cultures objectively we must first know the racism of our own. Unless you are mindful of the racial superiority inculcated in you by 500 years of colonisation and slavery you cannot come to our cultures objectively.

(1991, p. 41)

Ethnically sensitive practice is a *necessary* condition for good practice, but it is not a sufficient condition. Good practice must also be anti-racist (see Figure 11.2).

Figure 11.2   Ethnically sensitive and anti-racist practice

Gender

The development of the Women's Movement has helped to bring to our attention the unequal distribution of power and life chances between men and women. Interactions between men and women are thus strongly influenced by the power differences that are brought to bear. An uncritical approach to gender is therefore likely to lead to a number of problems:

○ Women's needs are likely to be overlooked.
○ Male dominance will be reinforced and legitimated.
○ Women's problems will be constructed in men's terms.
○ Stereotypical gender expectations will not be challenged.
○ Gender-related problems (depression or sexual abuse, for example) may pass unnoticed.

The notion that 'It's a man's world' is a significant and powerful one. And, of course, it will remain 'a man's world' unless the sexism inherent in society (including the people professions) is challenged and undermined.

There are also problems for men associated with sexism – problems arising from rigid stereotypes concerning how men are expected to think, feel and act (Lawler, 2008). This can be particularly problematic at certain times; for example, when a bereavement is experienced (Riches, 2002). There is, therefore, a pressing need for the significance of gender to be fully recognized and to be incorporated within the theory base that informs people work.

Women and men interact within a context of gender inequality. This inequality can be extremely significant in terms of:

○ creating barriers to positive interactions;
○ creating the potential for abuse and oppression;

○ exacerbating and/or reinforcing existing problems (for example, low self-esteem); and
○ supporting or reinforcing other forms of inequality.

It is therefore essential that people workers be sensitive to the significant role of gender.

Sexual orientation

Good practice in the people professions is premised on a non-judgemental approach. That is, people should be treated with dignity, respect and fairness without any judgement being made as to their social worth. This is particularly important with regard to a person's sexual orientation in view of the widespread prejudice against gay men, lesbians and bisexual or transsexual people.

It is important that our interactions with people are not beset with problems of discrimination and prejudice relating to sexual identity. Such discrimination has now come to be known as 'heterosexism' and is closely linked to sexism, in so far as it hinges, to a large extent, on stereotypical gender expectations.

As with other forms of discrimination, biology plays a significant role in that it is used as a justification for unequal treatment. If sexuality is seen purely or primarily in biological terms, then heterosexuality is deemed to be natural and 'normal', thereby defining homosexuality as unnatural or 'abnormal'. By ignoring or marginalizing the social and psychological dimensions of sexuality, a distorted view of sexual orientation is presented. And this distorted view mobilizes considerable prejudice and discrimination, which contributes to making gay men, lesbians, bisexual and transsexual people a stigmatized and oppressed group.

In working with people, the issue of sexual orientation can therefore be seen to be a very significant one. In view of this, it is necessary to avoid falling into the trap of seeing sexuality in narrow biological terms, for the following reasons:

○ It legitimates oppression by seeing a *different* sexual orientation as a problem, an illness to be cured. Indeed, for many years homosexuality was mistakenly defined as a psychiatric disorder.
○ It creates unnecessary barriers between worker and client. Prejudice stands in the way of effective interpersonal interactions.
○ It reinforces gender stereotypes and thereby contributes to the persistence of sexism as a form of oppression.

Good practice across the people professions is therefore premised on the need to avoid falling into the pseudobiological trap of heterosexism.

Age

Ageism is a term that is generally applied to discrimination against older people, although it is sometimes used to refer to discrimination against children (Sue Thompson, 2005). For present purposes I shall focus on older people.

Ageism can be seen to be characterized by a number of destructive forces:

○ *Marginalization.* Older people and their needs are rarely seen as a priority or a central concern. Older people tend to be pushed to the margins of society.
○ *Dehumanization.* Older people are often represented as 'past it', and of little use to society. They are seen as somehow less than human and treated as if their needs and rights are less valid than other people's.
○ *Infantilization.* Older people tend to be treated like children much of the time. This is reflected in the tendency to use first names without checking that this is acceptable to the person concerned.

In working with older members of our society, then, we need to be careful that we are not following the well-worn path of demeaning older people by allowing ageist stereotypes and assumptions to distort our interactions with them. In particular, we need to:

○ Avoid ageist language and patronizing terminology ('old dear').
○ Allow and encourage older people to participate in decision making.
○ Avoid seeing old age in unduly negative terms. The extent of illness, disability and related problems is generally greatly exaggerated.
○ Focus on empowerment, not dependency. It is important to ensure we do not allow the ageist stereotype of dependency to distract us from seeing possibilities for empowerment.
○ Value the experience of older people and recognize that they have not only needs but also a great deal to offer.

Although these issues apply specifically to older people as a socially disadvantaged group, there is a more general point to be made. That is, at all times we should seek to ensure that age discrimination does not act as a barrier to positive interaction with people of any age group.

Practice focus 11.2

Joan had worked with older people for a number of years in a variety of residential settings. She had always prided herself on how well she treated the people she cared for. However, after attending a workshop on anti-ageist practice, she became conscious that, in many ways, she had been contributing to ageism without realizing that she was doing so. In particular, she acknowledged that she had tended to concentrate on the basic physical needs of residents and had not considered issues of rights or choice.

(Source: Thompson 1995)

Disability

Disability is traditionally seen as a medical matter, a physical impairment that stands in the way of normal social functioning. However, a number of writers (for example, Oliver and Barnes, 2012) have shown this to be too narrow a view. In its place, they propose a social model of disability, one that emphasizes the destructive effects of social attitudes towards disability.

It can therefore be seen that it is the social attitudes that are disabling, rather than the impairment itself. For example, it is not the use of a wheelchair that denies access to certain buildings, but rather the failure/refusal to provide ramps. Failing to recognize the significant role of society in 'constructing' disability also means failing to recognize the discrimination and oppression disabled people experience.

The social model of disability therefore draws our attention to the prevalence of:

○ the tendency for disabled people to be marginalized, dehumanized and patronized (there is a strong parallel here with ageism);
○ a disabling focus on limitations rather than capabilities and potential;
○ a lack of awareness of the physical and attitudinal barriers that prevent disabled people from becoming fully integrated in mainstream society; and
○ a tendency to focus on dependency rather than empowerment (another parallel with ageism).

In working with disabled people, then, it is necessary to recognize the social roots of disability so that we can avoid:

○ allowing negative stereotypes to mar interpersonal interactions;
○ reinforcing or exacerbating the social disadvantages associated with disability; and
○ disempowering disabled people.

People workers need to be sensitive to the fact that disability acts as a form of social oppression, and our practice therefore needs to be geared towards challenging such oppression, rather than reinforcing it.

These, then, are some of the major aspects of diversity. I have presented them individually for ease of explanation, although it needs to be remembered that they do not occur in isolation. They intertwine in various combinations to act as dimensions of each individual's experience. In order to understand, and work with, the individual, we need to understand the aspects of diversity that apply to him or her. That is, we need to appreciate the social location of the individual, where and how he or she fits into society, in terms of both the social divisions highlighted here and any other such division – regional, urban/rural, educational background, intelligence and so on.

Affirming diversity

The picture I have sketched out in this chapter is one of considerable human diversity in which dignity and social worth are threatened by the dominance of mainstream ideas and attitudes that leave little room for variation from an assumed norm. These ideas are so powerful that they can make people feel guilty, inferior or inadequate for being different from the mainstream. In this way, the oppression becomes internalized, and this, in itself, contributes to the continuation of the status quo.

It is essential then that, as people workers, we are sensitive to the significance of diversity, and the inequalities that arise due to a failure to respect that diversity. This sensitivity does not arise overnight and needs to be carefully nurtured over an extended period of time. Each of us must take responsibility for developing our own awareness of these issues, but the following pointers can at least play a part in the process:

○ *Be wary of stereotypes.* We need to respond to the unique individual, not the oversimplified stereotype. This involves undertaking a thorough assessment in place of relying on assumptions (see Chapter 23).
○ *Take steps to learn about other perspectives, other life experiences.* This will help you to appreciate, for example, the values, beliefs and practices of cultures other than your own (see the 'Further learning' section at the end of the book).
○ *Focus on dignity.* This is an important concept that helps to ensure that people's rights, values and beliefs are respected and the individual is valued in his or her own right.
○ *Consider your own power.* In dealing with people from less powerful groups, it is important to understand the extent of your own power and influence. We can so easily take these for granted and fail to appreciate the impact we have on others.
○ *Review your practice.* If we are not careful, practice can become routine and uncritical, and thereby lose its sensitivity. By reviewing practice from

time to time, we can help to maintain a critical and sensitive edge (see Chapter 27).

○ *Ask for feedback.* By asking for feedback (from clients and colleagues, for example), we can monitor the effectiveness of our practice by matching the perceptions of others against our own. This helps to sharpen our awareness of other people's perspectives.

○ *Seek training.* The issues outlined in this chapter are complex and far reaching, and so it would be unrealistic to expect to address them fully simply by reading about them. Opportunities for discussing issues and applying them to practice situations can prove invaluable.

○ *Work together.* These issues affect all people workers, and so there is excellent scope for collaborating with colleagues in taking your learning forward. A supportive collective approach can achieve far more than an individual one (see Chapter 20).

These are not the only steps that can be taken, but they do provide a firm foundation for building a practice that respects, affirms and indeed celebrates, diversity.

These matters are very important underpinnings of people work, and will therefore feature again in later chapters, particularly Chapter 21 where there is a clear and explicit focus on anti-discriminatory practice.

Conclusion

Working with people involves empathy, the ability to appreciate the feelings and circumstances of others even though we do not necessarily share those feelings or circumstances. In order to develop and maintain empathy, we need to be able to understand, and respond appropriately to, the different cultural, linguistic and other aspects of a person's background. That is, we need to be sensitive to the role of diversity in shaping the situations we encounter in our work. In particular, we need to be aware of the ways in which difference comes to be seen in negative terms – we need to understand the discrimination and oppression that many people encounter in their lives.

Exercise 11

Mapping your Social Location

The importance of diversity and 'social location' has been stressed in this chapter. This exercise therefore asks you to consider your own social location, the ways in which human diversity applies to you. Consider your own background in terms of class, race and culture, gender and so on. What significance does each of these have for you? This should help you get a clearer picture of how important these issues are for each individual.

Use the space below to make some notes. You may find it helpful to do this exercise jointly with someone you know well and trust.

chapter **12**

Verbal communication

Introduction

This is the first of three chapters that address communication, a central feature of interaction. The major focus is on the spoken word, although account is also taken of the wider context that affects and influences the process of verbal communication.

Verbal communication can be divided into two elements: what is said and what is heard – the output and the input. I shall discuss each of these in turn before exploring a range of other important issues.

Output

Human speech is a complex matter that has been subject to extensive study and debate over a long period of time. No doubt we still have a lot to learn about language and speech, but there are some basic pointers that can be drawn upon to guide and develop practice in this important aspect of interpersonal interaction. I shall focus on five particular aspects.

Speed

The speed at which a person speaks can be very significant. This can apply in a number of ways, including the following:

○ Fast speech can indicate the emotional state of the speaker and can reflect anger, anxiety or excitement. In general, it indicates a state of arousal and can, in turn, create a state of arousal in the other party.
○ Fast speech can also be a source of annoyance and irritation, and this can prove to be a distraction for the listener, who may find it difficult to concentrate on what is being said.
○ A further problem associated with fast speech is that it can make it difficult for others to follow what is being said, particularly for people with a hearing impairment or whose first language is not the one being spoken.
○ Slow speech can also be an indicator of emotional state. In particular, it tends to reflect low spirits, tiredness or depression.

○ Slow speech can also indicate a degree of caution, defensiveness or a lack of confidence.

○ A further problem associated with slow speech is that it can be interpreted, rightly or wrongly, as a lack of interest in the conversation or in the person with whom you are conversing.

These, then, are some of the issues that relate to the speed at which we speak. They reinforce the point that we should be conscious of the speed at which we are speaking so that we can avoid some of the problems that arise.

Register

'Register' is a term for the degree of formality we use in speech at particular times or in particular circumstances. For example, the level of formality we use in a job interview is likely to be very different from that used when relaxing with friends. That is, we have the ability to 'switch registers' by deciding the appropriate level of formality for the situation in question. It is important that we use and develop this skill, as a failure to bring it to bear can prove problematic in one of (at least) three ways:

1 If we are formal in a situation that calls for a more informal approach, we run the risk of being seen as distant, unfeeling or arrogant. This creates unnecessary barriers to effective interaction, particularly when dealing with certain groups of people, such as children.

2 If we are informal in situations that call for a more formal approach, we are likely to undermine our own credibility. Positive interaction hinges on the ability to influence others (see Chapter 16), and so an inappropriately informal approach can stand in the way of effective communication.

3 An inconsistent use of registers in which a person switches between formality and informality within the same situation can achieve the worst of both worlds. That is, we can both alienate people and undermine our credibility by failing to maintain a level of formality appropriate to the situation.

Practice focus 12.1

When staff arrived each day at the centre where they worked, they wondered how their boss, Tony, would respond to them. This was because Tony had developed a reputation for being very inconsistent in the way he spoke to people. Sometimes, he would be very friendly and informal, but at others, he would be quite formal and distant – and his switches between the two did not appear to be related to any apparent changes in the circumstances. This inconsistency was a considerable source of irritation for staff and was generally interpreted as a lack of security and confidence on Tony's part.

Tone

Tone of voice is again an important indicator of emotional state. It gives important messages about how the person is feeling. It indicates a whole range of feelings: anger, sadness, joy, disappointment and so on. It can also indicate our attitude towards the other person. For example, tone of voice can communicate: approval/disapproval, closeness/distance, friendship/antagonism and so on.

We are often not aware of the tone of voice we are using. For example, at times it may only be when someone says: 'There's no need to shout', that we realize we actually were shouting. This is because there is a close relationship between our emotional state or attitude of mind and the tone of voice we are using. This is an important consideration when we are trying to influence the emotional state of another person. For example, there is little point urging someone to calm down, when our own tone of voice betrays that we are, ourselves, in an agitated state. There are therefore times when it is very important to be aware of tone of voice and to appreciate the significant impact it can have as part of the process of communication.

Pitch

Pitch is part of the 'tune' or intonation of speech, and tends to be described as either high or low. Pitch plays an important role in spoken language. For example, pitch is used to distinguish between a statement and a question. A question tends to end with a rising pitch.

Pitch in particular, and intonation in general, follow very complex rules to indicate subtle differences of meaning and emphasis. Once again, emotional state or attitude can be conveyed by this aspect of speech. For example, flat, unmodulated pitch can reflect a depressed mood, while high or fluctuating pitch can signal a state of arousal such as anger, fear or excitement.

Variations in pitch can be a source of irritation, particularly when speaking to people who are tense or distressed. This may then prove to be a barrier to effective communication.

Loudness

The loudness of a person's speech adds an extra dimension to the message being conveyed. Quiet speech can indicate:

○ a lack of confidence or assertiveness;
○ doubt about the value or validity of what is being communicated;
○ fear or anxiety; and/or
○ a reluctance to engage with the other party.

Similarly, loud speech can indicate:

○ an aggressive or domineering attitude;

○ a lack of sensitivity;
○ fear or anxiety; and/or
○ anger or disapproval.

Speech that is inappropriately quiet or loud can both hamper communication and act as a source of irritation and annoyance (which in turn acts as a barrier to communication).

Input

As communication is a two-way process, we need also to consider the issues relating to receiving communications. I shall explore some of these issues by addressing four particular aspects, as follows.

Listening

Perhaps the most important point to emphasize is that listening is an *active* process. It involves not only hearing what is being said, but also indicating to the other person that we have heard it. This provides reassurance for the speaker and encourages him or her to speak freely and openly. As Moss (2012) puts it: 'Active listening ensures that everything a person is trying to say is fully received and understood by the listener' (p. 15).

Active listening entails:

○ Acknowledging feelings (see Chapter 18); if we do not give a clear message that we are attuned to the other person's feelings, they are far less likely to believe that we are paying them adequate attention.
○ Appropriate use of body language (see Chapter 13); our nonverbal communication is very powerful; there is no point expecting people to feel that they are being listened to if our body language is giving them a message that we are not engaging with them.
○ Resisting the temptation to interrupt; this can be really difficult to do at times, but it is essential that we develop the patience to be able to do this, as interrupting someone totally destroys any sense of being listened to.
○ Paying careful attention to what is being said, to avoid misunderstanding; this can often be difficult too, especially if there are various distractions that can get in the way, but it is very important we make the effort to do this. How can we claim to have listened if we have not paid close enough attention to make sure that we have understood what is being said to us?
○ Avoiding jumping to conclusions or relying on stereotypes; we will struggle to connect with people in meaningful ways if we jump to conclusions or allow stereotyping to get in the way of genuinely understanding what is being said.

○ Reflecting back key points of what has been said, to confirm understanding; this is very simple but very effective in giving people the important message that we are taking them seriously and that we really do want to understand.

Active listening also requires time. That is, it cannot be done in a hurry. If we are to show that we value what is being said to us (and the person who is saying it), then we need to take the time to listen. The skills of listening are therefore intertwined with time management skills. But, if we do take the time to listen, the chances are that we will get that time back in terms of making progress faster, being more effective in getting to where we need to go.

Active listening is indeed a skilled activity and needs to be nurtured and developed with experience.

The environment

The environment in which communication takes place can have a significant bearing on the outcome of the interaction – that is, it can either help or hinder. This applies in a number of ways, including the following:

○ Confidential matters should not be discussed in front of others, and so care needs to be taken to ensure that the setting is appropriate to the nature of the conversation.
○ There are a number of aspects of the physical environment that can act as a distraction. These include: noise disturbances (having to compete with a television set is a common example); being involved in other activities at the same time (especially potentially hazardous ones such as cooking); constant changes in the environment (for example, people coming in and out).
○ The environment should match the formality of the communication. Trying to hold a formal discussion in informal surroundings may prove problematic for all concerned. Conversely, people may feel inhibited in trying to speak informally in a formal setting.
○ Seating arrangements can also be significant (see Chapter 13). For example, sitting at a higher level than the other party can reinforce power differences.

Overall, it is important to ensure that, as far as possible, the environment matches the nature, purpose and style of the communication being undertaken.

Emotional climate

Whilst the physical environment is important in setting the right context for effective communication, so too is the emotional climate. This involves being sensitive to the emotional dimension of your interactions in relation to both yourself (if you are anxious, angry or even elated, this can easily be interpreted as being preoccupied and therefore not listening) and the person or persons you are conversing with.

Our own emotional state can colour our perceptions of what is being said to us, or can even block the communicative process altogether. That is, if we are wrapped up in our own feelings or concerns, we will not be sensitive to the needs and feelings of others. It is generally not difficult for people to notice that we are preoccupied with our own feelings. However, when people are tense or distressed, as is so often the case in people work, they tend to be particularly sensitive to such matters.

Communication can be seriously hampered by a lack of attention to the emotional climate. We therefore need to be responsive to the feelings of those that we work with (colleagues as well as clients) so that the quality and effectiveness of our interactions can be maximized. These are very important issues that are addressed in more detail in Chapter 18.

Discrimination

As we saw in Chapter 11, contemporary society is characterized by discrimination against certain social groups. The power dynamics that underpin this discrimination also have a bearing on interpersonal communication in a variety of ways:

○ Gender is an important aspect of interpersonal dynamics. With regard to spoken language, gender differences play a major part. In particular, male dominance is reflected in language use in ways that reinforce the 'invisibility' of women. Tannen (1992) also points out that men and women use language differently, men focusing on 'status', women on 'connectedness'. This difference in focus can lead to misunderstandings if we are not sensitive to the gender dimension of language.
○ Differences in ethnic background can, in a similar fashion, lead to power differences being reinforced, barriers to effective communication, or both. A 'colour blind' approach that pays no attention to ethnic or racial differences will tend to produce poor or problematic communication.
○ Age differences can also be significant in terms of generational differences in styles of communication. For example, slang terms tend to be associated with particular age groups (see below).
○ The Disabled People's Movement has pointed out, amongst other things, that disabled people are often patronized or even treated like children. It is essential, then, that we do not allow ourselves to fall unthinkingly into such destructive patterns of communication.

Practice focus 12.2

Shama was part of a multidisciplinary team that had developed positive patterns of communication and collaboration. However, she was becoming increasingly aware that the team were having difficulty in communicating effectively with clients from ethnic minorities. She had made a positive contribution to previous discussions to ensure that issues of race and culture were not swept under the carpet by the predominantly white team. After thinking carefully about the situation for quite some time, Shama came to the conclusion that her colleagues were now able to understand cultural issues, but they had not yet learned the skills of using that understanding in practice. She therefore decided that this issue should be identified as a training need.

In listening to other people, we must make sure we actually *hear their voices*, rather than respond to discriminatory stereotypes. We need to respond with an open mind, not one that is closed by unquestioned assumptions.

Promoting effective communication

In addition to these factors, there are many others that need to be considered if the potential for positive communication is to be maximized. The topic is indeed a vast one, and so I shall limit myself to discussion of some of the key issues, beginning with a crucial one.

Clarity

As I shall stress in Chapter 14, a lack of clarity is a common problem associated with written communication. However, it is also a problem that can be seen to apply to verbal communication. There can be no guarantee that our communication will be characterized by clarity. However, there are certain steps that can be taken to minimize the risk of misunderstanding. These include the following:

1 *Don't be vague.* Try to be as precise and explicit as you can. For example, do not say 'I'll be with you in a few minutes' when what you really mean is half or three-quarters of an hour.
2 *Don't be ambiguous.* Try to avoid saying things that could be misinterpreted. For example, in 'Peter's doctor says he is pleased with the outcome', who is pleased, Peter or his doctor?
3 *Avoid slang or colloquialisms.* Slang is often local, and so people from other areas, or from different cultures, may not understand certain words or phrases that you use. Slang is also often 'generational', in so far as people of a different age group may not use or understand certain terms.

4 *Articulate carefully.* This means: do not mumble; speak loudly enough (without shouting); do not speak too fast and do not 'block' speech (for example, by putting your hand over your mouth).

5 *Think first.* Sometimes people cannot express things clearly because they have not got it clear in their minds what they are trying to say. In other words, if you are not sure what you are trying to say, do not be surprised when you fail to get your message across.

Time spent developing the skills of clear verbal communication should prove to be a very worthwhile investment. The benefits of clarity include:

○ fewer misunderstandings;
○ less time wasted;
○ greater self-confidence; and
○ the respect and confidence of others.

Developmental level

This applies primarily to communicating with children, but can, at times, have a bearing on interactions with adults. The basic point is that we need to become attuned to the developmental level of the person or persons with whom we are conversing. This relates to:

○ different levels of understanding between adults and children;
○ differences amongst children according to their level of maturity; and
○ differences amongst adults in terms of intelligence, educational attainment and life experience.

A failure to address these issues can seriously undermine any attempts to form a rapport. Also, it can actually make people's problems worse by alienating them in one of two ways: by speaking at a level above their heads (thereby undermining confidence and self-esteem), or by patronizing them through speaking down to them.

There are no simple formulas to follow in judging the appropriate developmental level, and so we need to become very sensitive to such matters. The question of developmental level is further discussed in Chapter 23.

Oppressive language

The potential of language to reinforce or exacerbate discrimination and oppression is often misunderstood and frequently trivialized. The central point that needs to be emphasized is that language not only reflects reality, but also contributes to creating and maintaining that reality (Thompson,

2011a). Language transmits the dominant ideas that perpetuate inequality and disadvantage (see Figure 12.1). For example, sexist language not only reflects the fact that we live in a sexist society, it also perpetuates sexism by:

o making women's subordinate position in society appear natural and legitimate; and
o socializing children into sexism by the transmission of sexist ideas and assumptions from one generation into the next.

Language is a very powerful vehicle for reinforcing social divisions and cultural expectations. We therefore have to recognize that an uncritical, insensitive use of language can contribute to maintaining current power imbalances in society.

One problem with developing a sensitivity to the discriminatory potential of language is that this complex area is often oversimplified and trivialized. Many people see it as a simple matter of identifying certain 'bad' words (such as 'chairman' or 'blackleg') and trying to avoid them, without necessarily understanding why they should be avoided.

Figure 12.1   Language and discrimination

This approach is characterized by the term 'political correctness'. But this in itself is indicative of the deeper problem. The fact that 'political correctness' has become a term of ridicule illustrates the basic point – the power of language to reinforce existing power structures. Because the development of anti-discriminatory practice has cast light on the oppressive potential of language and the need for linguistic sensitivity, a new term has been coined to decry and undermine the focus on the power of language. The term 'political correctness', then, is not the solution – indeed it is a clear example of the problem.

A simple list of taboo words is no substitute for sensitivity to language. Consider, for example, the term 'domestic'. In general this is an 'innocent', unproblematic term. However, when used as a noun to describe an assault on a woman by her partner, it has the effect of reducing the seriousness of the offence, and may actually be used to justify not taking the matter any further. What this illustrates, then, is that words in themselves are not problematic, but rather the ways in which they are used – and it is to this potential for discrimination that we must become sensitized if we are to ensure that our verbal communications are positive and constructive rather than oppressive (see Figure 12.1).

Conclusion

Although we speak to people more or less every day of our lives, the business of verbal communication can be seen to be a very complex matter. This means that there is considerable scope for learning and many opportunities for continuous professional development.

The guidance given here is not intended as a set of definitive, foolproof rules to follow, but rather as indicators of the kinds of steps that can be taken to develop understanding and improve practice. Verbal communication is a very skilled activity, and high-quality practice takes a long time to develop. It is to be hoped that the ideas put forward here will be of value to you in following that route.

Exercise 12

Observing Communication

This is an exercise that can be repeated a number of times – as often as you like, in fact. It involves noticing conversations (on radio, television or in 'real life') and noting the key features of the communication taking place. For example, how are features like pitch and tone used? Is active listening taking place?

You may find it helpful to use a recording (a video recording or DVD, for example) so that you can listen to it a number of times, concentrating on a different aspect each time. This exercise can be a very useful tool in helping you develop a better understanding of, and sensitivity to, verbal communications.

chapter **13**

Nonverbal communication

Introduction

In addition to the words we speak, we give very powerful messages through nonverbal communication. Our body language adds an extra layer of communication, an additional set of signals above and beyond the verbal messages given. An important aspect of interaction skills in people work, then, is the ability to send and receive nonverbal signals appropriately and to best effect. It is for this reason that this chapter explores some of the key issues relating to nonverbal communication – so that we can better understand, and use, this important dimension of human interaction.

How does nonverbal communication work?

Through people's gestures, facial expressions and other nonverbal behaviours, we are able to detect additional information about their feelings, intentions or state of mind. These nonverbal cues are in addition to the verbal communication and relate to the verbalizations in a variety of ways. Knapp (1978) identified six particular ways in which the two dimensions of communication interact. These are:

1 *Repetition.* This is where the nonverbal behaviour simply echoes what is being said. This has the effect of clarifying or reinforcing the verbal message.
2 *Contradiction.* This describes a situation in which there is inconsistency between the verbal and nonverbal dimensions, a case of mixed messages. An important point to note is that, where this does occur, the nonverbal component tends to be the more powerful. For example, if I say 'I don't mind', but my face shows clear signs of frustration and irritation, then the message likely to be received is that I do in fact mind.
3 *Substitution.* This term applies when a nonverbal communication is used to replace a verbal utterance. For example, a nod of the head may be used to indicate 'yes', without the word 'yes' actually being spoken.

4 *Complementing.* The nonverbal behaviours accompanying speech can complement or enhance the meaning being conveyed. For example, in giving someone some news, a broad smile will tend to indicate that we see the news as good news.

5 *Accentuation.* Nonverbal behaviours are often used to emphasize certain points or aspects of the spoken message. For example, a parent may forbid a child from doing a particular thing by saying 'No' and reinforcing this by shaking the head and wagging the index finger from side to side.

6 *Regulation.* The flow of conversation is often regulated by nonverbal communication. For example, gestures can be used to indicate: 'I've finished speaking now'; 'Please let me speak'; 'Hurry up'; 'Calm down', and so on.

These points will, it is to be hoped, help to develop sensitivity to, and understanding of, nonverbal communication (see also Exercise 13 at the end of this chapter).

Nonverbal communication is an aspect of interaction that is so commonplace that we tend to take it for granted. We are rarely aware that we are using it or that it is influencing us. In order to develop our people skills, we need to become more aware of it, more conscious of the powerful messages that are conveyed between people in such subtle ways.

As a precursor to developing this greater level of awareness and understanding, there are, however, a number of points that need to be made explicit. These are:

○ Nonverbal communication is a form of language. That is, it needs to be interpreted carefully and sensitively, rather than being seen as a simple form of code. For example, doodling may be a sign of boredom, but it could also be the opposite – it could be used as an aid to concentration. We need to understand the context in which the indicator occurs.

○ We need to look at overall patterns of nonverbal communication, rather than focus on individual indicators, as these can be misleading. For example, a sigh could indicate exasperation but, equally, it could indicate that the person concerned has breathing difficulties due to a condition such as asthma.

○ Nonverbal communication often tells us a great deal about the person's emotional state. The subject therefore needs to be dealt with sensitively, as an uncritical, unfeeling approach may cause considerable difficulties and inflame a problematic situation.

○ Nonverbal communication is an *interactive* process. That is, one person's nonverbal behaviours will influence, and be influenced by, the nonverbal behaviours of others. It is similar to a form of dancing in which one partner's movements reflect, and are reflected by, the other's. We therefore have to bear in mind our own 'steps' in the dance and not focus too narrowly on those of the others involved.

○ Culture is an important factor to bear in mind. Nonverbal communication tends to be culture specific, and so we need to be wary of applying our own meanings and norms to people from other cultures. Similar issues can also be seen to apply in terms of gender and class.

○ We need to remember the importance of working in partnership. We should not set ourselves up as 'experts' who are able to 'read' other people. If the people we work with feel that we are watching them closely and analysing their behaviour, they are likely to feel alienated by this, and so unnecessary barriers are created. We should use our understanding of nonverbal communication to work *with* people, not to work *on* them.

Aspects of nonverbal communication

This important dimension of human interaction can be seen to manifest itself in a number of ways. I shall discuss a number of these aspects in turn, although it needs to be emphasized that the coverage of these issues here is not intended to be either comprehensive or exhaustive.

Facial expression

Facial expressions are very powerful in conveying information. For example, on some occasions, a simple smile can express an enormous amount of information and can be a highly significant form of communication.

Sometimes facial expressions are deliberately used to convey a signal or message, for example, to show concern when someone is anxious or distressed. At other times, however, the facial expression may not be a deliberate attempt to communicate (for example, a look of fear, puzzlement or frustration) but will, none the less, succeed in conveying certain information, even if the person concerned did not wish or intend to do so. Indeed, this is a common characteristic of nonverbal communication, that we communicate a great deal of information without even trying to (and sometimes preferring that we had not done so).

Smiling is a particularly important form of facial expression, as Fontana confirms:

> Research shows that in both personal and professional life people who smile are rated as warm, empathetic and understanding. But the smile must be genuine. A false smile is seen as ingratiating, as submissive, as appeasing, and as associated with artificial or unassertive people ... The best kind of smile is one that comes spontaneously, from the pleasure of seeing someone. But in professional life people sometimes claim that what holds them back is a fear that smiles weaken their official and competent

image. There's no evidence this fear is justified. And most people who try smiling report how much more friendly everyone else suddenly seems to be.

(1990, p. 57)

Eye contact

The nature and degree of eye contact between people tends to be very socially significant. What tends to work most effectively is a balanced amount of eye contact, neither too little, nor too much. However, achieving such a balance is more easily said than done, and may require some degree of practice, especially when we consider that what constitutes an appropriate balance may vary according to culture and related factors.

However, too little eye contact can be problematic because there is a tendency for it to be interpreted as one or more of the following:

○ boredom, a lack of interest;
○ disapproval, antagonism;
○ a lack of confidence or assertiveness; and/or
○ shiftiness, untrustworthiness.

Excessive eye contact, by contrast, tends to suggest aggression or intimidation, and is often experienced as intrusive.

Practice focus 13.1

Sara was an experienced practitioner who was keen on working with students and helping them develop their knowledge and skills. But, she knew from the moment she met Tim that she was not going to enjoy working with him as much as she had with previous students. His intense eye contact was very unsettling for her and it made her feel very uneasy. She tried to understand this level of eye contact in terms of his eagerness to pay attention and learn. None the less, she found herself feeling very tense in his company.

The balance of eye contact may also be missing when there is frenetic eye contact. Sometimes people switch very quickly between eye contact and non-contact and this can be very unsettling and irritating.

Posture

The way we 'hold' our body also plays a part in communication. For example, a relaxed posture can indicate a relaxed frame of mind and tends to encourage others to relax. This can be very important in our interactions with others, whether clients or colleagues. A relaxed posture can help to release tension and defuse potentially fraught situations.

However, posture can also be problematic if it is not appropriate to the circumstances. As with any form of nonverbal communication, it is highly context dependent. For example, a very informal posture at a job interview may be interpreted as a lack of commitment or a degree of complacency, and may therefore prove to be counterproductive.

Orientation

This refers to the direction we face when we are conversing. It is usual to face in the direction of the person we are speaking to. It can therefore be very significant to do otherwise. For example, to face away from someone can be interpreted as a lack of interest, disapproval or even a direct snub.

Similarly, within a group context, orientation can be very significant and can make a major contribution to group dynamics. That is, the way groups interact in terms of orientation can be indicative of power relations, channels of influence, popularity, animosity and so on. The simple matter of the direction we face in interacting with others can therefore produce complex and highly significant patterns and dynamics.

Proximity

How close we get to people when conversing with them has important implications for how the other party perceives us and how they respond to us. If we stand too far away, we will come across as, quite literally, too distant. We will appear to lack interest or to be wary of the other person. This can cause unnecessary tensions, and thereby create barriers to effective communication.

However, what can be even more problematic is when we get too close to the other person, when we invade their personal space. This can be very intrusive and intimidating. This is particularly the case in terms of gender differences. For example, when a man invades the personal space of a woman, this may amount to sexual harassment (see below).

What constitutes an appropriate distance depends to a certain extent on the circumstances (rush hour public transport, for example) and/or cultural expectations. We therefore need to develop some degree of sensitivity to appropriate proximity so that we do not make others feel uncomfortable in our presence.

Touch

Touch is both a very significant and a very powerful form of nonverbal communication. All forms of nonverbal communication need to be used carefully and sensitively but this one particularly so in view of its potential for creating difficulties.

When used appropriately, touch can be very effective in:

○ providing comfort and reassurance when a person is in distress;
○ demonstrating solidarity;
○ calming someone who is agitated;
○ showing respect (a handshake, for example); and/or
○ praising or congratulating someone.

However, when it is used inappropriately or indiscriminately, it can:

○ invade privacy;
○ embarrass;
○ intimidate;
○ destroy trust; and/or
○ constitute sexual harassment.

This final point is of major significance. In a male-dominated society in which women are often portrayed primarily as sexual objects, inappropriate touching can be extremely problematic. This can create a situation where a woman either feels aggrieved at how she has been treated, but is reluctant to 'cause a fuss', or makes her grievance known and risks causing what can become a very tense and fraught situation. In either case, the situation is likely to be extremely distressing for the woman concerned. Touch is a very powerful communicative tool but, like any tool, it can also be abused, whether intentionally or through carelessness.

Clearly, then, touch is an important part of nonverbal communication, but one that needs to be used thoughtfully and cautiously.

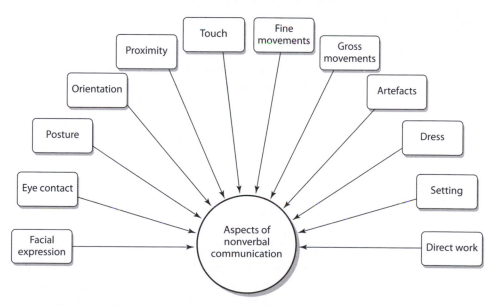

Figure 13.1　Aspects of nonverbal communication

Fine movements

This refers to the gestures and mannerisms that accompany spoken language. These can be seen to apply in one of two ways (or a mixture of the two). First, they can be used as deliberate signs or signals. Examples of this would include: beckoning, pointing, and nodding or shaking of the head. These can be very useful ways of getting a message across or reinforcing a particular point. We should note, however, that such gestures can be open to misinterpretation, particularly where cultural differences apply – gestures do not have the same universal meaning. For example, in some cultures, shaking one's head means 'yes', rather than 'no'.

Second, some fine movements can occur unwittingly. That is, we may not be aware that they occur. These may include certain hand movements, facial tics and so on. These mannerisms have little or no direct communicative content and can, in fact, act as barriers to communication, in so far as they may be distracting and/or irritating. This presents two challenges for us as people workers:

○ not allowing other people's mannerisms to distract us from our task; and
○ developing sufficient self-awareness to allow us to minimize or eliminate distracting or irritating mannerisms.

Gross movements

These are bodily movements on a larger scale. They include: walking away, pushing, grabbing and hitting. Gross movements tend to be largely, but not exclusively, associated with tense situations, possibly involving aggression. They often occur in more extreme situations where verbal communication has broken down or is in danger of doing so.

This form of nonverbal communication can often give us the message that feelings are running high, and it warns us that the situation may be getting out of hand. We should therefore be alerted by such movements, as we may need to take evasive or protective action. This is an important point, and one which relates to the discussions of violence and aggression in Chapter 19.

Practice focus 13.2

Jeff was one of many people who were outraged by the proposal for major organizational changes that were simply thinly disguised attempts to save money by cutting levels of service. However, Jeff was the person who made his feelings known most strongly at the meeting where these plans were announced – without actually saying anything. He picked up his papers, put them in his folder, stood up and walked out of the meeting – a clear example of actions speaking louder than words.

Of course, gross body movements are not always of a negative or worrying kind. Consider, for example, jumping for joy or hugging someone. However, once again these tend to be associated for the most part with situations that are, in some way, out of the ordinary. They therefore have a part to play in nonverbal communication.

Artefacts

The way in which objects or artefacts are held, worn or used can communicate a great deal of information about the person concerned. As with gestures and mannerisms, artefacts may be used deliberately to convey a message or emphasize a point, or may play an unwitting part in the process of communication.

An example of the former would be someone pointedly looking at his or her watch in order to convey the message: 'Hurry up' or 'You're late'. An example of the latter would be someone fidgeting with a ring, perhaps suggesting tension or anxiety. In either case, it can be beneficial to 'name the process', to make explicit what is happening so that communication can take place openly with less danger of misunderstanding. The notion of 'naming the process' is an important one and will be discussed further in Chapter 15.

Dress

The clothing that we wear, and the way that we wear it, can say a lot about us. It can give a lot of clues about our background, our values, and even our intentions. This can apply to our general style of dress or to specific clothing in specific circumstances. Certain situations call for certain styles of dress. There are unwritten social rules that can lead to complications if they are broken. For example, formal occasions require formal dress in most cases. Where this expectation is not met, difficulties may arise. If a probation officer were to attend court casually dressed, it is likely that the magistrates or judge would interpret this as a lack of respect. The choice of clothing would convey, intentionally or not, a message – communication would take place.

This has important implications for people work in terms of the impressions choice of dress can create. This relates to the meanings clients and other professionals may attach to our choice of clothing and the ways in which we may interpret theirs. In this respect, dress is an ever-present aspect of nonverbal communication. Whilst we may wish that dress were not so socially significant, it would be naive not to recognize that it is.

Setting

The setting or physical environment in which communication takes place adds a further dimension to the communicative process. This applies in a number of ways.

Where the setting is compatible with the message being conveyed, the effectiveness of the communication can be enhanced. However, there are also (at least) three ways in which the setting can be problematic, where the message implicit in the environment is not consistent with the verbal message being expressed:

○ The verbal communication may be undermined or contradicted, with the result that it is not accepted. For example, in the headteacher's office, a pupil is told 'I want to help you', but the strong association between the office and punishment leads the pupil to mistrust the message.
○ Similarly, incompatibility can lead to a confused message, where the person concerned is not sure whether to trust the verbal or nonverbal message. This could apply, for example, when a nurse, standing next to complex technological equipment, tells the patient: 'Your condition is not serious'.
○ The physical environment may distract the listener. For example, a worker undertaking a home visit may find that the client is distracted by a television set in the background.

Being aware of the importance of the setting, and being able to use it constructively are aspects of good practice in interviewing and so I shall return to this issue in Chapter 15.

Direct work

'Direct work' is a term used for attempts to communicate through play or other interactive activities. This is generally used with children who have experienced trauma in their lives, but it does not have to be restricted to this group of people.

A key element of this type of communication is the use of nonverbal channels to express painful or difficult sentiments when it may be too demanding emotionally to give vent to these feelings verbally. In this respect, the process can prove to be quite cathartic (see Chapter 18 for a discussion of 'catharsis').

Conclusion

It should be clear then, from this chapter, that nonverbal communication is a complex, multidimensional matter. However, we have the benefit of having learned a great deal about nonverbal communication as part and parcel of growing up and being a member of society. What is needed, then, is a sharper focus on interpersonal dynamics, a greater sensitivity to the subtle, but influential, processes that occur when people interact. Understanding nonverbal communication is not only an important tool for people workers, but also a fascinating undertaking in its own right.

Exercise 13

Observing Interactions

This exercise is designed to help you develop the sensitivity to nonverbal communication on which good practice is based. Refer back to Knapp's (1978) six functions of nonverbal communication. Watch carefully the interactions of other people and see whether you can identify at least one example of each of the six. You may wish to draw upon television, video or 'real-life' situations. Use the space below to make notes.

chapter **14**

Written communication

Introduction

It is not uncommon for members of the people professions to complain that too much time is spent on *paper* work and not enough on actual *people* work. Although this is quite a reasonable point of view, it also masks a potential danger. It runs the risk of presenting paper work as a relatively unimportant consideration. Written communication is a vitally important part of people work. Where it is done badly, or is not done at all, major problems can occur. If we see it as a chore and fail to recognize that it is an integral part of good practice, we are likely not to appreciate its significance or the dangers of neglecting it. This chapter addresses some of the key issues relating to written communication and, in so doing, underlines its importance as a basic aspect of good practice in people work.

Why do we rely on written communication?

A very basic reason tends to be that employers require it. That is, the vast majority of employers in the people work field require written records, and the small minority who do not are almost certain to use written communication in some form. However, there are also a number of other important reasons, chief among which are the following:

○ Written records act as the basis of reviewing and evaluating work – records describe the baseline from which progress can be measured (see Chapter 27).
○ Records act as an *aide-mémoire*, a helpful reminder to guide practice and provide an aid to continuity. For busy workers, relying on one's memory alone can be a risky business.
○ Written communication also provides the basis for justifying our actions. People workers are *accountable*. That is, we have to be able to account for what we do – for example, by justifying decisions taken. All this relies on appropriate forms of written communication.
○ Records may be used as evidence in a court of law, a tribunal or formal inquiry in some circumstances.

○ Written work can be the basis of learning. Discussion of written accounts of practice can help to develop understanding and enhance practice. See, for example, the discussion below of process records.

○ Written communication can also be used directly as a tool of intervention, a method of problem solving. For example, worker and client writing down together the strengths, weaknesses, opportunities and threats (SWOT analysis) can be a very fruitful exercise (see *The People Solutions Sourcebook*).

○ Written records also provide an important basis for future work. That is, accounts of work undertaken today may prove to be of great value in guiding and informing future intervention with the same individual, family or group. This also applies to records as the basis of multidisciplinary collaboration or networking.

Being able to communicate effectively in writing is therefore a fundamental part of good practice. If we skimp on this aspect of people work, we may be seriously undermining the overall process. Care therefore needs to be taken to ensure that the necessary levels of skills and understanding are developed.

Types of written communication

Different types of written communication require different approaches if they are to be used to best effect. I shall comment here on some of the many forms of written communication before going on to look at some of the key issues that apply more generally.

Letters

These tend to be short but important forms of communication. It is important to ensure that they are concise and to the point. If they are too long, with unnecessary padding, this may distract attention from important points you are trying to get across. It is also important that the level of formality is appropriate. See the section below on 'Purpose'.

Email

A new development in recent years has been the emergence of electronic mail (email) as a significant form of communication. Many people are not sure whether to treat emails as less formal letters or as written versions of telephone calls. Of course, the answer to this puzzle is that emails are neither of these.

We have to learn what the best uses of this new form of communication are rather than try and fit it inappropriately to existing modes of communication.

Running records

This is a term that refers to ongoing accounts of work. This can include contact records, a straightforward list of dates and times of contacts: personal visits, office appointments, letters and phone calls. It can also refer to more detailed records that 'tell the story' of the process of intervention. Here, there is a danger of getting bogged down in specific detail and losing sight of the overall aims and process.

Referrals

A referral is a request for an assessment or a service. As such, it needs to be clear what is being requested and why. A referral should therefore include the basic information needed to begin to form a picture of the situation. It is essential that such information is as accurate as possible, as a mistake at this stage could be very misleading and therefore highly problematic.

Reports

A written report may be required for a variety of reasons. The length, style, format and focus will therefore also vary considerably. A basic principle of report writing, then, is the need to match the report to the specific requirements, to ensure that it is appropriate to its purpose. Indeed, this is a general principle of written communication and one to which I shall return below.

Assessments

Chapter 23 is devoted to the process of assessment, and so the writing of assessments will be discussed in more detail there. However, for present purposes, it is important to note that the skills of writing an assessment can be critical. That is, high-quality work in undertaking an assessment can be undermined or even totally spoiled by poor written communication.

Summaries

Summaries play an important part in maintaining the thread of ongoing work by drawing together key themes and issues. They are also very useful when a piece of work comes to an end (see Chapter 28). Producing a brief but effective summary is quite a skilled job and requires the worker to be clear and focused in what he or she is doing. The effective use of summaries is therefore an important discipline to develop.

Agreements

Written agreements, or 'contracts' as they are often known, are a potentially very effective means of developing partnership and achieving change. Worker and client identify common areas of agreement in moving towards agreed goals (see Chapter 22). Again, this is a very skilled job, as the written agreement needs to reflect accurately and appropriately the precise terms of agreement. Vagueness in the way the agreement is phrased can lead to great difficulties later in the process.

Review documents

Some agencies use specific documents for recording the process and outcomes of reviews. These can play a major part in helping to review progress – see Chapter 27.

Messages

Taking a telephone message, for example, may seem a straightforward matter but is often problematic. To be effective, it is important to ensure that: the message is clear and unambiguous; the date is recorded (and time, if appropriate); and the telephone number or other contact point is included. It is also important to sign the note – relying on the other person recognizing your handwriting may lead to confusion. It is also less impersonal if the note is signed.

Practice focus 14.1

Kim returned to her desk after a long and difficult meeting. On her desk was a message which said: 'Chris rang. Please ring back within the next hour.' There were three problems with this message. First, she knew two Christines, three Christophers and one Christian – all known as Chris. Which one had actually rung? Second, there was no time on the message, and so she did not know when 'within the next hour' referred to, as she had been away from her desk for nearly three hours. Third, there was no name on the note and she did not recognize the handwriting. It was therefore going to be difficult and time consuming to trace who had left the note in order to clarify the message.

Process records

These are detailed records of an interview. The primary aim is to record the *process* of the interaction (hence the name). However, a common mistake is to regard them as verbatim recordings, word-for-word accounts of what happened. There is little point in making a verbatim record, whereas an account of the process that takes place between the participants helps to develop sensitivity to important aspects of interpersonal dynamics and also provides good learning material for training and staff development purposes.

Key issues

Despite the variety of forms of written communication, there are also common themes that emerge. Here I shall focus on a number of key issues that apply to a range of types of written communication.

Purpose

In undertaking written communication, it is vitally important to ask the question: 'Why?' We need to be clear about the purpose of writing. That is, we need to establish:

○ who will be reading the written work;
○ what it will be used for; and
○ what the writer hopes it will achieve.

For example, in writing a report, the worker needs to ensure that the tone, format, style and content are appropriate to the purpose of that report. A report prepared for a court hearing would need to be very different from one prepared for a review meeting (see Chapter 28). That is, what form a report (or other written communication) should take will depend to a large extent on the desired end product. In other words, the purpose of a particular piece of written work will be a major influence on the shape that work takes. It is therefore important to consider carefully the purpose of any piece of written work before writing begins. This should help to make the written output compatible with its intended purpose. Without this, a great deal of time and effort may be wasted and the results may be disappointing.

Relevance

A major question to consider for written work is: 'What shall I include and what shall I leave out?' There are, of course, two dangers that can be identified:

1 Too much information is included. Too much 'padding' is not only a waste of time and effort on the part of the writer, but can also distract attention from the actual central message that is being conveyed. That is, the provision of superfluous information or detail is counterproductive. Providing more information than is necessary is therefore more likely to hamper communication than to enhance it.
2 Too little information is included. If a key piece of information is omitted or glossed over, the end result may be less than satisfactory. That is, a written communication has to ensure that the essential points are conveyed if the process is to be an effective one.

Finding the balance between these two unhelpful extremes is not always an easy task. One principle that can help to guide us in finding this balance is: Provide the minimum of information necessary, not the maximum available. (This is also a principle that applies to the process of assessment, and so we shall revisit this theme in Chapter 23.) This basically involves focusing carefully on the information available and deciding which elements are necessary to convey the meaning intended. Of course, in order to decide what is necessary, we need to refer back to the *purpose* of the written communication.

In determining what is relevant, we need to ask the key question: relevant to what? The purpose of writing will therefore guide us in making the crucial distinction between 'need to know' and 'nice to know'. Too much of the latter will muddy the waters of the former.

Planning

Written communications can be confused, confusing and difficult to read if they are not planned in advance. Indeed, it takes a very skilled writer to produce high-quality work without first thinking through what is the best way of putting the ideas across (or even what those ideas are).

If people start to write without considering some key points, then the likelihood of a successful outcome will be seriously undermined. These include:

○ what points are to be made;
○ what order they should be in (see 'Structure' below); and
○ what level of formality is appropriate.

Time devoted to planning can be an important investment, as it may prevent time-consuming problems later and increase the likelihood of effective communication taking place. In addition, planning what needs to be written may actually convince you that writing is not the best means of communication for that particular situation. Perhaps, on reflection, a telephone call or a face-to-face meeting would be more appropriate.

Confidentiality

The topic of confidentiality is both very important and very complex. There are, however, a number of points that can help us deal with this aspect of practice appropriately. These are:

○ *Confidentiality is to the organization, not the individual.*   That is, workers should not promise to 'keep secrets', as they are acting on behalf of their employers, not in their own right. It is misleading to allow people to believe no one else will know the information given when it is likely to be available to others within the organization.
○ *Confidentiality is not absolute.*   That is, there are certain circumstances in which confidentiality has to be overridden. As Adams comments:

> Workers are accountable to their employers and not just to service users. In general, the appropriate response to the request: 'I'll tell you a secret if you'll promise not to tell anyone', is along the lines of, 'I'm prepared to

listen to you. But if what you tell me involves harm to you or to another person, I may *have* to tell somebody.'

(1994, p. 16)

An example of this would be a situation in which it appears that child abuse may be taking place (see Practice Focus 14.2).

○ *Confidentiality has to be taken seriously.* A tokenistic approach that simply 'goes through the motions' is potentially very harmful. An unnecessary breach of confidentiality can do a great deal of damage in terms of trust, respect and positive working relations.

Practice focus 14.2

Gina had worked with the Taylor family for over a year, dealing with a number of problems relating to the children's health. During this time, the family had often confided in her, as they had come to trust her and respect her professionalism. However, the situation changed quite drastically when Gina had cause to suspect that one of the children had been abused. She followed the guidance given in the Child Protection Procedures and informed the duty social worker of her concerns, as a result of which a child protection investigation was undertaken, subsequently confirming that abuse had taken place. Gina had felt quite guilty about not respecting the family's confidentiality, but she was reassured by knowing that the children's safety was the paramount concern.

Structure

Written work benefits considerably from having a clear, logical structure. This helps to prevent confusion and makes the reader's task that little bit easier. This is particularly the case with lengthier communications such as reports.

One very common, and very useful, way of structuring a report is to divide it into three parts, with each part serving a separate function. The three sections of the report are as follows:

1 *Introduction.* The purpose of the introduction is to orient the reader, to 'set the scene' for what is to come in the remainder of the report. It helps the reader form a picture of what ground the report is to cover. It should give a brief overview of the report's contents and focus.

2 *The main body.* This is the main substantive part of the report in which the key points are made. These should be presented in a logical order, with a clear flow from one point to the next, thereby helping the reader digest the information being conveyed. This is not to say that there is one 'right' order for presenting the points you are making. There is

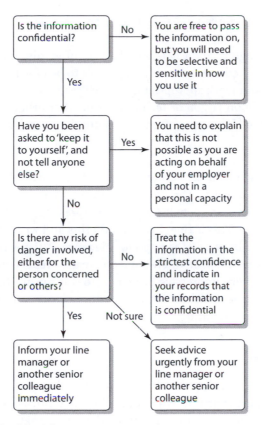

Figure 14.1 *Confidentiality*

often more than one effective way to present the material but a little time spent planning the order in which you intend to write should help prevent a confused and confusing report being produced. That is, the order in which the points are presented can be either a help or a hindrance.

3 *Conclusion.* The purpose of this section is to draw the report to a logical close. It should briefly summarize the message that the report was intended to convey. If appropriate, this section should contain any recommendations that are to be made.

By structuring a report in this way, it is possible to provide a clear, easily understood written communication. Without a clear structure, reports are more likely to be jumbled, vague and confusing.

Clarity

Effective written communication depends to a large extent on clarity. It is therefore important that you:

○ Avoid long, cumbersome sentences that are confusing and difficult to follow.

○ Avoid ambiguity and vagueness. Beware of words or phrases that can be misinterpreted or that are too imprecise to be of value.

○ Present your work appropriately – see 'Presentation' below.

○ Do not rely on jargon or technical terms that others may not be able to understand. Jargon can often be a useful shorthand, but it can also reduce clarity.

To prevent misunderstanding, then, it is essential to make clarity of expression a priority. The basic rule here is to ensure that you express yourself clearly. Some people try hard to express themselves in an elegant or impressive way. This is fine if you can do this and write clearly but the very real danger to be wary of is to go for elegance at the expense of clarity. An example of this would be where someone reads a report and then comments: 'This sounds very impressive but what does it mean?' Similarly, beware of flowery language. This can not only reduce clarity but also come across as pretentious and irritating.

Fact and opinion

An important distinction to be drawn is that between facts and opinions. It is important that the two should not be confused as this can be very misleading. Good practice therefore demands that, where you give an opinion, it is clear that this is what you are doing. For example, opinions should be prefaced by comments like 'I believe . . .' or 'In my view . . .'. Similarly, where a confirmed fact is being stated, it is helpful to explain or justify its factual basis. For example, instead of writing what could be seen as a judgemental statement: 'Mr Hughes is a violent man', it is better to state the precise facts: 'Mr Hughes has three convictions for grievous bodily harm'.

Presentation

The way written work is presented is very important for two main reasons:

1 *Making an impression.* Poor presentation of written work can create a very negative impression. Errors of spelling, grammar, punctuation and so on can give the impression of sloppy and careless work. Poor presentation can therefore undermine what is, in other respects, high-quality work.

2 *Getting your message across.* Poor presentation can reduce clarity and therefore hamper communication. This applies in terms of:

○ poor use of paragraphs spoiling the flow of what is being conveyed;
○ grammatical or spelling errors changing the meaning of a sentence (or rendering it meaningless); and
○ omitted words or incorrect punctuation affecting the meaning of a sentence.

In trying to avoid these problems, it is helpful to:

○ Carefully check over what you have written. This type of proofreading can prevent a lot of problems.
○ Ask someone to read it over for you.
○ Read it out loud. This can often help to identify problems of punctuation or sentence construction.

Access

Many forms of written communication will be available to clients if they request access to it. It is therefore very important indeed that this is borne in mind when writing. A useful general principle is that it is best not to write anything down that you would not be prepared to show the client, unless there is a particular reason why it is important to do so.

If this principle is not adhered to, a great deal of conflict, tension and ill feeling can arise if a client gains access to a report or other records that are inaccurate, insensitive or judgemental.

Conclusion

While all forms of communication have an important part to play in people work, written communication has the added dimension that it is more permanent. While other forms of communication may come and go, written work can remain available 'on file' for many, many years, and can therefore go on influencing actions and interactions years after it was first recorded. This emphasizes and reinforces the need to make sure that our use of the written word is appropriate and as effective as possible.

Written communication can at times be complex and demanding but it is not without its rewards, and so the time and effort that have to be devoted to developing the necessary skills are a worthwhile investment that should pay dividends in both the short and long term.

Exercise 14

Report Writing

For this exercise you will need to take a report (or other form of written communication) that you have written. Read it through carefully and, on the basis of what you have studied in this chapter, evaluate it. That is, look at it carefully and identify its strengths and also those aspects that you would improve if you were to rewrite the report. This should help you consolidate your understanding of some of the key issues relating to written forms of communication. Use the space below to make some notes.

chapter 15

Interviewing

Introduction

First of all, it is necessary to clarify that the term 'interview' is being used to refer to any formal or semi-formal discussion between a worker and client(s). That is, it is not being used in the narrower sense of a job-selection interview.

An interview is much more than a chat. It is often the means by which people work is undertaken, the channel through which change begins to take place. As such, an interview needs to be focused, with a clear purpose, forming part of a systematic process geared towards achieving identified objectives (see Chapter 22). Effective interviewing is therefore a highly skilled job, and is best not left to chance. This chapter therefore concentrates on the skills involved in successful interviewing and addresses some of the pitfalls that can stand in the way of good practice.

First, however, it is important to consider what needs to be done prior to the interview.

Before the interview

Good practice in interviewing does not begin when the interview does. Effective interviewing is premised on a degree of advance planning and prior preparation. This involves considering a number of issues that are worthy of attention before launching into the interview.

Time and place

Choosing the appropriate time for an interview can be very important. For many interviews, the time at which it takes place is not a significant issue to consider. However, in some cases, timing can be crucial. For example, it may not be appropriate to interview a child who has just arrived home from school and has not yet had the chance to adjust from school to home life.

Time can also be important in terms of the length of the interview. Short, hurried interviews and long, drawn-out ones can both be very problematic or even counterproductive.

It was noted earlier that the setting is an important aspect of communication. The place in which an interview takes place can therefore be very significant. There is no hard and fast rule about what is the best place to conduct an interview, but the question of appropriate setting is one that does need to be considered, particularly for the more sensitive or potentially problematic interviews.

Purpose

Interviews are, by definition, discussions with a purpose. It is therefore helpful to bear this in mind in planning for the interview. Being clear about the purpose of an interview helps to retain a sharp focus and facilitate progress towards the desired outcomes.

Making the purpose clear also helps the client(s) feel more comfortable about what is going on and less suspicious or mistrustful of the worker's motives in carrying out the interview.

Are you the right person?

For some types of interview, it is important, if not essential, to ensure an appropriate match of worker and client in terms of gender and/or culture. For example, a woman who has been sexually assaulted may well find it very distressing to be interviewed by a man. Even if the interviewer is highly skilled, simply being the wrong person for the job can mean that the interview does more harm than good.

Linguistic sensitivity

In some cases, it may be necessary to call upon the services of an interpreter. Where the need for this arises, careful consideration must be given to the situation. For example, using a family member in a situation that is characterized by family tensions, may lead to a distorted representation of what is being said (whether deliberately or unwittingly). Similarly, using a child to interpret may mean that he or she is exposed to information that is not appropriate for a child.

Who should be involved?

Interviews are often on a one-to-one basis, but may also involve a number of people simultaneously. At times, it may be important to consider who should (or should not) be involved. Once again, there is no simple, hard and fast rule about this. However, if no thought is given to the matter, the interview may be ineffective or even make the situation worse. The actual purpose of the interview can be a useful guide as to who needs to be involved in it.

Contingency plans

While it would be unrealistic to make contingency plans for every interview, it is a good idea to do so for some situations. For example, for some high-profile interviews, it would be very unwise not to have an alternative strategy to fall back on. Urgent problems or potential emergency situations tend to fall into this category.

Key skills

In conducting interviews, a range of important skills apply. I shall focus here on some of the main skills needed and comment on each of these in turn.

Listening

The importance of active listening was emphasized in Chapter 12. The interview situation is where this skill really comes into its own. Indeed, it is highly unlikely that an interview could be effective without good listening.

Part of this is the ability and willingness to acknowledge feelings. For example, if a person is feeling angry, it is unlikely that progress will be made until the feelings of anger are acknowledged or addressed in some way. Listening therefore involves 'tuning in' to feelings and responding appropriately and constructively. This is a significant skill in its own right.

Also important in the context of interviewing is the ability to recognize nonverbal communication, to 'hear' what the body language is saying. Without this sensitivity, much of the important interaction in an interview will be missed.

Directing

In order to ensure that the interview is focused, and in line with its purpose, some degree of 'directing' is called for. This does not mean that we should order people about. However, it does mean that we need to have some degree of control over the direction of the interview.

This is an example of assertiveness, as discussed in Chapter 5. That is, the aim is to achieve a win–win situation. We should not attempt to bully others into submission, but neither should we allow ourselves to be pressurized into losing track of why we are there or what we are trying to achieve.

Directing is therefore a subtle skill that allows some degree of control over the interview without being intrusive or domineering. It entails being responsive to people's wishes, needs and feelings, but without necessarily abandoning the process of work of which the interview forms a part.

Partnership

If people work is to be effective, it needs to be based on partnership. This is because imposed change is far less likely to be successful than change to which the person concerned is committed, and for which he or she takes ownership. Working together in this way depends on our ability to earn people's trust and gain their confidence.

The skills involved in this should not be underestimated, as it is a complex and intricate task. These skills can be developed with experience but some useful pointers would be:

○ Do not do most of the talking. Make sure the interview is a two-way process.
○ Do not put words into other people's mouths. It is better to ask than to tell.
○ Help people to feel comfortable and at ease so that they feel able to talk freely.
○ Make it explicit that you want to work together. Make it clear that you are not there to make all the running.

Partnership is an important concept and will be a key feature of some of the discussions in Part III.

Empowerment

As discussed earlier, this is another important concept for people workers. It refers to the process of enabling people to take greater control over their lives. Through empowerment, people can become better equipped to deal with their problems and pursue their goals. Appropriate interviewing can make an important contribution to this process, while inappropriate interviewing may do a great deal of harm to it. That is, interviewing is a focal point for empowerment.

In order to promote empowerment, it is important to ensure that:

○ Self-esteem is not undermined and, where possible, is boosted.
○ Barriers to progress are identified and steps taken towards removing them.
○ Discrimination and oppression are recognized as significant aspects of people's lives in general and interpersonal dynamics in particular (see Chapters 11 and 21).

Empowering interviews are those that help to build on strengths and overcome weaknesses or, better still, turn the latter into strengths too.

Practice focus 15.1

As part of her training course, Jackie was required to role play an interview with a prospective client. The result was not a happy one for Jackie. The feedback she received was that her style of interviewing was perceived by others as overbearing and lacking in sensitivity – a style that contributed more to disempowerment than empowerment. Jackie had, up to that point, perceived her style as being firm and businesslike. However, by watching the videotape of the interview, she was able to see that she had dominated and had not allowed the interviewee to play an active role in the interview.

Use of self

Interviews are not simply a technical exercise. They necessarily draw on the personality, experience and background of the worker. Seeking to make positive use of these factors is what is known as 'use of self'. This may include giving examples from one's own experience to help people understand a particular situation or see a way forward. However, two dangers here that need to be avoided are:

1 Trying to impose one's own perspective or values on the situation without taking adequate account of how the other person's experience differs from one's own.
2 Trying to play down people's problems by comparing them with our own. This can easily be interpreted as a sign that we are not taking the situation seriously or are trivializing it.

We all have aspects of our personality and experience that can be used to good effect, and recognizing this fact can help to give us the confidence we need to do so.

Tolerating silence

Some interviews, particularly those where emotional issues are to the fore, may involve periods of silence. This can occur when the person is too upset to speak or needs time to reflect. When such a silence occurs, we can feel very uncomfortable indeed. We can feel under immense pressure to 'fill the gap', to say something simply to break the uncomfortable silence. However, despite this pressure, it is very important that the temptation to fill the silence is resisted. People workers have to learn to tolerate silences because:

○ This shows respect for the client and sensitivity to his or her feelings.
○ Failing to do so can make the client withdraw, and feel reluctant to trust the worker.
○ Handling silences well tends to be perceived by clients as very supportive.

Difficult though it may be, tolerating silence and using it as a supportive space is a very worthwhile capacity to develop.

Maintaining boundaries

Interactions between people operate at different levels and in different spheres, and there are 'social rules' concerning what is appropriate in differing circumstances. Interviews can, if we are not careful, transgress these rules. This applies in a number of ways, including the following:

○ Confidentiality is an important issue (see Chapter 14). The boundaries of confidentiality need to be recognized.

○ Good relationships with clients are an important aspect of people work. However, this is different from friendship, which can get in the way of the professional task at times. It is therefore important to maintain a boundary between professional and personal relationships.

○ People workers are part of a network of other professional and voluntary workers. There is a danger, then, that in our eagerness to be helpful, we may take on someone else's responsibility. This can be problematic in four ways:

1 The other worker is likely to be better equipped to undertake their own duties.
2 This type of 'encroachment' may cause resentment and hamper working in partnership.
3 Spending time doing other people's jobs leaves us less time to do our own.
4 If we are doing things that are not formally part of our job, our employer or professional insurance may not cover us if anything goes wrong.

Structure

As with written communication, as discussed in Chapter 14, interviews benefit from having a clear structure. This follows broadly the same pattern as written reports, namely a three-part structure as follows:

1 *Introductory stage.* This is the opening phase of the interview and often includes a few pleasantries to help people relax and settle into their roles. However, it is also important to establish the purpose and focus of the interview at this stage. If these are not clarified early on, then the whole process can be distorted by the mystique and suspicion that can be generated.
2 *The main body.* This middle stage is where the main business of the interview is carried out. It involves the exchange of information, problem-solving activities and a whole range of other forms of interaction. This is often the crux of people work, the focal point at which decisions and agreements are made, conflicts addressed and progress made or halted.
3 *The conclusion.* Drawing an interview to a close is a skilled activity that involves summarizing (see below), identifying what is likely to happen next in the process (the time and date of a further interview, for example) and making sure that the client is clear about what has been agreed, and so on. Some informal chatting can also be useful at this stage, to 'round off' the interview.

A structured approach helps to maintain a clear focus, and contributes to creating a professional impression. However, it is important not to confuse structure with rigidity. Adopting a structured approach is not the same as adopting a regimented one. A degree of flexibility is called for. Indeed, the constructive balance between structure and flexibility is a key theme of Chapter 22.

Summary and feedback

As mentioned above, summarizing is an important part of concluding an interview. However, it can also be helpful at other points in an interview. To feed back, in summary form, the key points of what has been said can be useful in terms of:

- confirming that we have been listening;
- identifying any misunderstandings that may have occurred;
- clarifying points of agreement and disagreement;
- gaining an overview of the situation, pulling different strands together;
- 'punctuating' the interview, giving time and space to think, or digest what has been said;
- encouraging the development of partnership by focusing on a shared perspective; and
- helping to ensure that the interview does not lose focus and begin to drift.

Pitfalls to avoid

While the development of the skills outlined above is an important part of effective interviewing, there are also some pitfalls that need to be avoided. Navigating a way round these pitfalls represents a significant set of skills in its own right. Having a clear grasp of what the danger points are is therefore a worthwhile goal to pursue. I shall encourage movement in that direction by commenting on some of the more significant pitfalls that apply to interviewing.

Collusive games

In a classic text Berne (1968) describes many of the various 'games' that can develop in interpersonal interactions. Such games can prevent positive and constructive interviews taking place. They can act as a barrier to open and honest communication.

Such games often include an element of collusion. For example, there may be a tacit agreement along the lines of: 'I won't challenge you if you don't challenge me'. Such agreements are rarely expressed openly but often develop through a complex set of subtle manoeuvrings. Where such situations occur, the potential for effective interviewing, based on partnership and empowerment, is greatly restricted.

Structure blindness

This is a term used to refer to the tendency not to notice or address issues that relate to the structure of society. This includes 'colour blindness', a failure to take account of cultural differences and the effects of racism, and 'gender blindness', a one-sided view of the world that presents men and masculinity as the social norm, with little or no attention paid to women's issues or perspectives.

People workers need to be sensitive to issues of ethnicity, gender, age, disability and any other factor that can form the basis of discrimination and oppression. Interviews that take insufficient account of human diversity run the risk of reinforcing existing patterns of inequality.

Jargon

The need for clarity has already been stressed. However, one particular aspect that needs to be emphasized is the difficulty that can arise in using jargon in interviews. Jargon can be a very useful form of shorthand and a good way of making technical distinctions that day-to-day language does not recognize. However, when used inappropriately, it acts as a significant barrier to communication.

One important point to recognize is that we often use jargon without realizing that we are doing so. For example, to a professional worker, the term 'assessment' may be a clear and well-established concept, whereas, to others, it may come across as a vague and indeterminate term that is only fairly loosely grasped, if at all. A simple term like 'assessment' can therefore generate a great deal of mystique and suspicion if we are not sensitive to the differences between jargon and everyday speech.

Promises

It is very tempting to make promises in interviews, but this is a temptation that is very much to be resisted. This is because there is rarely any guarantee that such a promise can be kept – and broken promises can so easily destroy trust and confidence in the worker.

Even simple promises can sometimes prove impossible to keep, for example due to illness. Furthermore, people workers operate in the context of competing demands, and so it is quite possible that certain promises will be overtaken by other priorities. The maxim: 'Don't make promises you can't keep' is a good one but, in people work, there are few promises that we can guarantee we will be able to keep. We therefore need to be very careful and selective in making promises.

False reassurances

This follows on from the previous point. It is dangerous to give false reassurances, as these may later be thrown back in our faces when trust and respect are destroyed. When someone is distressed, it is very tempting to say something like: 'Everything's going to be all right'. However, we need to consider what happens in those circumstances where things do not turn out to be 'all right'. At a time of crisis, someone may place a lot of store in what a trusted worker has to say. It is important, then, that the worker does not fall into the trap of giving false reassurances (especially in working with children, who are more likely than adults to take what we say literally). It is perfectly possible to give realistic reassurances without having to rely on false ones.

Unfocused chats

The need to be focused and clear about the purpose of the interview has become a recurring theme in this chapter. The danger of allowing an interview to drift into an unfocused chat is therefore one to be taken quite seriously. This is not to say that there is no place for pleasantries and informal chats within the context of an interview, but it does mean that these should not be allowed to take over and undermine the central tasks of the interview.

Figure 15.1 Pitfalls to avoid

Practice focus 15.2

Barbara was a student on placement who, as part of her induction, was accompanying experienced workers as they undertook their day-to-day tasks. After a visit to one particular family, Barbara was quite confused, as she could not understand the purpose of the interview. It seemed to be a general discussion about the family's situation with no apparent focus or purpose. Barbara plucked up the courage to comment that she was unclear as to the purpose or focus of the visit. She was to be very disheartened by the reply: 'I don't like to be regimented in what I do; I like to take things as they come.' Barbara read this as confirmation of a lack of clarity and planning in this particular worker's practice.

Conclusion

Interviewing is a crucial process within people work and, as we have seen, is a highly skilled activity beset with a range of potential difficulties. With practice, particularly practice informed by clear principles, the necessary skills can be developed and refined, and the worker can take significant steps towards safeguarding him- or herself from the pitfalls that abound. With experience, workers can develop specific skills relating to particular situations or tasks, for example conversing with a diffident teenager or making people feel secure enough to talk openly.

Interviewing is one of the aspects of practice that offers scope for the development of excellence and an extremely high level of job satisfaction. It is therefore a topic worthy of careful, detailed and sustained attention.

Exercise 15

Planning an Interview

For this exercise you are asked to prepare a detailed plan of an interview, either a real one that you intend to carry out or an imaginary one for the purposes of this exercise. Refer to the 'Before the interview' section of this chapter and use the space below to make notes.

chapter **16**

Influencing skills

Introduction

When we communicate with one another, it is, of course, not simply a matter of people conveying information to each other. What also happens is that people seek to influence each other – this is a common aspect of day-to-day interactions. This may be at a very simple level. For example, if we want someone to smile, we smile at them first. It may not always work, but it none the less remains the case that we are daily trying to influence the behaviour of others. And, of course, other people are seeking to influence us, to persuade us to do what they want us to do or to fit in with their plans. An example of this would be when someone reminds us of a deadline for a particular piece of work to be completed. Of course, they are not simply doing us a favour in reminding us, they are also trying to make sure that we meet that deadline. Influencing skills are basic components of working life (and, of course, of our private lives – interactions based on influencing do not end when the working day does!).

When it comes to interaction skills, then, we should bear in mind just how important influencing skills are in helping us achieve our objectives and make progress (Cialdini, 2009). Without them we would really struggle to get anywhere in the context of people work. Consequently, this chapter explores what is involved in one person seeking to influence one or more others in a particular direction, and highlights a number of strategies that can be used to maximize our effectiveness.

Working in partnership

Before looking at what is involved in influencing other people, one important point we need to bear in mind is that people work is based on working in partnership – that is, my success depends on other people, and some people's success relies on mine (see Chapter 20). We are not isolated individuals who can just do as we please without consequences for ourselves and the people we work with.

In view of this, before we go any further in exploring influencing skills, there is an important distinction to be drawn, namely that between influencing and manipulating.

The latter term implies that we are attempting to influence people in ways that will benefit *us* but disadvantage *them*, while the former (in the sense I am using it here at least) implies that we can benefit from what we are hoping they will do, but so can they – or, at least, they should not suffer as a result of it. For example, if I persuade a colleague to join me in a particular project because I know their involvement will be a significant benefit for me, is that influencing or manipulation? Well, it depends. If he or she also benefits from being involved in the project (or at the very least suffers no disadvantage from being involved in it), then I would regard that as influencing and thus as legitimate. However, if I persuade him or her to get involved, knowing that he or she will suffer problems or difficulties or otherwise be disadvantaged by being involved, then that amounts to manipulation – getting what I want at his or her expense.

This has much in common with the philosophy of assertiveness presented in Chapter 5, where the aim is to achieve a 'win–win' situation, and not for one party to gain at the other's expense. Manipulation, then, is one form of influencing but one I would regard as not only unethical but also counterproductive, in so far as achieving our ends at other people's expense simply gives them grounds for trying to achieve their ends at our expense. Influencing skills in general are part and parcel of working in partnership and can play a fully legitimate part, as long as we do not stray into the territory of manipulation instead of staying on the firmer ground of seeking to influence others for mutual advantage.

Practice focus 16.1

Shabnam was keen to meet with Keith, her opposite number from the South region, when he took up post. However, she was very disappointed when she did get to meet with him. This was because he made some very transparent efforts to manipulate her into doing what he wanted (taking on some of his responsibilities, for example). It was quite clear that he was not interested in forming a positive and mutually beneficial working relationship; he simply wanted to pressurize Shabnam into taking more than her fair share of work. Shabnam decided she would now steer well clear of him and have as little to do with him as possible, thus leaving him without the benefit of her extensive experience and in-depth knowledge of the area and the job. His crude attempt to manipulate her had cost him dear.

Strategies for influencing

What, then, is involved in seeking to influence others? What can we actually do to make ourselves effective in this regard? Let us now look at some of the strategies or 'tools of the trade' that can be drawn upon. The following list is not exhaustive but should be sufficient to paint a picture of what is involved and how we can develop our skills.

Connection

This refers to the basic idea of 'connecting' or engaging with people. At its simplest level, this may simply be smiling, asking somebody how they are and so on. Now, while that may seem fairly obvious, it is amazing how often these basics are forgotten. If you deliberately look out for an example of this, it will not take long to find one (for example, somebody trying to sell something without making any effort to 'connect').

There are also more sophisticated levels of connection, but the basis of them all is having the ability to form a rapport with someone. Note, however, that this should not be tokenistic. 'Making the right noises' fools nobody. Making people feel at ease because you are taking a genuine interest in them, person to person, by contrast, is far more likely to produce a good working relationship in which your views will be listened to. In other words, a good rapport provides a sound platform from which to influence situations.

This idea of connection can also be broadened out to apply to such issues as connecting with someone from a different culture from your own. Being able to communicate across cultures is an important skill or set of skills, and its significance should not be underestimated if we are to take seriously the importance of valuing diversity, as discussed in Chapter 11. See also the 'Guide to further learning' section for details of helpful literature for promoting such skills.

Putting cards on the table

This refers to being open about what you are trying to achieve and encouraging the other person(s) to do likewise. This can then set the scene for being able to identify overlapping areas of interest. That is, even where there are significant areas of conflict between you and one or more people, it may still be possible for you to work together and for them to assist you in achieving your ends. Initially this may seem a strange idea as it means that you may be influencing (and being influenced by) someone with whom you have a significant conflict of interest. However, by 'putting your cards on the table', you may be able to reach a position where you can agree to disagree on some things but be able to support one another in other areas.

Another advantage to this approach is that it may actually reveal that some conflicts of interest are more apparent than real. That is, by attempting to find areas of common ground, you may come to realize that you have far more such overlapping areas of interest than you had initially realized.

Giving solutions not problems

'I've raised this with my boss several times but still nothing's been done' is a common refrain. One way round this is to offer your boss (or anyone else, for that matter) solutions rather than problems. That is, rather than identifying problems and then giving somebody else the problem of solving them and feeling frustrated when they do not do so, an alternative is to decide what you think the solution should be and then present both problem and solution together. For example, instead of saying: 'Here is Problem X, can you please solve it?' we could try: 'Here is Problem X, we think the solution is Y because Z. Is it OK if we try to get this sorted?' Experience suggests that this latter approach is far more likely to influence what the other person does (see Practice Focus 16.2 below). Put it this way: which would be more likely to influence you, if you were the person somebody was trying to influence by using this strategy – being presented with a problem or being presented with a proposed solution?

Practice focus 16.2

The team had been concerned about the poor quality of the reception area for some time and had raised it with the team leader a number of times, but without any satisfactory response. However, one day when the team leader was unable to attend the monthly team meeting because he was on leave, the team discussed the problem in his absence. In the course of the meeting a number of possible solutions to the problem were suggested and the team narrowed this down to two. On his return to work after his holidays the team leader was presented not with another moan about the reception area but with two possible ways of tackling it. He could see problems with one of the suggested solutions but not the other, and so he agreed to raise this at the next district management team meeting. By presenting solutions instead of problems, the team had made progress and therefore felt much happier about the situation.

Giving feedback

One of the skills needed to be an effective staff supervisor is the ability to give feedback constructively and appropriately. However, this is applicable to not only the use of supervision, but also any situation where it is important for people to know where they stand in relation to one another – which basically means a very wide range of situations indeed.

Giving feedback can involve either positive or negative feedback. Positive feedback is where we praise someone or show our appreciation for something. This can be helpful in forming a positive rapport based on mutual respect. However, praising somebody just to influence them is likely to have very limited success – it does not take much for someone to see through this type of superficial approach. Negative feedback is where we express our concerns about someone or something. This is not simply a matter of criticizing someone, as that is hardly a skilled activity. What it involves is having the tact and subtlety to express negative feedback appropriately and constructively (see Thompson and Gilbert, 2011). This is not a simple matter or an easy set of skills to develop but, if you are able to do it, it can be very helpful in gaining respect – and being respected is a fundamental part of being able to influence others.

Speaking the same language

This can mean literally speaking the same language. If you are able to speak to someone in their first language, this is something they are likely to value, but again this is something that should not be done tokenistically. It must be part of a genuine commitment to forming a positive rapport, and not a cheap or empty gesture.

Speaking the same language can also refer to speaking the same type of language. In Chapter 12 we saw that it is important to match our 'register' to the situation – for example, to use a formal style of speech in formal situations, and an informal style in informal situations. The same approach can be taken in relation to matching the style of language not only to the formality or otherwise of the situation, but also to the preferred speech style of the person. For example, using a lot of jargon in a conversation with someone who is unfamiliar with such jargon or is averse to its use is not likely to help when it comes to seeking to influence that person. By contrast, using a sporting metaphor to get your message across to someone who is very keen on sport is likely to be a much more favourable strategy. Neurolinguistic programming (or NLP for short) is an approach to communication and influencing which places great emphasis on the idea of 'speaking the same language' (see the 'Guide to further learning' section).

Dealing with objections

Lambert (1996) argues that it is important to handle objections when trying to influence people. That is, we have to recognize that there may be resistance to what we are trying to do or say. If so, then we should be clear about what the specific objections are, perhaps by making them explicit and then attempting to respond to them where we can. For example, if someone has anxieties about a particular aspect of what you are proposing, making this explicit will give you the opportunity to give them reassurances or to make changes to what you had in mind in order to accommodate their concerns.

This is clearly preferable to meeting objections or resistance and just trying to sweep them under the carpet, in the hope that they will go away. In fact, it could be argued that it is precisely in those situations where we meet objections that we are most going to need to be on our mettle when using our influencing skills. It is also perhaps in dealing skilfully and fairly with objections that we have major opportunities for gaining the respect and credibility we need in order to be effective influencers.

Listening and empathy

In Chapter 12 the importance of active listening as part of effective communication was emphasized. We can now also see that being a good listener is a further part of being a good influencer. That is, if we want people to listen to what we have to say, then we have to return the favour – we have to show that we too are prepared to listen.

However, it is not simply listening in a direct sense; we also have to be able to put ourselves in the other person's shoes, as it were. We have to have empathy, the ability to understand the other person's perspective, if we wish to develop a good working relationship in which we are respected and our views have credibility. Understanding where the other person is coming from (and where they are heading for) can give us a fuller understanding of the situation and make us much better equipped to deal with the situation in a way that is acceptable and advantageous to all concerned – a 'win–win' situation.

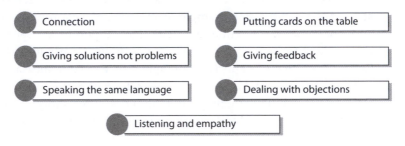

Connection	Putting cards on the table
Giving solutions not problems	Giving feedback
Speaking the same language	Dealing with objections
Listening and empathy	

Figure 16.1   Strategies for influencing

Conclusion

This chapter is not intended to turn you into one of those slimy, manipulative people that everybody gives a wide berth. As we have seen, influencing is one of the basic building blocks of social interaction. When people are together, the chances are that somebody is trying to influence somebody else or indeed that they are seeking to influence one another (Pink, 2013). These are basic skills that we develop as we grow up and learn the 'rules' of our society and culture. However, as with so many people skills, we learn the basics from our day-to-day social lives, but to use those skills at the advanced level required for effective people work, we need to work at them, learn more about them and develop them further. It is to be hoped that the discussions in this chapter will help you to do just that.

By raising awareness of some of the issues and processes involved and exploring a range of strategies, this chapter can play a part in helping you improve your understanding and your effectiveness as a people worker. I hope I have managed to influence you enough to realize just how important influencing skills are, and therefore to appreciate the need to keep learning about them and developing them as far as you can.

Exercise 16

Influencing Strategies

This is an exercise that can be used many times over. It involves observing social interactions (either 'live' or in representational form in film, television and so on) and seeing whether you can identify the various influencing strategies being used. Begin by trying to relate the ones discussed in this chapter. However, after a while you may be able to identify other strategies not included in this chapter (the list here is far from exhaustive). Use the space below to make some notes.

chapter **17**

Leadership

Introduction

The first point to emphasize about leadership is that, while it is closely allied to the notion of management, it is not only managers who can be leaders. Leadership is a process that involves motivating and inspiring others to achieve their best and, while that can be seen as an important task for managers, in principle anyone can be a leader. Figure 17.1 below shows the significance of this.

In this chapter, we shall explore the significance of leadership as a set of people skills. I shall begin by defining leadership, then move on to examine what leaders actually do, before finally exploring what is involved in developing our own leadership skills so that we can put them to good use in our professional endeavours.

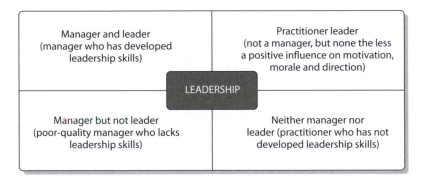

Manager and leader (manager who has developed leadership skills)	Practitioner leader (not a manager, but none the less a positive influence on motivation, morale and direction)
Manager but not leader (poor-quality manager who lacks leadership skills)	Neither manager nor leader (practitioner who has not developed leadership skills)

Figure 17.1 Leadership and management

What is leadership?

Being a leader involves having a vision of where you and the people you are responsible for are heading, and communicating that vision effectively. It involves developing a shared view of the destination you are aiming for and the route you intend to follow to get there. Having a vision involves developing a set of goals to achieve, and this in itself is a significant source of motivation (there is a strong link here with the idea of systematic practice to be explored in Part III of this book). A leader, then, is somebody who has clarity about where the group is going and makes sure that everyone is clear about this, so that they are motivated to move forward constructively together. In this way, leadership is an important foundation for teamwork. This is a point to which I shall return below.

The idea of leadership can be understood by considering its derivation:

> 'Leadership' is derived from the Old English *laedan*. The *Oxford English Dictionary* defines 'lead' as: 'to show the way to (an individual or group) by going with or ahead; to guide, control and direct; to direct the course of; to give an example for others to follow'. . . . The Anglo-Saxon *laed* means a path or road, related to the verb *lithan*, to travel or proceed. . . . So their concepts of leader would be around: pathfinder, helmsperson, navigator, steersperson, explorer, educator.
>
> (Gilbert, 2005, p. 4)

Leadership, then, involves clarifying pathways for moving forward. As such, it involves the idea of a vision, as mentioned earlier – that is, a conception of where it is you are trying to get to so that you can then decide what path(s) to follow to maximize your chances of achieving your ends.

As a 'visionary' process, leadership is a matter of pulling rather than pushing. That is, a good leader is somebody who is able to motivate – or even inspire – staff and others to move forward without having to push or coerce them. To a certain extent, it is a matter of carrot rather than stick. But it goes beyond this, in so far as the inducement of a 'carrot' is likely to produce only a superficial commitment to the team's goals, whereas effective leadership is likely to produce a much fuller and deeper commitment to achieving those goals. This is because people who are fortunate enough to work with an effective leader are likely to share the goals and thereby develop a personal commitment to achieving them, rather than their compliance having been bought by a 'reward'.

Traditional
command and control
(push)

Leadership based on
motivating and inspiring
(pull)

Figure 17.2 Pulling and pushing

In this way, a good leader 'pulls' the team by motivating and inspiring members to pursue the shared goals. There is therefore no need to 'push' people (except as a last resort), in the sense of putting them under pressure to complete a particular task or pursue a particular course of action. One important consequence of this is that it can create a sense of security. Followers of a leader are likely to be keen to do their best and to achieve their goals because they feel that they are part of a greater whole, the leader of which is someone they have faith in, somebody who helps them develop a sense of safety and security in what they are doing.

A key part of this is trust. Where there is no trust, there is no real leadership. Leaders therefore have to develop the skills of winning trust and also have to make sure that their actions are consistent with their values, as someone whose behaviour is seen to lack integrity (that is, is not value driven) will not generally be regarded as a person who can be trusted.

As Stephen Webb points out, trust is easily lost:

> Trust is fragile; once it has been violated it is difficult to re-establish (Slovic, 1999). It is typically created in a slow sequential order, but is damaged in an instant by accident or mistake. Thus once lost it takes time before it can be regained.
>
> (2006, p. 103)

Leaders therefore have to be very careful to ensure that they do not lose trust – for example, by letting people down. This means that leadership is quite a significant challenge, and is not something that can be developed overnight. However, we should be careful not to go to the other extreme and assume that leaders are born, not made – a point to which I shall return below.

What leaders do

The primary role of a leader is to shape the 'culture' – the team or organizational culture which he or she is responsible for or is a part of. For example, if there is a culture of defeatism and low morale, then this is likely to prevent the individuals concerned from pulling together as a team and meeting their goals of achieving their vision. A leader will therefore rise to the challenge of trying to shape a more positive culture.

A culture is a set of habits, unwritten rules and taken-for-granted assumptions. The idea is captured by the phrase: 'the way we do things round here'. A good leader does his or her level best to ensure that they are encouraging a positive and supportive culture and discouraging aspects of a culture that are counterproductive – negativity and cynicism, for example.

Practice focus 17.1

The team would often make decisions about how to improve their practice but, unfortunately, any changes they made would be short lived and they would quickly return to their old habits and established ways of working. Liz found this frustrating but accepted it as a fact of organizational life: 'Teams make decisions but don't stick to them; that's life.' However, she was very interested to note what happened when the team had a new manager, Andy. His influence as a leader proved to be quite significant. When the team made any decisions after his arrival, he would watch closely to make sure that team members were sticking to what they had agreed, and every time someone began to revert to the old pattern of working, he would gently remind them that the team had decided that wasn't the way they were going to do it anymore. This proved to be very effective, as this gentle 'policing' of the team's decisions enabled change to be carried through and become established as new patterns of working. This made the team much happier about their ability, with Andy's leadership support, to improve their practice. Indeed, they felt much happier about the team overall as Andy's approach had created a sense of trust and security. This helped to generate a sense of well-being within the team, as each member felt that they had a leader that they could rely on. This simple process on Andy's part of making sure that the team carried through the changes agreed was extremely effective in creating a culture of positive change. Liz realized now that the team's previous laxity in carrying decisions through was not 'just one of those things that happen in organizations', but, rather, was an indication of the previous team manager's lack of leadership skills in allowing the team to lose sight of its decisions and the need to implement them effectively.

Having a clear vision and communicating it effectively are at the heart of shaping a culture. To break existing habits and develop new ones that are more productive and more conducive to achieving job satisfaction, it is necessary to offer something more positive in their place. Having clarity about what the team is all about (its aims, its values, its distinctive features) can readily serve the purpose of creating the motivation to move forward positively and, in doing so, create new habits, working practices and attitudes and thus establish a new culture.

A significant part of this is developing approaches based on empowerment, rather than simply relying on traditional command and control mechanisms. If the leader simply gives instructions that amount to a message of: 'I am the boss; do as I say', then this is unlikely to have any positive or beneficial impact on the culture, which may be destructive, obstructive or otherwise unhelpful. However, it should be noted that empowerment is not simply a matter of delegation. Empowerment is quite a skilled process in the context of the workplace. It involves helping people to have the confidence to move forward together, with clear goals to aim for that they are committed to. If employees perceive a leader's efforts in the direction of empowerment as simply having the boss's work dumped on them, the result will be disempowerment, disaffection and quite a mountain to climb for the leader to win people over. Empowerment therefore needs to be thought through very carefully to avoid the very common dangers of oversimplification associated with it (see Thompson, 2007, for a discussion of this).

One of the most significant skill sets that a leader needs is the ability to influence people (see Chapter 16). For a leader, however, it is a much broader role than simply influencing individuals; it also involves influencing the overall atmosphere and context in which people work (the culture). This can be done in a number of ways, but what it all amounts to fundamentally is being successful in developing and communicating a clear vision and thus a set of strategic goals to aim for.

Leaders have a particularly important role to play at times of change. One of the important things leaders do, therefore, is to manage change effectively. It involves helping people to maintain a sense of security during what can be unsettling times. A leader therefore has to have a good understanding of the processes involved in change and how to influence these positively to ensure that the benefits of change are capitalized upon and the costs and dangers of change are kept to a minimum (see the discussion of 'force-field analysis' in *The People Solutions Sourcebook*).

One important thing to recognize in relation to leadership is that it does not operate in a social vacuum. We therefore have to be wary of stereotypes of leadership which portray leaders as white, male and macho – even military figures. The reality of leadership is much more complex than this. It is therefore important that we do not adopt a simplistic view of leadership that discourages women, black people and other non-dominant groups from fulfilling their leadership potential. This would be entirely contrary to the principles of valuing diversity (see Chapter 11) and anti-discriminatory practice (see Chapter 21).

This is an important ethical dimension of leadership. Another significant such dimension is the need for leaders to earn respect and, in part, do so by showing genuine appreciation and offering support. Bearing this in mind, we can see that, in order to achieve their goals, leaders need to 'get people on board' – to make them feel part of the team, part of an important shared endeavour – and this is done primarily through earning and showing respect and, in addition, valuing the contribution that every team member makes. In doing this, they are exploiting opportunities and situations and not exploiting people – an important basis for *ethical* leadership, in so far as it does not involve abusing or misusing power.

Developing leadership

As noted above, one significant obstacle to the development of leadership is the assumption that leaders are born, not made. The reality is that the skills of leadership can be learned over time. The people skills discussed in this book form a significant foundation for what is required in order to be an effective leader.

This is one of four myths about leadership that Gilbert challenges. He offers an important set of insights into how leadership can easily be misconceived or misrepresented:

> There are indeed quite a few misunderstandings about leadership:
>
> ○ That 'leadership' and 'management' are the same.
> ○ 'Leadership' is so superior to 'management' that once you have the former you do not need the latter.
> ○ 'Leadership' is tied to specific roles, rather than being a quality required at all levels and in all groups: e.g. users, carers, professionals and all staff.
> ○ Leaders have to be a charismatic hybrid of Alexander the Great, Queen Elizabeth I, General Norman Schwartzkopf and Florence Nightingale!
>
> (2005, p. 4)

In terms of the first point, we have already established that you do not have to be a manager to be a leader and not all managers are leaders (see Figure 17.1). In relation to the second point, management is about keeping the wheels turning, while leadership is about making sure that they are turning in the right direction, so clearly both are needed within organizations. The third point again relates to our earlier discussion encapsulated in Figure 17.1. The fourth point is important in emphasizing that perfectly ordinary people can be effective leaders. Charisma is a great asset if you have it (or can develop it), but it is not an essential prerequisite. We should therefore not allow stereotypes or other misrepresentations to dissuade us from fulfilling our leadership potential by developing the skills over time.

One central set of such skills is that of communication. An effective leader needs to be an excellent communicator, not only of the vision that is fundamental to the group's project, but also more generally in terms of interacting with others. Communication is about giving and receiving messages. A leader therefore needs to be clear about what messages he or she is giving, through:

○ *Actions.* What are we doing that convinces people that we are worthy of respect, that we value their contribution and that we can be trusted to lead them through difficult territory towards the identified goals?
○ *Inactions.* If there are things that we are failing to do, are we undermining our role as leaders, in so far as we are failing to create the sense of security and trust that is so essential?

○ *Interactions.* Are we relating to people within our team or group and also key figures outside of the group in effective ways? Are we showing our commitment to moving forward constructively through these interactions?

○ *Reactions.* Do we panic or do we keep calm in difficult situations? It is important to develop and maintain a sense of security if we are to be effective leaders, and so we have to be on our mettle when it comes to reacting to difficult or demanding circumstances.

Leadership encourages creativity, professionalism and reflective practice and helps to act as an antidote to rigid, formalized bureaucracy based on unthinking routines and 'following orders'. As such, it has a great deal to offer. Developing the skills involved can be quite a daunting challenge, but it is not one that needs to be achieved urgently. It is something that can be developed over time. Indeed, leadership can be seen as quite a significant challenge throughout our career because, as I mentioned at the beginning of the chapter, it is not only managers who can be leaders. As practitioners in the people professions we all have the potential to build up our leadership skills and capitalize on them in whatever ways we can – acting as a positive influence on the people we are seeking to help and on our colleagues, particularly colleagues less experienced or less confident than ourselves.

Practice focus 17.2

Jess was disappointed when she joined her new team. This was because, in her previous job, she had been part of an enthusiastic and supportive team, but her new team was quite the opposite; it was a very negative team, with lots of moaning and cynical comments. It was as if the team had given up on itself and resigned itself to low-quality work premised on low morale. Jess wondered how she was going to cope with this. Already she could feel herself losing heart and sinking into negativity and defeatism. However, she then noticed that Marian, the team manager was trying to make efforts to instil a more positive culture, to undermine the cynicism that had crept in. After considering the situation very carefully for a while, she decided that she would try and support Marian in these efforts. In a supervision session with Marian she therefore raised the question of what she could do to help tackle the team's problems. She was a bit anxious in raising the issue in case Marian objected to her 'treading on her toes', but her concerns quickly showed themselves to be unfounded, in so far as Marian warmly welcomed her support. After this Jess played an important part in trying to challenge the culture of negativity. Although she didn't think of it directly in such terms, she was in fact beginning to develop her leadership skills.

Conclusion

Leadership is by no means an organizational panacea, but it is certainly a significant asset. Often the key difference between a team of staff being successful and satisfied in their work and being unsuccessful and dissatisfied is the quality of leadership. A good leader can bring out the best in people, while a poor leader can add to people's pressures by making them feel undervalued, unsupported and unclear about where they are supposed to be going.

It is to be hoped that this chapter, brief though it is, has given you a foundation of understanding and a desire to develop that understanding through further reading and discussion. You, and the people you work with, potentially have much to gain by the development of your leadership skills.

So, to make the most of the opportunities presented, you may want to start by considering who you regard as a good leader and see if you can work out what it is that makes them a good leader in your eyes. Thinking about what that tells you about your own leadership potential and learning needs could be an excellent step in the right direction.

Exercise 17

Influencing Culture

Think about the culture you currently work in (or where you are currently studying). How would you describe that culture? Is it mainly positive and constructive or are there strong elements of negativity and low morale? How could the culture be improved?

What does considering these questions teach you about leadership?

chapter **18**

Handling feelings

Introduction

At the beginning of the book, the point was made that people work can be understood in terms of three dimensions: thoughts, feelings and actions – 'Think–Feel–Do'. This chapter focuses specifically on the second of these – the ways in which feelings affect practice.

There are two main sets of issues to be addressed: dealing with other people's feelings, and dealing with our own. The emotional dimension is often one that may be neglected and, where it is considered, it may well be that only the first aspect is addressed – the feelings of others. In a sense, this is not surprising, as it can be quite unsettling to delve into our own emotional responses. It can make us feel very uncomfortable, and therefore reluctant to consider them at anything beyond a superficial level. However, as I shall argue below, it is important that our own feelings are taken into account, as a failure to do so can lead to a number of problems, both for ourselves and for the people we work with.

Feelings can often have a subtle effect on our practice without our realizing. They can colour our perceptions and shape our actions. In this respect, actions and attitudes can often be 'feelings in disguise'. That is, they can stem from an emotional response to a particular situation. This can apply in one of two ways. First, feelings can act as an 'accelerator'. They can push us forward into doing certain things. That is, feelings act as motivators, although they can sometimes motivate us too much, in the sense that they can make us act rashly.

Second, feelings can act as a 'brake'. That is, they can demotivate us and stand in the way of us achieving our goals. For example, feelings of loss and sadness can rob us of our energy and commitment, and leave us struggling to cope with the demands made upon us (Thompson, 2012b).

Clearly, then, the emotional dimension of human experience raises a number of important issues for people workers. A better understanding of the role of feelings can therefore help to equip us for the demands of the job. I shall first of all address some of the important questions that arise in attempting to deal appropriately and constructively with the feelings of others, before moving on to consider the complexities of handling our own feelings.

Other people's feelings

Perhaps the first point that should be emphasized is the importance of being able to recognize feelings, to be able to detect their sometimes subtle influences. Sensitivity to feelings is an essential part of good practice but this can often be blunted, particularly at times when people are busy or under pressure (or, as I shall argue below, when we are preoccupied with our own feelings). It is therefore important that we do not allow pressures of work or other concerns to reduce 'Think–Feel–Do' to a simple matter of 'Think–Do'.

However, it is often the case that feelings are expressed openly and explicitly, and so there is no question of not recognizing them. When this occurs, there is a very strong temptation to acknowledge this by saying something along the lines of: 'I know how you feel'. However, as many practitioners have found to their great cost, comments such as this can be disastrous when feelings are running high. It can provoke a very strong reaction. This is because it fails to recognize that a bland response to intense feelings is likely to be experienced by the client as an intrusion that alienates the individual and serves to invalidate his or her feelings.

A more helpful or appropriate comment would be something like: 'I can see that this is upsetting ...', or 'I realize you must be angry about this'. Such comments acknowledge that there are strong feelings but do not give the impression that we 'know' what is inside the other person's head or heart.

This raises a key distinction that we should bear in mind, namely that between sympathy and empathy. Sympathy entails sharing the same feelings as the other person at a particular time or in particular circumstances. Empathy, by contrast, refers to recognizing the other person's feelings (and responding accordingly) without actually feeling them ourselves.

Sympathy

Sharing the other person's feelings

- If they are sad you are sad. You run the risk of being overwhelmed by other people's feelings

Empathy

You recognize the other person's feelings but you do not share them

- You are better equipped to help them with their sadness (without necessarily feeling sad yourself)

Figure 18.1 Sympathy and empathy

Of course, empathy rarely occurs in a pure form. It is perhaps inevitable at times that we feel at least a hint of the feelings the other person is displaying. However, if we were to take on board all of the feelings that we encounter in undertaking people work, we would very quickly become swamped and overwhelmed. The essential task, then, is to remain sensitive to people's feelings so that we do not become callous or unfeeling, but without being so sensitive that we become disabled by the welter of emotions that we come face to face with. That is, we need to nurture the skills of empathy, rather than run the risk of allowing sympathy to disempower us, thereby rendering us of little use or value to people at the very point when they may need us most.

Other people's feelings can make us feel very uncomfortable, and this can sometimes lead some workers to gloss over the feelings dimension and give it as little attention as possible. One of the ways in which this can manifest itself is through a 'macho' attitude in which feelings come to be seen as an encumbrance, a barrier to 'getting on with the job' – as if feelings were not part of 'the job'. This 'be tough' approach can be a misguided attempt to deal with the pressures of the work. As such, it is very destructive, as it reduces effectiveness, increases the likelihood of mistakes being made and creates an unsupportive atmosphere by excluding or marginalizing the emotional dimension.

A 'macho' approach, although more closely associated with men, can none the less apply to women. A 'be tough' attitude is not an exclusively male phenomenon, but can be equally problematic wherever it is adopted. Similarly, we should avoid the stereotype that men are not capable of sensitivity and emotional responsiveness. The idea that emotional issues are 'best left to the women' is a very unhelpful one, as it places an unnecessary burden on women and devalues the part that men can play in high-quality people work.

At the opposite extreme from the macho approach is what I would describe as a self-indulgent voyeurism. This is where a worker may become preoccupied with the feelings issues involved in a particular situation at the expense of other important aspects. This can extend to the point where the worker seems to get some sort of psychological benefit from working closely with other people's feelings. It becomes a type of 'voyeurism' in which close exposure to someone's intimate personal feelings provides a form of gratification. This is not to say that dealing with feelings should not be enjoyable and bring job satisfaction, but there are dangers involved when the process becomes one characterized by a degree of self-indulgence.

Where this occurs, it may indicate that the worker has unmet emotional needs of his or her own. Its results are potentially very serious as the client may experience the situation as intrusive and oppressive, and therefore be very distressed by it, in what is already likely to be a distressing situation.

The situation may also prove to be damaging for the worker, especially if the client rejects him or her, or makes a complaint.

Thankfully, this type of emotional over-involvement is relatively rare but, when it does arise, it is potentially disastrous. Clearly, then, it is extremely important to ensure that we do not allow ourselves to be drawn into this type of situation. Similarly, we should be ready to support colleagues when we suspect that they may be becoming entrapped in such a destructive scenario.

Practice focus 18.1

Kay worked very closely with Mrs King and would often visit her in her own time. Kay felt she had a good relationship with Mrs King and was therefore quite concerned when she was told that her involvement would soon have to come to an end due to a reorganization of the workload. She had made a major emotional commitment to this particular client and felt very unhappy about not continuing her work. Kay explained her feelings to Mrs King who, at first, was touched by Kay's loyalty to her. However, this feeling was shortly to be replaced by anxiety as Kay stressed more and more how unhappy she was. Mrs King felt very distressed by the strength of Kay's response to this situation, a fact which came to light later when she discussed her concerns with the worker who had taken over from Kay.

Responding appropriately to other people's feelings is a complex and demanding task. Furthermore, particular emotions may require a particular response, rather than a blanket approach. Some examples of this would be:

○ *Loss.* When a person experiences a significant loss, his or her emotional needs will be different at different stages in the process of adjusting to the loss. For example, in the early stages of a loss reaction, there is little point in trying to advise people or give them information, as they are likely to be in a state of shock in which they are unable to take very much in. All that may be possible initially is simply 'to be there' and thereby provide what may be an important source of moral support (Thompson, 2012b).
○ *Anger.* When someone is feeling very angry, there is a danger that saying the wrong thing may inflame the situation even further. Words therefore have to be chosen very carefully in such situations. This is one of the skills associated with handling aggression and will be discussed further in Chapter 19.
○ *Guilt.* Feelings of guilt can arise when someone genuinely has something to feel guilty about. However, they can also arise in response to a loss, even where the person concerned has nothing to feel guilty about. For

example, when someone dies, a common response from a person grieving is to keep saying things like: 'If only I'd . . .', as if he or she were in some way responsible for the death. It is important to remember, then, that guilt is often an irrational response to a painful situation. Providing reassurance can be helpful, but it is unlikely to be enough in itself, as a person in this situation is likely to need time to work through their feelings.

○ *Joy.*   We also need to consider responses to positive emotions such as joy. At certain times, we may have to help keep such feelings in perspective without being seen as a 'killjoy'. For example, in a situation where someone is 'counting their chickens before they're hatched', the worker may need to help him or her adopt a more realistic perspective in order to avoid the pain of disappointment. In this respect, even responding to positive emotions needs to be a skilled activity.

○ *Anxiety.*   Anxiety is a state of generalized emotional discomfort. It is similar to fear, but also different in so far as fear tends to be more specific – we tend to know what it is that we are afraid of. Anxiety is less specific, a less focused sense of unease. It is this that makes anxiety more difficult to deal with. But this also gives us a means of dealing with anxiety – by 'translating' it into fear. That is, we can help clients develop a better understanding of what is causing their anxiety and, by identifying specific fears, outline a way forward for tackling them.

One very important concept in relation to dealing with feelings is that of 'catharsis'. This refers to the process of setting people free when they have encountered an emotional 'blockage', for example as a result of bereavement. Sometimes, people's lives can be highly problematic because they have reached an emotional impasse. This can be very disabling, leaving people ill-equipped for the day-to-day demands that they face.

There can therefore be a very significant role for the worker in unpicking the lock of this impasse in order to allow people to regain control of their lives and come to terms with the emotional pain and difficulties they have encountered. Helping someone to achieve catharsis can therefore be a task of major importance, a significant form of empowerment.

Our own feelings

Although people workers should aim for some degree of objectivity and detachment, it is of course inevitable that our own feelings will have at least a small part to play in influencing the complex interactions that characterize people work. Indeed, in many cases our own feelings can be very much to the fore and can play a major part in influencing the outcome of the intervention. It is therefore important that we address the question of the impact of our feelings on practice (and, of course, the impact of practice on our feelings).

People work involves a set of processes in which workers engage with, and respond to, a range of other people – clients, colleagues, staff from other organizations and so on. When people come together in this way, a variety of emotional responses will be generated, including jealousy, hope, anger, frustration, disappointment, joy and anguish; we could not possibly predict what emotion will arise in what situation, but there are some guidelines or general principles that can help us to appreciate the significance of the emotional dimension.

One such principle is the need to avoid adopting a 'stoic' response. This is the equivalent of adopting a macho approach to other people's feelings. Once again, it entails a 'be tough' attitude that seeks to play down or marginalize the role of feelings in human interactions. The stoic approach attempts to bypass or repress one's own feelings, rather than deal with them openly or constructively.

There are three main problems associated with a stoic approach. These are:

1 Often the energy it takes to repress the feelings leaves less energy for tackling the problems that gave rise to the feelings in the first place. That is, it is counterproductive in so far as it distracts attention from the main task at hand.
2 Our own feelings can be a source of positive and constructive energy, a tool to be used to promote change and enhance problem solving in people work. That is, the process of repressing feelings not only wastes personal resources in itself, but also stifles what can be an important contribution to effective practice.
3 If feelings are repressed over a long period of time, the result can be that 'burnout' is experienced. This is an important point to which I shall return below.

An important issue in relation to the stoic response is the extent to which the organization in which one works encourages or discourages it. The key concept here is 'organizational culture', the shared values and practices that characterize an organization (Northouse, 2010). If the atmosphere in which we work is a 'stoic' one, then the expression of feelings may prove difficult. If, however, the atmosphere is a positive one that accepts and acknowledges the emotional demands of people work, then the expression of feelings will be much easier, and may even be positively valued.

Each of us can play a positive role in creating or maintaining an 'ethos of permission', a work environment that permits or even encourages expression and discussion of feelings. We can do this by:

○ not being afraid to express our own feelings;

○ not disapproving of other people expressing or discussing their feelings;
○ recognizing when someone is distressed, and offering them support; and
○ including the emotional dimension in discussions of work.

An ethos of permission can be very supportive, whereas an ethos of stoicism can produce an oppressive atmosphere that can be experienced as stressful. This is particularly important for people workers due to the tendency to regard such workers as 'special people' who are good copers and resilient in response to life's pressures, with little need for support.

A concept closely linked to stress, and very relevant in this context, is that of burnout. This refers to a condition in which the worker becomes numb to the emotional aspects of his or her work, and practises in a routine, unfeeling way. This tends to arise as a response to prolonged exposure to the stresses associated with a job in which the emotional demands are high.

Burnout represents a highly problematic situation in a number of ways, including the following:

○ *For the worker.* Burnout minimizes or destroys job satisfaction and can, in extreme cases, lead to mental health problems such as depression.
○ *For clients.* Effectiveness is reduced by burnout and many clients will recognize that there is little or no sense of commitment on the part of the worker.
○ *For colleagues.* A person experiencing burnout can be quite a damper for colleagues, undermining positive attitudes and team spirit. This can have a detrimental effect on a whole group of staff.
○ *For the organization.* A burnt out worker can destroy an organization's reputation for high-quality work through poor quality, insensitive practice.

The key issue with regard to burnout is that, if our own emotional needs are not met, then we shall be ill-equipped to deal with the feelings of others in a responsive and constructive way. It is therefore vitally important to ensure that we pay heed to our own emotional needs in order to minimize the risk of falling victim to burnout.

The concept of 'counter-transference' is also relevant to the question of dealing with our own feelings. As we noted in Chapter 1, 'transference' refers to the process whereby the client imports feelings about a previous relationship into his or her relationship with the worker. 'Counter-transference' is where this operates in reverse. That is, it describes a process whereby a previous relationship influences the worker's attitude and response to the client.

This usually happens because there is something about the client that reminds the worker of someone who is well known to him or her. For example, if the client looks or acts like a person the worker dislikes, then the worker may have to guard against transferring the negative feelings on to the client. Similarly, if the client reminds the worker of positive associations, then he or she may well have to guard against being uncritically positive. Counter-transference can therefore lead us into adopting an unbalanced attitude towards particular clients. In this respect, we need to be very conscious of our feelings towards the people we work with in order to ensure that our practice is not coloured by prejudices caused by counter-transference.

One principle that can help us to guard against such difficulties is that of 'unconditional positive regard'. As noted earlier, this is an idea to be found in the work of Carl Rogers (1961) which is used to describe an attitude of mind that ensures that we are positive towards the people we work with, regardless of our personal feelings towards them. That is, good practice is premised on doing our best for all clients, not only the ones that we like.

This is particularly important in certain types of people work. For example, in working with perpetrators of child abuse, what they have done may fill us with revulsion. However, if we allow this to colour the extent to which we help them deal with their problems, we are, in effect, reducing our own effectiveness. In this way, a failure to adopt unconditional positive regard is likely to result in less effective child protection practice. Unconditional positive regard is therefore not only a moral ideal, but also a fundamental principle of good practice.

This does not mean that we have to like everyone we work with, or that we are 'not allowed' to have negative feelings, but it does mean that we need to be as effective as possible with all the people we work with, regardless of our feelings towards them or what they may have done. Difficult though it may be to be positive towards people we do not like, good practice requires us to overcome these difficulties.

The emotional dimension of people work can also affect our relationship with our line manager. Tony Morrison (2013) discusses two ways in which this can occur. First, he comments on the process of 'mirroring', which he describes as developing a parallel with the subtle process by which the dynamics of the people we are working with are reproduced in the relationship between worker and supervisor. Mirroring arises from the ways in which individuals, groups or whole organisations adopt particular defence mechanisms in response to stressful feelings.

An example of this would be where a client subtly makes it clear that he or she is not happy about discussing emotional issues. This can then be mirrored in the worker's own approach. Because the feelings dimension has not been addressed, the worker may feel very uncomfortable in discussing such issues with his or her supervisor, thereby reinforcing the tendency for emotional issues to be neglected. When this process takes hold, it can be very difficult to untangle the emotional issues and make positive progress.

In this way, the worker can become cut off from supervision as an important source of support.

Second, Morrison discusses the 'Professional Accommodation Syndrome'. This describes the process by which an insensitive response to emotional pressures on the part of a worker's employer can amplify the distress experienced. It is unrealistic in many people-work settings to expect their work to be pain free. However, what can be highly problematic is the insensitive response of so many organizations when staff talk about the effects of their work on them. This produces a situation in which there are *primary* pressures from the nature of the work itself, but it tends to be the *secondary* pressures arising from their organization's unsupportive response that create stress and distress.

Practice focus 18.2

Ceris was returning to the office after a long and particularly difficult assessment visit to a client with mental health problems. It was 6.30 and Ceris felt quite drained. The client had threatened violence, his family had been very upset and she felt tired and very isolated. As she let herself into the office, she noticed there was still someone in her team room. She discovered that two colleagues and her team leader had stayed behind specifically to give her the opportunity to talk through her difficult visit. She cried, feeling looked after, supported and so much better.

[Source: Thompson, Murphy and Stradling, 1994]

Conclusion

The feelings dimension of people work is perhaps one of the most difficult aspects to deal with. This is, as we have seen, partly because the feelings of others can be so intense and powerful, and partly because our own feelings can be intertwined with our practice in complex and subtle ways. Consequently, it is not surprising that many workers seek to ignore or minimize the role of feelings in people work.

However, the dangers associated with the failure to grasp the nettle of feelings should, by now, be quite clear. If we try to turn our back on the emotional issues involved in people work, we not only reduce our chances of being effective, we also run the risk of doing more harm than good, to ourselves and to the people we are trying to help.

Exercise 18

Perception Check

Johnson discusses what he calls a 'perception check', a strategy for trying to make sure we have understood the other person's feelings. He describes it in the following terms:

> The best way to check out whether or not you accurately understand how a person is feeling is through a perception check. A *perception check* has three parts:
>
> 1 You describe what you think the other person's feelings are.
> 2 You ask whether or not your perception is accurate.
> 3 You refrain from expressing approval or disapproval of the feelings.
>
> (1993, p. 152)

This is a technique that you can use to good effect in your work. However, before doing so, it may be as well to try it out on a colleague, your partner or a friend. You may find it useful to seek feedback as to whether your use of this technique was helpful to the person concerned. Use the space below to make notes for future reference.

chapter **19**

Managing conflict

Introduction

People work often involves an element of conflict, sometimes a major element. This can be a significant source of anxiety, a serious concern for staff involved in this type of work. It is therefore important that we explore what is involved in the process of managing conflict and consider some of the issues that contribute to good practice.

Often the role of the worker is to avoid or resolve conflict though negotiation. The skills involved in this are very important because, as Johnson recognized some time ago: 'You cannot not negotiate' (1993, p. 205). That is, the process of negotiation will tend to occur in situations of conflict, even if we do not begin it deliberately. The task, then, is to become more aware of what happens during negotiations so that we are better equipped to handle them constructively.

But we also need to go beyond this, to consider what happens when negotiation fails and an aggressive response ensues. We need to identify the key factors that apply in situations characterized by aggression and/or violence, and identify strategies for dealing effectively with the challenges that such situations present. This is a key task in terms of:

- ensuring that aggressive responses do not undermine our effectiveness by sidetracking us from pursuing our agreed goals;
- protecting ourselves from harm in potentially volatile situations; and
- boosting our confidence in dealing with such situations in future.

The chapter is divided into two main sections. The first deals with the process of negotiation and therefore has a preventative focus (preventing conflict from overspilling into aggression). The second addresses issues of aggression and violence and offers guidelines on how to respond appropriately when faced with aggression and actual or potential violence.

Negotiation

According to Pruitt and Carnevale:

> Negotiation . . . can be defined as a discussion between two or more parties aimed at resolving incompatible goals. The parties involved may be individuals, groups, organizations, or political units such as countries or the UN Security Council. When there are incompatible goals, a state of social conflict exists. Hence, negotiation is a way of dealing with social conflict.
>
> (1993, p. xv)

Negotiation involves working in partnership with a view to agreeing a way forward. This can sometimes be a straightforward co-operative endeavour. However, it can also be a very fraught and difficult process involving a great deal of tension. How it turns out depends partly, but not exclusively, on the knowledge and skills of the worker.

One aspect that is particularly important to understand is the role of power. Indeed, power is a significant aspect of human interactions in general, but particularly in people work. Power is not a simple, one-way process in which the strong dominate the weak. It is a much more complex matter of subtle and intricate interactions operating at a number of levels. For example, while the worker may have certain powers not available to the client, the latter is not entirely powerless. He or she may resist or not co-operate, or may even sabotage what the worker is trying to achieve. This is what is sometimes known as 'countervailing' power – the power to say no.

Power is an important issue with regard to negotiation because:

○ Attempts by a powerful party to 'bully' the other party into submission will make a negotiated agreement all the more difficult to achieve – see Chapter 6.
○ Countervailing power can be used to sabotage negotiation, especially where there is a lack of trust.
○ Successful negotiation can be a process of empowerment in terms of achieving greater control over one's own circumstances.

In addition, we also need to recognize that knowledge is a form of power. Providing information and helping people to understand can therefore be important aspects of negotiation, in so far as they can help to encourage co-operation and collaboration. Using the power of knowledge to empower others can help to develop trust and respect, factors commonly recognized to be important elements in successful negotiation.

Isaac argues that: 'the ability to negotiate is an essential part of working in partnership' (1991, p. 201). If we are not able to deal constructively with conflicts, then the basis of partnership is likely to be quite fragile and insubstantial, especially in people work where conflicts are far from uncommon. Isaac recognizes the importance of negotiation: 'The task of negotiation, as part of partnership, is for each partner to signal their needs or wishes of the other so that both can search for common ground and agreement' (p. 201). From this he goes on to propose a model of what he terms 'principled negotiation'.

Principled negotiation involves four main aspects:

1 *Separate the people from the problem.* We need to make a distinction between the needs of the individuals concerned and the objectives of the partnership. The needs of individual participants may be more appropriately addressed outside the negotiation arena, as the concerns of one individual may dominate proceedings at the expense of developing an overall consensus.

2 *Focus on interests, not positions.* Negotiation should be more than a form of 'positional bargaining', as this can lead to a vicious circle in which people become more and more entrenched in their positions, thereby increasing, rather than reducing, conflict. It is therefore important that people involved in the process of negotiation are enabled to explain what their interests are (what they hope to gain from the process). These interests then need to be acknowledged and confirmed as legitimate.

3 *Generate possible options to further mutual interest.* This involves a form of brainstorming in which the shared task is to produce a number of possible options for moving forward in a way that will be acceptable to all concerned. As with brainstorming in general, the aim is not to produce a clear solution, but rather to generate a wide range of possibilities. This encourages creativity and avoids the problem of too narrow a focus.

4 *Agree criteria for evaluating results.* The potential solutions generated will need to be evaluated so that inappropriate ones can be discarded and workable options chosen. After agreement has been reached about how to move forward, the more precise details can be worked out so that the necessary steps can be taken.

This model offers a structured framework for dealing with what can often be a difficult process.

An important set of skills associated with negotiation are those of assertiveness, as discussed in Chapter 5. The aim of assertiveness is to achieve a balance in which each party respects the needs and wishes of the other(s) in and through the process of creating 'win–win' situations. Indeed, the parallel between developing assertiveness and negotiation is a very strong and clear one.

Practice focus 19.1

Jan's efforts to achieve agreement across the whole group were fraught with difficulties. At one point she was ready to give it all up and accept that a consensus was not going to be possible. It was then that she hit on the idea of using assertiveness as a way of tackling the situation. At the next group meeting she explained the basic ideas underpinning assertiveness, particularly the notion of seeking 'win–win' situations. She was then able to use this as a basic framework for helping the group identify possible ways of achieving an assertive balance. The group struggled with the idea at first but then began to make major steps forward.

Central to both assertiveness and negotiation is an emphasis on co-operation, rather than the exercise of power. As Johnson comments:

> Co-operators resolve conflict as partners, side-by-side, not as adversaries. They are partners in a hard-headed side-by-side search for a fair agreement advantageous to both sides. Otherwise, you have to be careful when you pass dark alleys! One-sided settlements, imposed by who has the most power at the moment, are rarely stable or long lasting and typically damage the relationship.
>
> (1993, p. 226)

Negotiation is part and parcel of people work, whether part of a deliberate strategy of intervention, or an implicit aspect of day-to-day interactions. However, one point that needs to be recognized is that there are limits to negotiation. That is, some things are simply not negotiable. There are two main ways in which this can be seen to apply:

1 *Official requirements.* Legal or policy requirements mean that some things are not open to negotiation. Certain things have to be respected, regardless of the wishes of the people concerned, for example, health and safety requirements.
2 *Personal values.* At certain times, an individual may, due to personal values or principles, be unwilling to enter into negotiations about a certain issue. We should be wary, then, of trying to coerce people into a process of negotiation.

Aggression and violence

It is often at times when negotiation has broken down, or has not had a chance to get started, that situations involving aggression and violence occur.

But, just as negotiation is a skilled process, so too is dealing with aggression and violence. Indeed, as we shall see, there is considerable overlap between the two sets of skills.

Before considering the reality of aggression and violence, it is worth identifying some situations that could be misread as aggressive scenarios but which are not. These include:

○ *Mock aggression.* In some contexts the language a person uses may imply aggression where no aggressive intention is meant. Examples would include the use of swearing and superficially aggressive comments. Someone may say, for example: 'If you tell anyone this, I'll kill you.' In some circumstances, this may well be a genuine threat, but in others, it may be a rather clumsy attempt to seek reassurance of confidentiality.

○ *Testing behaviour.* Sometimes, people may seek to test us out, perhaps to ensure that we are made of stern enough stuff to earn their respect. When this occurs, it often takes the form of a test of how easily shocked we are. When we encounter this type of behaviour, we can easily interpret it as a form of aggression, unless we are sensitive to the fact that testing behaviour is more to do with defence than attack.

○ *Unchannelled anger.* When someone is feeling angry, he or she may act in such a way as to make us feel that our safety is at risk. In some circumstances, this may well be the case. However, we should not fall into the trap of making the automatic assumption that an expression of anger is a form of aggression or a necessary precursor to violence.

An important point underpinning these three examples, and indeed the whole topic of aggression and violence, is the need to assess situations carefully. Recognizing the potential for aggression and violence is an important people work skill, and is not simply a matter of 'common sense'.

What, then, are the factors we should be sensitive to, in assessing the risk of an aggressive or violent outburst? Breakwell identifies a number of factors that make such an incidence more likely to occur:

Generally, the risk is greater if:

○ The person is a member of a group or subculture where physical violence is the norm. A violent person will therefore experience no loss of face (and may, in fact, gain social approval).

○ The person has a history of violence – violence is then assumed to be a preferred strategy for dealing with problems.

○ The person is aroused by something unpleasant (especially if this is interpreted as a deliberate attempt to hurt and as directed specifically at him or her).

○ The person is disinhibited (through drugs, alcohol . . . physical illness such as brain damage, etc.).

○ The person expects the violence to be rewarded (either materially or through social approval).

○ The person believes no other action is possible. This may be associated with a belief that the person is not in control of his or her own action (this owes something to the instinct theories of aggression).

(1989, p. 53)

Clearly, then, an important aspect of dealing with violence and aggression is that of *anticipation*. This means that a balance needs to be struck between, on the one hand, failing to notice important warning signs and, on the other, over-reacting to aspects of a situation, and thereby causing an escalation of tensions (see Figure 19.1).

Dangerous	Safe	Dangerous
Lacking sensitivity to danger signs	A balanced approach	Prone to over-reacting

Figure 19.1   Responding to aggression

It is important, then, to be aware of what the 'warning signs' are, so that the situation can be carefully assessed and an appropriate and balanced response determined. In addition to the pointers identified by Breakwell above, the following are issues worthy of note:

Nonverbal communication.   More identifies a number of important nonverbal cues:

○ agitation, restlessness and making frequent movements
○ threatening gestures, provocative behaviour
○ holding the gaze – eyeball-to-eyeball confrontation
○ invasion of 'personal space' – coming too close
○ banging table or other furniture
○ clenched fists
○ towering posture
○ obvious facial muscle tension
○ poking fingers or pushing
○ unusual or inconsistent behaviour, e.g. the noisy client who becomes quiet and withdrawn.

(1990, p. 34)

Verbal communication.   This can be quite overt as, for example, in the case of a raised voice (or even verbal abuse), or by more subtle means, such as 'depersonalization' – the process by which someone may seek to undermine your status as a person.

Although anticipation of aggression in interpersonal interactions is important, we should not neglect the need to be aware of the potential for aggression more broadly, so that we can be prepared for, or avoid, such situations. That is, if we know in advance that we may face an aggressive response (for example, in denying a request or exercising a legal duty), then we would be well advised to consider some practical techniques and strategies *before* becoming involved in the situation. These would include:

○ *Not going alone.* The presence of another person can help to protect you from harm, although the situation needs to be handled sensitively, as the presence of another may make the situation more tense.
○ *Having access to help.* Mobile phones may, at times, be a much needed means of getting help. 'Panic buttons' in certain areas are also not uncommon – knowing that access to help is available can give you confidence, and discourage the potential attacker.
○ *Avoid cornering.* Having someone 'cornered' can increase their levels of tension and frustration, and should therefore be avoided. However, balanced against this is the need not to allow yourself to be cornered – to ensure you are within reach of a safe exit. Consequently, it is necessary to be sensitive to positioning. This can also be applied more broadly in terms of car parking. That is, having one's car parked in an accessible place for ease of exit may prove to be of value at times.

'Cornering' is also something to be avoided in a less literal sense. That is, to corner someone psychologically is a dangerous tactic, as it is likely to provoke a strong reaction, possibly an aggressive or violent one. It is therefore necessary to make sure that people have avenues out of situations without losing face. If such exits are blocked, it is not surprising that the person concerned may resort to violence.

Similarly, we need to be wary of antagonizing people in any way, as this may amount to 'skating on thin ice'. This is particularly the case when working with people that we do not know very well. The longer we work with a particular person, the more attuned we should become to his or her likely 'flashpoints'. That is, we should become sensitive to points or issues that may produce a strong response.

What happens before and during interactions can be crucial in terms of the development or otherwise of aggressive or violent encounters. However, what is also of great importance is what happens *after* the event. There are a number of important points to take into account, including the following:

1 Exposure to aggression and/or violence can be very traumatic, leading to a significant experience of stress (see Chapter 3). This means that a great deal of support is likely to be needed if the situation is not to prove detrimental on a longer-term basis. This support will often take the form of 'debriefing'. This involves having the opportunity to talk through the incident, and give vent to one's feelings about it. It is essential that such a discussion does not become an 'inquest' in which attempts are made to allot blame. This is because such a discussion would not only fail in its purpose of providing support but would also run the risk of exacerbating the feelings of guilt that are often generated by such incidents.

Practice focus 19.2

Rhys had been subjected to verbal threats a number of times in the past but these had always passed without incident. This time, however, was different. Although he was not injured, he was very shaken when a client grabbed hold of his tie and pulled him towards himself. Fortunately, Rhys was able to break away and make his escape without further physical contact. Rhys was extremely distraught by the incident, and was not sure that he would be able to deal with potentially difficult situations in future – in short, he had lost his confidence. It was therefore very fortunate that Rhys had a very skilled and sensitive line manager who was able to give him the opportunity to talk in detail about what had happened and how he felt about it. This 'debriefing' was precisely what he needed and made a significant positive difference to how he coped with the situation.

Guilt is an irrational response to situations involving loss. And aggressive encounters can entail a number of losses including the loss of trust, security and confidence. In view of this, it is important that we do not allow a strong sense of guilt to dominate our thinking and distort our perception of the situation. An insensitive approach to debriefing can therefore do more harm than good.

2 In parallel fashion, it is important that we offer support to others when they have encountered a situation involving aggression or violence. This helps to create a supportive environment, an 'ethos of permission', as discussed in Chapter 18. Employers should have policies concerning aggression and violence as part of their health and safety responsibilities.

Understanding the demands of dealing with aggression and violence is important for each of us so that we can both protect ourselves and support our colleagues.

3 In the aftermath of such traumatic incidents, there is a great deal to be learned. We can draw out the main learning points in order to equip

ourselves better to deal with such situations in future. (This is an example of reflective practice, a topic to be discussed in Chapter 30.) In this way, we are able to draw some positives from what otherwise remains a negative and detrimental situation.

However, in view of the comments made in Point 1 above, it is vitally important that this process is handled sensitively. If not, then attempts to draw positive benefits from the experience may actually be a source of further harm. That is, an insensitive approach to attempting to learn from the experience can leave the worker feeling demoralized – blamed and unsupported by someone who translates 'What can we learn from what happened?' into 'What did you do wrong?' There is, then, a clear danger in rushing into attempts to learn without first carefully thinking through how best to do this, or even whether it is appropriate in the circumstances.

4 Although the client may have resorted to aggression or violence, he or she may still require intervention, for example, a person in an Accident and Emergency Unit requiring medical attention. Indeed, intervention may be needed more than ever in the circumstances. The situation coming to a head in this way may produce a crisis in which people are more responsive to intervention, and more committed to bringing about change (Thompson, 2011c). However, if staff are to be exposed to risk of harm, a decision may have to be made as to whether it is safe for work to continue. Sometimes, work may have to be continued (due to a court order, for example), while at other times work may have to be suspended as the level of risk is unacceptable.

If the work is to continue, then a further decision has to be made as to whether the original worker is the best person to remain involved. This will need to be assessed carefully, and, of course, the worker should be given the option of no longer being involved.

Clearly, the events that occur *after* an aggressive or violent incident raise a number of important questions that need to be considered carefully. Indeed, the whole topic of aggression and violence is a complex one that requires careful and sensitive handling. Like so many aspects of people work, there are no simple or straightforward solutions.

Conclusion

Negotiation is a basic feature of interpersonal interactions and is therefore a significant aspect of people work. Negotiation involves a set of skills that can be developed through practice and reflection upon the subtle processes involved. Where negotiations break down, or do not have the opportunity to get started, an aggressive or violent response can be the likely outcome. When this arises, the situation can be a major challenge and a significant source of trauma (see Chapter 29). It is therefore important that ways and means are found to avoid potentially violent situations where possible: anticipate likely aggressive responses; defuse tense situations; and respond positively and supportively in the aftermath of such incidents.

Exercise 19

Trigger Points

For this exercise you will need to consider one or more incidents in which there was an aggressive response. Think carefully about what the 'trigger points' were, what factors played a part in the development of the situation. Use the space below to make some notes.

If you have no experience of such a situation arising, seek out a colleague or friend who has. Discuss with this person what he or she thought were the factors leading to the aggressive response.

chapter **20**

Multidisciplinary working

Introduction

In *The People Solutions Sourcebook* I refer to PRECISE practice, with each letter of this acronym referring to a particular aspect of good practice. It is the 'p' of PRECISE practice that concerns us here, as this refers to partnership-based practice. It can be understood to refer to two types of partnership: one between the helper and the helped (that is, between the worker and the client), and also to the network of helpers – that is, to the multidisciplinary context of the people professions. This chapter focuses on the latter of these two and explores what is involved in developing effective working relationships with fellow professionals from other disciplines.

Partnership is in effect a form of conflict management (see Chapter 19). This is because multidisciplinary collaborations involve a number of differences that can easily clash. Being able to work effectively in partnership therefore requires us to have the skills of working with differences positively and constructively, rather than allowing them to stand in the way of progress. These differences are primarily, but not exclusively:

- *Values.* Different professional groups may have a lot in common in terms of their values, but there can also be major differences. For example, a probation officer and a nurse may have significantly different values in some respects (Moss, 2007).
- *Perspectives.* While someone's perspective will owe much to their values, there can also be other ways in which perspectives differ. For example, a youth worker may be focusing on keeping a young person out of the criminal justice system, while a police officer may be trying to secure a conviction.
- *Priorities.* A hospital doctor may be very keen to discharge an elderly patient because he or she needs that bed for another patient, while the hospital social worker may be reluctant to be part of such a move if it is felt that the support measures the elderly person would need at home are not yet in place.

○ *Expectations.* Professional groups can have very varied expectations from the situations they encounter and the work they do. Some professionals will have a very high success rate in what they do, while others may have quite a low success rate, depending not so much on the competence of the particular workers, but more on the nature of the work. For example, someone involved in mediation can reasonably expect a success rate in the region of 80 per cent, while a youth justice worker trying to prevent a young person from committing offences may perhaps expect a much lower success rate.

○ *Norms.* Different professional groups will have different traditions and thus different approaches. Consequently, their respective organizations will have developed varying norms. That is, what is considered normal in one organization or professional group may be considered not at all normal in other groups. Dress code would be a good example of this, as would norms relating to whether first names or title plus surname are used in addressing senior officers.

○ *Budgets.* What may be a significant outlay to, say, a voluntary organization, may be small beer to a large, private company. What is considered a reasonable level of expenditure by one professional may therefore be considered far from reasonable by someone from a different professional background or setting.

○ *Protocols.* Organizations differ in their level of bureaucracy. So, what may be a relatively simple, flexible protocol in one organization may be horrendously complex and bureaucratic in another. Conflict can therefore arise if someone from an organization that is relatively flexible is waiting for someone from a more bureaucratic organization to follow through on a procedure, and is becoming impatient about the delay.

○ *Experiences.* Some professional groups will quickly develop experience in certain aspects of practice, while others may encounter such situations far less frequently. For example, a worker in an Accident and Emergency Unit may quickly develop experience, knowledge and skills in dealing with aggression and violence, whereas a counsellor may take much longer to have sufficient experience of such occasions to develop the confidence in dealing with them.

These examples show that, when people from different professional backgrounds are called upon to work together in tandem, there are various complicating factors that we need to be aware of. With this in mind, in this chapter we explore why multidisciplinary working is important, and the principles of good practice that should underpin it.

Why is multidisciplinary working important?

Primarily, this form of working partnership is important because of the need to avoid the following three sets of problems:

○ *Falling between two stools.* People may lose out in situations where they could potentially receive help from two or more places, but may actually end up not receiving help from anywhere.
○ *Wasteful overlap.* This refers to situations where people may be receiving overlapping help from more than one source, leading to an inefficient use of resources, as well as other potential problems in terms of the respective organizations getting in each other's way.
○ *Pulling in different directions.* Where there is a need for more than one agency to be involved, then there can be significant problems if representatives of those agencies are not 'singing from the same hymn sheet'. This is problematic for professionals when they find themselves in such situations, as the conflicts and tensions can be quite unpleasant and difficult to deal with. But, what we have to remember is that it is even worse for clients where they are not receiving the help they need because of the failure of the professionals involved to 'get their act together' in terms of effective partnership working.

Figure 20.1 The importance of partnership

In some of these situations, clients may receive contradictory advice, with one person undermining the efforts of another. In many situations this will happen unwittingly – that is, there will be no deliberate attempt to undermine a fellow professional. But, unfortunately, there are cases on record of this happening intentionally – clearly very poor, unethical practice.

A fundamental part of multidisciplinary collaboration is the need for understanding and valuing each other's roles. This can work in terms of people from different discipline areas – for example, various health professionals all being involved with the same patient. Or, it could be within the same organization where people have different disciplinary roles – for example, a coach and a manager could 'tread on each other's toes' if they are not sufficiently aware of their respective roles and boundaries. Unless people have a good understanding of the role of fellow professionals, then there is always the danger that problems will arise, and then multidisciplinary working will not be effective or, at least, will be less effective than it could have been.

Practice focus 20.1

Sarah was very committed to her job, always determined to do the best she could in the circumstances. She didn't like wasting time and was always keen to press on and get things done. She felt she did well in her work and enjoyed good working relationships with colleagues within her own office and with the other professionals she worked with. She was therefore very surprised when she was told by her manager, Jo, that a complaint had been made against her following a recent multidisciplinary meeting. She sat down with Jo to go through the details of the complaint and could hardly believe her ears. A number of colleagues had described her as 'pushy' and difficult to deal with, claiming that she did not take account of their point of view.

As it was an informal complaint at this stage, Jo was able to speak directly to the people concerned to get more information about their concerns and to feed them back to Sarah so she had a clearer picture of why people had been unhappy with her. What emerged from these discussions was a range of concerns about Sarah being single minded about what she wanted and not really taking on board other people's views and perspectives. Jo knew Sarah well enough to be aware that she was very committed to doing what was right by her client, but what was beginning to emerge was a concern that perhaps she was not taking a broad enough perspective on this and was therefore alienating fellow professionals by failing to take on board their views and their issues. It was as if Sarah's enthusiasm to do a good job was preventing her from seeing the overall picture more clearly. Jo was confident, though, that she would be able to help Sarah make the necessary changes in her approach.

Principles of working together

As we have seen, multidisciplinary collaboration is an important, if not essential, feature of 'people work'. Many of the duties undertaken in the people professions involve the need to co-operate with staff from other disciplines. It is therefore worth considering some of the elements of good practice in multidisciplinary collaboration.

Avoid stereotypes

One of the pitfalls that can block effective co-operation is a reliance on stereotypes. The bossy nurse, the aloof doctor, the naive social worker, the uncaring manager – these are all distortions of reality that create barriers to good practice. We have to be careful to ensure that our interactions with other professionals relate to real people and not to stereotypes or other false or distorted impressions. Stereotypes are unfortunately all too common, so we have to be quite sensitive and 'tuned in' to how such assumptions can cause problems (see the discussion of reflective practice in Chapter 30).

Understand each other's roles

A basic element of collaboration is an understanding of the roles of other professionals involved. Unless we are attuned to the roles and duties of staff from other disciplines, we will not appreciate the pressures they face, and will therefore not be in the best position to work together. A failure to understand each other's roles can lead to misunderstandings as well as, at times, considerable ill-feeling. It is therefore vitally important that each person in the multiprofessional network takes the trouble to find out more about the roles and duties of the other professionals involved.

Be sensitive to different values, priorities, norms and so on

As we noted earlier, different professional groups tend to develop different values, priorities and so on. This touches on a set of complex and thorny issues relating to values, but one point remains clear – we must not allow differences of perspective to undermine the quality of service available. However challenging it may be for professionals with very different outlooks to work effectively together, we owe it to our clients to do the best we can to provide as close to a 'seamless' service as we can get.

Avoid hierarchies

When groups of people work together, there is always the danger that a hierarchy will develop in which some people are seen as more important or influential than others. This can produce a situation in which professional rivalry and power bids detract from the primary tasks of people work. Partnership is very much to be preferred to hierarchies. This means that, for the benefit of maximizing the help we can give people, all professionals involved need to show respect to other professionals and not 'look down' on other groups. Everyone has an important part to play.

Avoid preciousness

Because people work so often hinges on relationships and 'use of self', we can sometimes feel quite close to the people we work with. However, we must not allow this to develop into a situation in which we feel precious about 'our' client. It is not unusual for a number of professionals to be working with the same client. A precious approach which 'claims ownership' of clients is therefore highly problematic. The example given below in Practice Focus 20.2 may perhaps be showing elements of preciousness creeping in.

Focus on communication

Where professionals are working together, good communication becomes a priority. If communication channels across the disciplines are not effective, there may be significant gaps in the services provided, or, as we noted above, there may be duplications that are wasteful of scarce resources. Also, poor communication can contribute to problems such as the ones outlined above: stereotypes, misunderstandings about roles and expectations, and unhelpful hierarchies.

One further principle that is worth exploring in a little more depth is the need to be 'person centred'. What I mean by this is making sure that our efforts are geared primarily towards the needs and interests of the person (or persons) we are trying to help. In terms of the importance of self-care, we must also take account of our own needs and interests, but it is important to ensure that these do not predominate at the expense of the client's. Similarly, organizations have needs and interests (making the books balance, for example), and it is important that we do not fail in fulfilling our role and duties by allowing ourselves to lose sight of our primary focus on the client.

Practice focus 20.2

When Karim became head of department, he was concerned that the staff group had become quite institutionalized, heavily into following procedures and protocols and often losing sight of what the department was trying to do. Consequently, morale was low and the number of complaints received was high. Flexibility was not part of the culture of the department at all, even though other parts of the wider organization did not have any problems with rigid approaches. Karim thought carefully about the situation and came to the conclusion that a major part of the problem was that the department was not person centred. Bureaucratic routines had come to dominate under the management of his predecessor and this had had the effect of the staff team losing sight of the people they were there to serve. The clients had to fit in with the bureaucracy, rather than the organization trying to meet its clientele's needs as flexibly and effectively as possible. Karim realized that he had a major challenge on his hands, as he knew he would have to try and change that culture to make it more person centred – in other words, to make it more responsive to the needs of clients. Without this change, he recognized, there would continue to be problems of job satisfaction (morale) and client satisfaction (quality of professional practice).

I use 'person centred' as a general term for this type of approach to fit with the breadth of usage of similar terms across different professions. For example, counsellors may talk of being 'client centred', health professionals will often refer to themselves as being 'patient centred', while teachers and lecturers may think in terms of being 'student centred'. 'Person centred' as a term tries to capture the same commitment to putting the people we serve first, but without making the terminology specific to a particular disciplinary group.

Being person centred is important for two reasons:

○ We are being paid and the people we serve are not. The term 'professional' means different things in different circumstances, but one significant point to note is the fact that professionals are paid for their efforts. It is therefore important that we make sure that what happens is geared towards meeting the needs of the client and is not bogged down in the needs of professionals or their petty squabbles. As Alinsky (1989) put it many years ago, we need to 'start where the person is at'. If we do not, then the result is very unethical practice, in so far as we are taking the money that is intended to help people and using the work time it buys to focus on our own needs rather than the needs of the clientele we serve.
○ It provides a focal point for co-operative efforts. Having the person we are trying to help as our central focus provides a unifying force that channels efforts in the direction of the individual's needs and interests. In this way, we are much less likely to get sidetracked into issues that arise from differences between the various aspects of the professional agendas. Being person centred therefore helps to promote effective multiprofessional co-operation.

This brief foray into the principles of multidisciplinary collaboration should serve to illustrate its complexity and underline the need to invest time and energy in developing effective co-operation across the full range of disciplines involved in people work. Different disciplines bring different perspectives to bear, and this more holistic picture can be of much more value than the narrower view of any professional. As we shall see, in Chapter 24, planning in particular can benefit considerably from the development of high-quality multidisciplinary collaboration.

Conclusion

Multidisciplinary collaboration has always been important in the people professions, but in recent years it has gained a renewed emphasis, partly because of developments in law and policy and partly because more and more people are recognizing that it is not helpful to clients to have people from different helping agencies getting in each other's way, undermining one another or failing to provide a seamless service.

The partnership work involved in developing effective multiprofessional working is premised on a number of important skills that feature in other chapters: communication; conflict management; handling feelings; reflective practice; and so on. Working towards multidisciplinary partnership can therefore be seen to rely on a range of people skills, and so, in some ways, it is a crossroads at which a number of skills issues come together.

It is to be hoped, then, that the comments provided in this chapter provide a good foundation for building effective multidisciplinary working relationships. It has to be recognized that it is not necessarily an easy goal to reach, but it is certainly one worth working towards.

Exercise 20

Professional Stereotypes

Think about your own professional group. How are you and your colleagues seen by other professionals? What stereotypes of your profession exist that might get in the way of working effectively together? What can you do to prevent reinforcing such stereotypical assumptions?

What stereotypes exist in relation to the professional groups you work alongside? How can you make sure that you do not allow such distortions to affect your partnership working?

part **III**

Intervention skills

Chapters

Introduction to Part III

Both the personal effectiveness skills discussed in Part I, and the interaction skills discussed in Part II, are geared towards 'problem solving', by which I mean the various tasks people workers become involved in with a view to making a difference in someone's life in a positive and constructive way (see *People Problems* for a fuller discussion of these issues). They are, however, indirectly linked to the question of intervention, while the issues to be discussed in this third and final part are more directly associated with the process of intervention – they represent some of the basic building blocks of people work.

Chapter 21 focuses specifically on developing anti-discriminatory practice, as part of the process of countering the discrimination and oppression many clients experience. As such, it builds on the foundations laid in Chapter 11 in addressing the importance of recognizing and valuing diversity.

Chapter 22 explains the importance of being 'systematic'. It demonstrates the value of being clear about the outcomes we are working towards and the strategies we use to bring such objectives to fruition. This sets the scene for Chapter 23, in which the process of assessment is outlined, and its significance as the basis of good practice is emphasized.

Chapter 24 focuses on planning as an important aspect of attempting to meet people's needs and address their problems, while Chapter 25 explores the related area of decision-making skills. Chapter 26 is concerned with managing risk. Working with people invariably involves a degree of risk, and so being well informed about risk issues is important.

Chapter 27 explores the important processes of reviewing and evaluating intervention, and Chapter 28 identifies some of the key issues associated with ending intervention.

Chapter 29 addresses the significance of trauma in people's lives, and maps out how we can play an important role in helping people recover from it and, ideally, achieve healing.

Chapter 30 relates to a recurring theme throughout this book, namely the importance of integrating theory and practice. This final chapter addresses the difficult but worthwhile task of developing reflective practice, a form of practice that avoids working in a routine, uncritical way.

Part III has a strong emphasis on a problem-solving approach based on identifying clear objectives. It has to be recognized that this approach can be applied directly to many situations, but may have to be adapted to apply to others. For example, some problems cannot be solved, and so the focus has to be on managing the problem, rather than solving it. However, the sort of problems that cannot be solved – terminal illness, for example – tend to generate a number of other problems (for both the client and the worker). The problem-solving approach advocated here can therefore be applied to these problems, and this makes it an appropriate approach even to problems that have to be managed rather than solved.

chapter 21

Anti-discriminatory practice

Introduction

The main theme of Chapter 11 was 'valuing diversity' – the moral and professional requirement to recognize and respond positively to the significant differences of culture, language, gender and so on. These differences are important aspects of interpersonal interactions for, without due sensitivity to their differences, the potential for effective and appropriate interactions is seriously reduced.

We can now revisit these issues, but this time with a different focus. Instead of concentrating on diversity as a factor in interpersonal interactions, I shall address the question of how the discrimination and oppression associated with diversity can be tackled in and by the process of intervention. That is, I shall examine some of the ways in which our practice in people work can:

- recognize the impact of discrimination and oppression on people's lives;
- avoid the pitfall of reinforcing or exacerbating such discrimination and oppression; and
- challenge and undermine the oppressive structures, attitudes and actions that disadvantage certain groups in society.

The basic starting point is that developing anti-discriminatory practice is an *essential* part of good practice. If we are not sensitive to issues of discrimination, we run the risk of condoning, reinforcing or even amplifying the oppression to which such discrimination leads. If we practise in ways that take no account of discrimination, we may find that we are actually doing more harm than good. That is, instead of our work empowering people and promoting equality, it can actually have the opposite effect by taking away people's power and control and reinforcing, or even exacerbating, existing inequalities. For example, if a worker does not take account of racism in working with black clients, then the actions and attitudes of the worker may make the client feel even more devalued and alienated in a white-dominated society.

The chapter is divided into three main parts. The first looks at ways in which, as individual practitioners, we can move in the direction of anti-discriminatory practice. The second part outlines the organizational context and considers aspects of organizational policy and culture that are significant. The third part explores ways in which groups of practitioners can work together to influence the direction of change for both individual practice and the organizational context. In this way, part three links together parts one and two.

Individual practice

There is a strong element of professionalism in people work, in the sense that people workers tend to have a degree of autonomy in terms of decision making, choosing how we tackle problems and so on. This gives us a considerable degree of responsibility for our actions, and so it is very important that we consider the likely consequences of our actions. As people workers, we are generally in a position of power in relation to the people we seek to help, and so we have to make sure that such power is used positively and constructively, and is not abused, or used irresponsibly.

In view of this, we need to look carefully at the use of power in society and its effects on disadvantaged or minority groups. I shall do this by addressing three sets of issues: recognizing oppression, power sharing through partnership and participation, and empowerment.

Recognizing oppression

Many aspects of oppression are so deeply ingrained in everyday life that many people do not notice them at all – they become taken for granted. For example, many disabled people are seriously disadvantaged by access difficulties due to environmental barriers. This problem is clearly visible for all to see but, unless we are 'tuned in' to issues of discrimination and oppression, we are unlikely to notice. A key task, then, is to become more aware of discrimination, so that we are able to recognize oppression and its consequences.

There are a number of processes that are associated with discrimination and oppression. These include:

○ *Marginalization.* Many people are pushed to the margins of society and excluded from the mainstream where important decisions are made. Consider, for example, the predominance of white, non-disabled men in positions of power, and the predominance of black people, women and disabled people in low-paid work and the unemployment figures. This can also be seen at a micro level. For example, it may be assumed by a worker that the man is the 'head of the household'. Another example would be forms that ask for the person's 'Christian' name, rather than first name, thereby marginalizing people of other religious backgrounds or indeed no religious background at all.
○ *Group closure.* This is a process similar to marginalization, in so far as it hinges on an 'us–them' mentality. The term refers to situations whereby people define themselves as a group and, in so doing, exclude other people unfairly. For example, many clubs seek to exclude women in order to maintain an all-male membership.
○ *Stereotyping.* Rigid views of what particular individuals or groups are like are not helpful in people work, as they reflect and reinforce

the discrimination some groups of people experience. As Pickering comments:

> Stereotyping may operate as a way of imposing a sense of order on the social world in the same way as categories, but with the crucial difference that stereotyping attempts to deny any flexible thinking with categories. It denies this in the interests of the structures of power which it upholds. It attempts to maintain these structures as they are, or to realign them in the face of a perceived threat. The comfort of inflexibility which stereotypes provide reinforces the conviction that existing relations of power are necessary and fixed.
>
> (2001, p. 3)

We therefore need to ensure that we do not allow our own thinking to rely on oppressive stereotypes, and that we challenge them in the thinking of others.

○ *Stigmatization.* Some individuals or groups tend to be 'stigmatized'. That is, they are automatically seen in negative terms because of who they are or some aspect of their circumstances. For example, people living on a housing estate with a higher than average crime rate may all be 'tarred with the same brush' and assumed to be untrustworthy and unreliable. Stigma is therefore closely associated with stereotyping.

○ *Scapegoating.* An individual within a family or group can become the person who takes the blame for the problems of that family or group. Often it is a relatively powerless person within a group who bears the brunt of the group's difficulties. He or she becomes a valve for releasing group tensions. This can also apply at a macro level. A group of people can become the scapegoat for a whole society. For example, black people in Britain are sometimes seen as the cause of social problems, rather than the potential victims.

Figure 21.1 Discriminatory processes

Practice focus 21.1

Malik was the only black youngster who attended the centre. At first, he seemed to be well liked and accepted by the rest of the group. However, when the group went through a period of tension and conflict, the situation changed quite markedly. Some of the more influential members of the group began to take out their frustrations on Malik. The situation very quickly accelerated into one of open conflict, with Malik being blamed for a variety of problems. This clear example of scapegoating gave the staff a major challenge to face, but one that they had to tackle because of the gross unfairness of the situation.

These are just some of the negative and destructive processes that reflect and illustrate experiences of oppression arising from misuses of social power. They are part and parcel of everyday life, and so we can so easily fail to notice them if we do not make the effort to bear them in mind and consider their implications for the people we work with, and for our own practice.

Partnership

The importance of working in partnership has been a recurring theme at various stages in the book. This is not without good cause, as partnership is an essential feature of good practice in people work. This is because a failure to work in partnership is likely to result in:

○ *Resentment and non-co-operation.* If people are not involved in planning what is to happen, or not consulted about what they want or need, we should not be surprised when they respond with resentment and/or a low level of co-operation. An approach based on partnership, by contrast, is likely to produce a much higher level of commitment. A lack of consultation only serves to reinforce existing inequalities and power imbalances.
○ *Mystification.* Partnership is based on openness and sharing of information and plans. If people are kept in the dark, the work becomes shrouded in mystery. This tends to have the effect of creating suspicion and mistrust, and therefore creates barriers to positive interactions and effective practice. Once again, this serves to reinforce existing inequalities.
○ *Dependency.* If clients are not involved in partnership, then they will have little or no control over what is happening to them. This is a situation that is likely to increase, rather than decrease, the likelihood of dependency. Dependency, in turn, increases a sense of powerlessness.
○ *Short-lived success.* Even if some degree of success is achieved without partnership, in many cases it is unlikely to be sustained over a period of time. This is because, unless the person or persons concerned have played an active part in solving the problem, they are unlikely to understand

what made the difference, and will therefore be less well equipped to deal with the situation in future. Similarly, if someone has co-operated with change due to the pressure we have put them under, it is likely that old patterns and old habits will be resumed, once we are no longer involved.

Partnership not only avoids these, and related problems, it also provides a much firmer foundation for practising in ways that play a part in countering discrimination and oppression. Indeed, partnership helps to lay the foundations for empowerment.

Empowerment

The basic idea underpinning empowerment is that people should be helped to gain power and control over their own lives and circumstances. This is important for all individuals, but it is particularly so for members of oppressed groups in order to counter the negative effects of discrimination and marginalization. For example, the effects of sexism are such that women are likely to have to fight harder to make their voices heard in a male-dominated world.

Indeed, one important aspect of empowerment is to help people have a voice, to have opportunities for putting forward their point of view. This is a key element of client participation and a point to which I shall return later.

Other aspects of empowerment include:

○ working in partnership to avoid creating dependency;
○ boosting confidence and self-esteem, where necessary;
○ a collective approach – bringing together people with similar problems, concerns and strengths; and
○ consciousness raising – helping people to see their problems in their broader context, with less emphasis on 'personal failings' and more on the destructive effects of the way society is organized.

Of course, a central feature of work geared towards empowerment must be that we do not, in any way, contribute to the discrimination and oppression people experience. That is, we must ensure that our own attitudes and actions, including the language we use, are not discriminatory or oppressive. This involves a degree of self-awareness (Chapter 1), use of supervision (Chapter 7), continuous professional development (Chapter 9), understanding of diversity (Chapter 11) and reflective practice (Chapter 30). Tackling discrimination and oppression, then, is not a discrete activity in its own right. Rather, it is a part of most, if not all, of our activities as people workers. In view of this, we need to recognize that empowerment is not a simple skill, but rather a complex set of activities linked into a wide range of aspects of people work.

It is also important to note that empowerment has become a fashionable concept that receives a lot of attention. As Gomm (1993) acknowledged, it has become something of a 'buzzword'. However, we should be careful not to allow this to distract us from its central importance as an essential feature of good practice in people work. Empowerment has indeed become fashionable, but this is not to say that it is nothing more than a fashion (see Thompson, 2007).

The organizational context

Anti-discriminatory practice is not simply a matter of individual practice. The organizational context in which such practice takes place is also vitally important in terms of the success or otherwise of our efforts to challenge and undermine discrimination and oppression. There are ways in which this context can facilitate anti-discriminatory practice, and ways in which it can hinder it.

In considering the organizational context, there are some fundamental questions that need to be asked:

○ Are there equal opportunities or diversity policies in place?
○ If so, do they relate only to staffing, or also to service delivery?
○ Are such policies simply 'paper' policies, or are they actually implemented at an operational level?
○ Are senior managers committed to organizational change, or are they resistant to it?

These are important questions that have a significant bearing on the extent to which anti-discriminatory practice will be supported or facilitated. Answers to these questions will help to provide a picture of the organizational context.

An important concept in this regard is that of organizational culture, which Johannsen and Page define as:

> Values, beliefs and customs of a group or type of people. In a company or co-operation, its culture is demonstrated by its management style, including the degree of autocracy or participation practised, and the expectations of employees.
>
> (1990, p. 79)

An organization's culture strongly influences 'the way we do things round here'. That is, common working practices, attitudes and approaches are shaped to a large extent by dominant cultural expectations within the organization concerned.

Such a culture will also be a significant issue in terms of tackling discrimination. Some cultures are strongly rooted in tradition, and are therefore unlikely to be responsive to equality initiatives. Other cultures, by contrast, are more flexible, and are therefore amenable to change in the direction of anti-discriminatory policy and practice. In order to promote anti-discriminatory practice, it is therefore important to get to know the organization in which we work, particularly in terms of cultural norms and expectations. That is, if workers are to influence the direction of change positively in an organization, we must first understand how that organization works.

However, we must also understand the context in which organizations operate, namely the legal context. There are a number of Acts of Parliament that outlaw discrimination and provide a basis from which to tackle inequality. See Leighton (2004) for an overview.

A knowledge of legal requirements with regard to discrimination and equality can prove very useful in seeking to influence an organization that is reluctant to embrace the importance of equality and diversity. It can be used to influence policy and practice within an organization. However, such attempts to bring influence to bear are likely to be far more potent when undertaken collectively, at the level of the group.

Group influence

The impact a single individual can have on an organization's approach to discrimination is inevitably quite limited. However, groups of people working collectively can be far more effective in promoting change. It is therefore worth considering some of the ways in which groups can influence both the organization at a macro level and individual practice at a micro level. These include:

○ *Staff meetings.* Some staff groups promote anti-discriminatory practice by including it as a standing item on team meeting agendas. This can be used to enhance practice within the team, and issues can also be fed through management channels to express concerns and make suggestions.

○ *Training.* Staff groups can apply pressure to have appropriate equality and diversity training provided. Also, such training can be used to identify organizational changes that need to be made, and again these can be fed back through management channels. Indeed, training can be an important vehicle for promoting organizational development.

○ *Support groups.* Members of staff with a particular background can usefully come together to support each other and act as a pressure group. For example, many organizations have a black workers' support group and/or a women's group. Such groups can be of benefit not only to the members of those groups, but also to other workers and the organization by providing important insights into the experience of discrimination and oppression.

○ *Development groups.* There is much to be gained from like-minded people banding together to discuss, and implement, possibilities for developing anti-discriminatory practice. Such groups can play a valuable role by identifying problems to be addressed, exploring potential solutions and generally raising awareness of the need to work within an anti-discriminatory framework.

Development groups can be specific (for example, addressing a specific form of oppression, such as racism or ageism) or general (addressing all forms of oppression).

○ *User participation.* The notion of partnership discussed earlier involves the participation of clients in the assessment of their needs and the attempts to meet them. However, participation can also apply at a broader level. Where clients are empowered to contribute their views on planning, developing and evaluating services, the result can be a very positive one in terms of ensuring responsiveness to need and identifying barriers to good practice, including aspects of discrimination and oppression.

Practice focus 21.2

After attending a course on anti-discriminatory practice, a group of colleagues decided it would be very useful to create a support group to work together on issues of inequality, discrimination and oppression. They agreed to meet on a monthly basis to compare notes, support one another and seek to influence practice and policy. Within a year some managers were using the group as a source of advice and consultation on important matters relating to equality and diversity. The group were delighted that their collective approach had achieved far more than any individual actions could have done.

Each of these group strategies for promoting anti-discriminatory practice can be instrumental in raising awareness and making positive progress towards challenging oppression. However, in addition to this, the very fact of working in groups can, in itself, be a tremendous source of empowerment.

Group-based approaches to anti-discriminatory practice can be very effective in influencing both individual practice and the organizational context. Consequently, each individual worker can make a positive contribution by playing a part in forming groups and supporting existing groups. Each worker can be part of a network geared towards challenging discrimination, an anti-oppressive alliance.

Conclusion

A commonly held value in the helping professions is the recognition of the uniqueness of the individual. This is clearly a value that has an important part to play in ensuring that people are treated with dignity, with their rights as individuals respected. However, there is also another side to this coin, namely the need to recognize the significance of broader social factors in shaping the experience of the individual:

> Whilst ['individualisation'] clearly has distinct advantages and much to commend it, it also has the disadvantage of discouraging practitioners from seeing clients in their broader social context – specifically within the context of membership of oppressed groups. For example, in dealing with a woman experiencing depression, the significance of gender can be highlighted (Brown and Harris, 1978) and aspects of depression can be related to expectations of female roles in society. In this way, the classic mistake of encouraging women to be more 'feminine' can be avoided. They can be helped to understand their feelings in the context of finding a positive thread of meaning rather than simply slotting into an accepted social role – especially when it may very well be that such oppressive gender expectations played a significant part in the onset of the depression, for example in terms of domestic violence, restricted opportunities for personal fulfilment, or sexual abuse.
>
> (Thompson, Osada and Anderson, 1994, pp. 17–18)

In a way, this point captures a basic feature of anti-discriminatory practice – a valuing of the uniqueness and individuality of the person, but set in the context of structured inequalities, discrimination and oppression.

That is, if we do not take account of social factors such as sexism, racism, ageism and disablism, we will be able to do justice to only those individuals who are fortunate enough not to be subject to any form of oppression. For those who do experience oppression, we shall be ill-equipped to respond appropriately to the reality of their experience, and will therefore run the risk of actually adding to their oppression.

We can conclude, then, that all practice needs to be anti-discriminatory practice, in so far as approaches that are not sensitive to discrimination will not only miss significant aspects of the situation, but may actually do a great deal of harm.

Exercise 21

Developing Empowerment

For this exercise you should re-read the section on empowerment, paying particular attention to the four 'bullet points'. Consider how each of these relates to your own work. How could you put these into practice? Try to give an example of each. Use the space below to make notes.

chapter **22**

Being systematic

Introduction

A systematic approach to practice is one that is clear and focused, with little or no tendency to vagueness or drift. That is, systematic practice involves having clear objectives and a firm focus on the actions being taken and their effects.

This is an important approach to all aspects of people work, and seeks to avoid some traditional forms of practice that are characterized by drift and uncertainty. 'Drift' is an important term that refers to the tendency to lose sight of what we are doing and why we are doing it: to 'lose the plot'. When drift occurs, it can be highly problematic, as we shall see below. Systematic practice is therefore an important 'antidote' to the destructive effects of drift and vagueness.

This chapter is in two main parts. The first explores many of the dangers and pitfalls associated with drift and an unfocused approach to practice. The problems identified here serve to reinforce the importance and value of adopting a systematic approach to practice. The second part introduces a simple but effective model for facilitating systematic practice. The basic framework is described and some of the key issues associated with its use are addressed.

Problems of drift and vagueness

There are many problems associated with drift and a lack of focus. I shall outline some of the more important ones and consider their negative impact on the quality of practice. Such problems include:

○ Clients are often in a state of confusion by virtue of the particular problems they face. If we are not careful, we can add to this state of confusion by being vague and unfocused. In situations characterized by confusion and a lack of direction, the people worker's role is often that of an 'anchor', providing a degree of stability, security and clarity. An unfocused approach can therefore not only fail to fulfil this important role, but also add to the confusion and instability.

○ A lack of focus and role clarity is recognized as an important potential source of stress. If we are unable to develop and maintain a clear role, then we bring upon ourselves additional sources of pressure, and thereby make ourselves more prone to stress. Systematic practice is therefore an important aspect of stress management. This applies on both an individual and a collective basis. That is, a lack of focus on our part increases not only our own pressure, but also that of our colleagues.

○ Vagueness and drift are also problematic, in so far as they give us fewer opportunities for learning. That is, if we lose sight of what we are trying to achieve, we are also likely to lose sight of opportunities for learning. We are less likely to enhance our knowledge and skills if we are subject to drift. For example, if we are not clear what we are trying to achieve – what desired outcomes we are working towards – then it will be difficult, if not impossible, to establish what helps and what does not.

○ A similar argument applies to the evaluation of practice. How can we measure our effectiveness, or consider our strengths and weaknesses, if we are unable to relate these to the progress (or lack of progress) being made? This is a point to which I shall return in Chapter 27.

○ A lack of focus can also make us vulnerable to being sidetracked into other issues that are not rightfully our concern. That is, if our role is not clear, then we are more prone to being drawn into other, perhaps inappropriate roles. This may simply emerge in the confusion of the situation, or there may be a deliberate attempt by someone involved to influence the situation in a particular direction.

○ Being open to the influence of others can also be a problem in another sense. If the situation is one characterized by conflict, an unfocused approach will leave the worker in a weak position to negotiate or have an influence on the outcome of interactions. Dealing with conflict situations can be difficult enough without having the added burden of coping with drift and vagueness.

○ Setting priorities and managing one's workload are also likely to be hampered by an unfocused approach. Consequently, a great deal of time and energy can be wasted through a failure to set priorities. This also means that some very important work may not get done because its significance was not appreciated.

○ In similar vein, judging when is the appropriate time to bring intervention to a close becomes very difficult when we lose sight of what we are trying to achieve. I shall return to this point in Chapter 27.

○ Drift also stands in the way of continuity and progress within a particular programme of intervention. That is, structured, step-by-step programmes become difficult, if not impossible, to implement, unless we are able to maintain a clear focus on objectives and strategies for achieving them.

○ A vague, unfocused approach is likely to undermine professional credibility. If we are not able to convince people we know what we are doing and why we are doing it, then we should not be surprised when we fail to win their respect and earn their trust. Systematic practice enhances professional credibility.

○ Systematic practice also enhances job satisfaction, in so far as it removes the drift and vagueness that can stand in the way of gaining satisfaction from our work. That is, an unfocused approach removes or minimizes opportunities for job satisfaction.

Practice focus 22.1

When his new line manager took up post, Andrew was pleased to find that she was very supportive. However, he was taken aback when she told him that she wanted a summary of what work he was doing, including a definition of the identified problem, agreed action plan and proposed timescale for each piece of work he was undertaking. At first, he found this highly systematic approach quite unsettling, threatening, in fact. However, once he became used to it and accepted it as a constructive process, he found it very helpful indeed as a means of managing a heavy workload through maintaining a clear focus. This approach helped to increase his sense of security, confidence and job satisfaction.

It should be abundantly clear, then, that the problem of drift is a very costly one, and the investment in developing systematic practice a worthwhile one. It is therefore worth exploring a framework for promoting systematic practice, and it is to this that we now turn.

A framework for systematic practice

The framework I am proposing is simple but effective. It hinges on three key questions (see Figure 22.1), and I shall address each of these in turn.

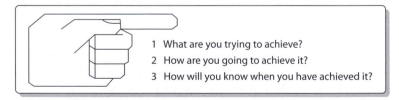

1 What are you trying to achieve?
2 How are you going to achieve it?
3 How will you know when you have achieved it?

Figure 22.1   Systematic practice

What are you trying to achieve?

This refers to the process of goal setting and involves identifying the appropriate objectives to be pursued. These can be divided up into immediate or short-term objectives, medium-term objectives or long-term ones (sometimes referred to as final outcomes). These objectives need to be:

○ *Realistic and achievable.*   There is little point in setting objectives that are unlikely to be met. Unrealistic objectives will serve only to demotivate, and therefore act as a barrier to progress. Realistic objectives, by contrast, can motivate us and spur us from success to success ('Nothing succeeds like success'). For this reason, it is also important to ensure that, where possible, objectives are arranged in an appropriate order, with the easier tasks coming first.

○ *Firm but flexible.*   If objectives are too loose and ill defined, then they will be of little value in guiding and supporting practice. However, if, by the same token, the objectives set are too rigid and inflexible, they can become more of a hindrance than a help, leaving us little or no room for manoeuvre. Finding the appropriate balance between flexibility and firmness can be a difficult task, but one that becomes easier with the development of skill and experience.

○ *Negotiated.*   Objectives need to be shared, in the sense that they should be negotiated and agreed amongst the parties involved. It is not the worker's job to determine what the objectives should be, as if playing the role of an 'expert'. This is because people need to take ownership of their problems and demonstrate a commitment to solving them, if their attempts to make progress are to be effective. People who have objectives imposed upon them are far less likely to make the effort to achieve those objectives. We are often in a position of authority with regard to the people we seek to help, but this does not preclude the possibility of working in partnership as far as possible. It is clear, then, that objectives need to be worked out in partnership so that all concerned have a commitment to bringing them about.

○ *Measurable.*   There is no need for objectives to be measurable in any precise or mathematical way – this can make for too rigid an approach. However, it is helpful if objectives can be framed in such a way as to make it relatively easy to determine whether or not they have been achieved. For example, if an objective is phrased in a vague way, then there may be no way of establishing whether or not it has been achieved. In this respect, 'To improve group functioning' is an example of an objective that has little meaning or value.

An important part of the process of deciding what needs to be achieved is the question of determining what the problem is, and who it is a problem for.

A classic mistake in people work is to start thinking about solutions without first clarifying what the problem is (or what the problems are). This is understandable, in so far as the emotional dimension (the 'feel' of Think–

Feel–Do) can often put us under pressure to resolve the situation very quickly. However, we need to be able to resist this temptation, as it can:

○ lead to a short-lived, superficial solution;
○ produce considerable confusion and vagueness;
○ do more harm than good, if we do not appreciate the significance of the situation we are dealing with;
○ distort our priorities; and
○ act as a barrier to establishing more appropriate solutions.

It is also important that we do not lose sight of the question of who it is a problem for. For example, in dealing with a family, what may be a problem for one member of the family, may not be so for others. In fact, one person's problem may be another's solution (and vice versa). In view of this, it is essential that we give careful consideration to the problem situation and take into account differences of perspective.

This is an important aspect of working in partnership, as it means that we have to engage with the people concerned and gauge their perceptions, rather than simply attempt to impose our own view of the situation.

In determining what it is that we are trying to achieve, we are beginning the process of assessment (to be discussed in more detail in Chapter 23). An important element of assessment is effective and appropriate recording of information. This is particularly important with regard to setting objectives, because, if we are lax or careless in keeping a record of what we are trying to achieve, later stages of the process may be undermined by forgetting what the objectives were, or by a dispute as to what the agreed objectives were.

How are you going to achieve it?

Once a set of objectives has been agreed, these become the targets that we need to aim for in planning our intervention. These help to guide our actions by giving us a clear focus and an overall framework within which to work.

The objectives represent the points we wish to arrive at; it is towards these that we must work. What is needed, then, is the plotting of a route from where we are now (the problem situation) to where we want to be (having achieved our objectives – the final outcome). This route is what is known as a *strategy*. A strategy is a plan of action that plots the route between our current situation and where we want to be.

This strategic approach has much in common with task-centred practice (Marsh and Doel, 2005), in which emphasis is placed on the specific tasks that will lead us, step by step, from the current problem to the identified goals. Much of the skill involved in this type of work relates to being able to determine the appropriate steps for making progress. Being able to agree appropriate and workable objectives is an essential stage in the process, but so too is being able to identify the steps to be taken to achieve the goals set. Indeed, if we are not able to move forward, then the hope and commitment generated by agreeing objectives can very soon dissipate.

There is no single prescribed way of moving forward, and this is a distinct advantage of a systematic approach – a balance between a focused and structured framework and the flexibility of a wide choice of methods and strategies for achieving one's aims within that framework. Consequently, we can draw on a wide range of methods of problem solving and promoting change without losing the clarity and focus inherent in a systematic approach.

As with the process of goal setting, good practice hinges on being able to work in partnership. If people are not actively involved in the process of change, then they are less likely to take ownership of the problems and the steps towards a solution. This can create a degree of dependency on the worker, and thereby serves to disempower clients – giving them less control over their life and circumstances, undermining confidence and so on. The skills of working in partnership are therefore essential aspects of effective people work.

One of the problems associated with attempting to move towards our objectives is, ironically, that we can become so embroiled in implementing our strategy that we lose sight of our objectives. That is, we become so engrossed in what we are doing that we lose track of why we are doing it. This emphasizes the need to keep a clear focus and avoid drift. It also emphasizes the need constantly to review our work (see Chapter 27), and measure progress against the objectives set.

Practice focus 22.2

Brenda was very highly regarded as a practitioner, particularly in terms of her assessment skills. Colleagues would often go to her for advice on dealing with complex and demanding assessments. Brenda was highly skilled at identifying problem areas and potential strengths in the situations she dealt with.

However, when her employers introduced an appraisal scheme, Brenda's first formal appraisal was mixed. While she was highly praised for her assessment skills in terms of identifying, in partnership with clients, what needed to be achieved, it became clear that she was far less skilled and experienced in developing action plans – identifying the steps needed to meet needs or resolve problems. Filling this 'gap' in her professional skills repertoire she now saw as a challenge, and she set about meeting that challenge with enthusiasm.

How will you know when you have achieved it?

In order to measure progress against agreed objectives, we need to have clear criteria for judging success. That is, if we do not know what success looks like, how will we know whether or not we have been successful?

This relates back to the point made earlier about the value of making objectives measurable, phrasing them in such a way as to make it easy to determine whether or not they have been achieved. For example, consider a situation in which a child's health, welfare, education or development were being adversely affected by the home situation. On investigation, it may emerge that a very fraught marital relationship between the parents appears to be a significant factor. The tension in the relationship may act as an obstacle to discussing childcare issues, and so reducing tension between the parents may be recognized as an important aim. However, 'To reduce tension in the relationship between parents' would be a difficult objective to measure, and would therefore be of little value in determining success. By contrast, 'To reduce tension in the relationship between the parents, to the point where childcare issues can be discussed calmly and constructively' is much more helpful as a target to be aimed for.

Being clear about how we will know when we have achieved each of our objectives is important in a number of ways. These include:

○ Recognizing success provides opportunities for praise and positive reinforcement. This can be an important source of motivation to provide some of the energy and commitment needed to pursue the other objectives.
○ Review and evaluation of practice become much easier to achieve (see Chapter 27).
○ Decisions can be made about ending our work (see Chapter 25).
○ Objectives can be changed as and when required.

This last point is a particularly important one, as it is often necessary to change objectives. This is because objectives which seem realistic and achievable in the first place may turn out to be far more difficult to achieve than was originally anticipated. Alternatively, new information may come to light that makes it appropriate to abandon certain objectives and possibly add or amend others. In short, objectives need to be flexible enough to be workable tools.

In parallel fashion, the strategy (or strategies) chosen to meet the objectives may also need to be changed, as the process of intervention proceeds. In both cases, reviewing objectives and reviewing strategies, it is important that we are clear about how we will know when we have achieved those objectives.

Conclusion

A systematic approach to practice offers a number of significant benefits, not least among which can be included:

○ Greater control over one's work, and therefore greater confidence in being able to deal with it appropriately and effectively.

○ Greater professional credibility and, with it, the respect and trust that can be so important in influencing others in people work.
○ More opportunities for learning and thereby maintaining a profile of continuous professional development (CPD – see Chapter 9).

Perhaps one of the most important benefits of a systematic approach is that it can give the client a degree of confidence, faith and trust – and therefore a greater degree of security. This can be particularly significant for people who, for whatever reason, are distressed, under pressure or struggling to cope. As mentioned earlier, an important role for the worker can be to act as an anchor for people whose circumstances resemble uncertain and turbulent waters.

It has been important to emphasize the importance of systematic practice, as this sets the scene for the chapters that follow. This is because systematic practice facilitates (and is facilitated by – the two are mutually supportive) an approach to practice premised on a clear process, beginning with assessment, through intervention, to review, evaluation and ending (see Figure 22.2).

Assessment involves gathering information with a view to forming an overview of the situation, a holistic perspective on the circumstances that have a bearing on the problem situation. This provides the basis from which a plan of action can be developed. That is, it facilitates the process of goal setting which, in turn, forms the basis of intervention.

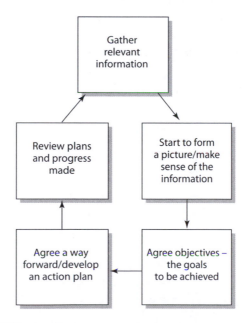

Figure 22.2   The assessment cycle

Once intervention is under way, it needs to be reviewed from time to time to ensure that the objectives and strategies are still appropriate. This paves the way for *ending*, drawing the intervention to a close because the objectives have been met, or it has been agreed that they are no longer appropriate, and *evaluation*, the process whereby the strengths and weaknesses of our practice are identified and the lessons that can be learned are drawn out. This is an iterative process. That is, it is not a simple, linear process, but rather one that 'loops' back to earlier stages. For example, when intervention is reviewed, this review forms the basis of a new stage of assessment. In this way, the overall process is cyclical, rather than linear.

It is therefore to the question of assessment that we now turn. We begin to explore this process in more detail in Chapter 23 in which a number of key issues relating to assessment are identified and discussed.

Exercise 22

Using Systematic Practice

Consider a piece of work that you are currently involved with or have previously undertaken. In relation to this piece of work, consider the three key questions of systematic practice:

- What are you trying to achieve?
- How are you going to achieve it?
- How will you know when you have achieved it?

Use the space below to make some notes.

chapter **23**

Assessment

Introduction

Assessment is an essential part of the process of people work. It involves gathering relevant information, developing an overview of the situation, and planning what needs to be done to resolve the problems identified and build on the strengths that become apparent.

In this respect, assessment acts as a preparatory stage to establish firm ground on which to base later stages of the process of helping. This applies in terms of:

- *Intervention.*   Assessment acts as the basis of an action plan which guides and informs the process of intervention. It sets the objectives that intervention is geared towards meeting.
- *Review and evaluation.*   Assessment becomes the basis for subsequent review and also acts as the baseline from which evaluation operates.
- *Ending.*   In so far as assessment sets the objectives for intervention, determining to what extent they have been met becomes a significant factor in considering when to bring intervention to a close.

Because assessment relates so closely to these other stages of the process of helping, we need to remember that it is a cyclical process, rather than a one-off event – that is, it is iterative (see Figure 23.1).

Another important point to remember with regard to assessment is that the term refers to a process, and not simply to a document. That is, although the process of assessment may lead to a document being produced (a written report or set of forms, for example), the assessment is more than simply the written outcome. If we are not aware of this, assessment can easily come to be seen as simply a bureaucratic exercise, a process of form filling. It needs to be emphasized that, as we shall see in this chapter, assessment is a vitally important professional activity and an essential part of the helping process.

The remainder of this chapter consists of a consideration of some of the key issues that relate to assessment. This is by no means a comprehensive list but should provide a sufficient overview of assessment to help workers to begin to develop their practice in this area.

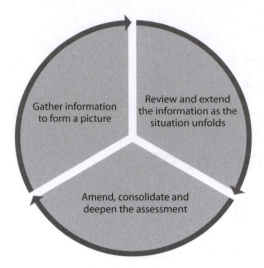

Figure 23.1 Assessment as an iterative process

Practice focus 23.1

Lisa had worked for many years as an unqualified worker before undertaking her professional training. Filling in assessment forms had been a major part of her work. However, when, as part of her course, she undertook a project on assessment, she began to realize that it was a very complex subject. She looked back over her previous experience of assessment work and felt angry that no one had ever taught her how complex and important assessment was. She realized that her earlier work had only scratched the surface of the situations she had dealt with. She worried that, at times, her involvement might actually have made the situation worse by failing to take into account key issues such as culture and language.

Key issues in assessment

Begin with social location

In undertaking an assessment, it is important to *begin* with a consideration of aspects of the person's 'social location' – that is, where he or she fits into society (notwithstanding immediate threat to life or limb – for example, in some nursing situations). This can be seen to apply in terms of:

○ *Race.*   Is the person concerned likely to be exposed to racism?
○ *Ethnicity.*   Does he or she have particular cultural or religious needs or practices that need to be taken into consideration?
○ *Gender.*   To what extent, and in what ways, is sexism relevant to the situation?

○ *Language.*   Is linguistic sensitivity an issue? Is an interpreter needed?
○ *Disability.*   Does the person concerned have a physical or mental impairment that leaves him or her vulnerable to the disempowering effects of disablism?
○ *Age.*   Is the person's age likely to make him or her subject to social disadvantage and denial of rights (Sue Thompson, 2005)?

It is important that we address such questions right from the start, as our assessment may turn out to be completely off target if we have not taken such basic issues into account from the outset.

Legislative and policy requirements

What people workers can do, and what we must do, depends to a large extent on legislative and policy requirements. That is, various Acts of Parliament and related policies lay down:

○ *Powers.*   What workers are empowered to do in certain circumstances.
○ *Duties.*   What workers must do in certain circumstances.
○ *Restrictions.*   Limitations on what workers are allowed to do.

Each of these needs to be taken into account in undertaking an assessment, as they may have a significant bearing on what the worker can or must do. It is therefore dangerous to ignore the ramifications of such factors.

Gathering information

In order to develop an overview of the situation, it is necessary to gather relevant information. Success in this owes much to our powers of observation, and these can be seen to be significant in a number of ways:

Nonverbal communication.   As we noted in Chapter 11, the ability to 'read' nonverbal communication is an important aspect of people skills.

Power and authority.   These are basic elements of interpersonal dynamics and therefore have an important part to play in assessment. This applies in a variety of ways, including:

– *Deference.*   Sometimes, one or more members of a family or group may show undue deference to another member – for example, by constantly seeking permission from him or her.
– *Balance of contribution.*   Power in families or groups is often reflected in terms of the extent to which individuals contribute to discussion, with the more powerful people having more to say.

- *Exclusion.* Sometimes, a relatively powerless person may not be able to contribute at all. For example, someone may constantly speak for or over him or her.
- *Decision making.* Noting who makes the decisions in a family or group can tell us a lot about how power and authority operate.

Frozen watchfulness. This is a term that applies primarily to children, but can refer to other age groups. It describes the way fear of a particular individual can be manifested by an extreme wariness of that person. For example, children who have been abused often 'freeze' when the abuser enters the room, and watch him or her very carefully.

Developmentally inappropriate behaviour. Sometimes, people display behaviour that is atypical of their stage of development (see Chapter 24). For example, a young girl who has been sexually abused may display 'sexualized' behaviour, perhaps by trying to touch someone's genitals. Where a person's behaviour is not consistent with his or her level of development, this may prove to be very significant. As with frozen watchfulness, this point applies primarily to working with children but can refer to other age groups.

Minimum necessary, not maximum available. One mistake sometimes made in undertaking an assessment is to gather as much information as possible within the time available. There are three problems associated with this:

1 It is an intrusion into people's privacy, in so far as it involves gathering information above and beyond what is necessary for the task. It can therefore be seen as a civil liberties issue.
2 It is a waste of time. Gathering more information than is necessary involves expending valuable time and energy in a wasteful way.
3 Having more information than we need only serves to confuse the issues. We can easily become 'flooded' with information (see Chapter 4).

The basic task, then, is to gather as much information as we need for the particular purpose. This introduces the need to be focused and clear about the purpose of the assessment – a skill entirely consistent with systematic practice as discussed in Chapter 22.

Define the problem

I earlier made the point that, in pressurized situations, we can sometimes fall into the trap of seeking a solution before first clarifying what the problem is. As Compton and Galaway comment:

We are reminded of the professor who regularly met her freshman classes by writing

$$\frac{3}{2}$$

in large bold print on the blackboard. She then turned and smiled expectantly at her class. A few braver souls responded 5, to which the professor shook her head negatively, and then a few more would indicate 1, to which there was also a negative head shake. Then, in a veritable chorus, the class shouted out 6, to which the professor commented, 'but, you see, you have given the answer before you knew the problem.' Having answers before we know the problem is a common temptation to which many inexperienced and even some experienced ... workers succumb.

(1989, pp. 9–10)

It is an essential part of assessment, then, to define the problem (or problems) in clear terms, and begin to spell out the implications that arise from this. If we lose this focus on the nature, extent and implications of the problem(s) identified, there is a danger that the solutions proposed will be inaccurate and inappropriate, and therefore ineffective.

Partnership, not paternalism

People work involves the coming together of individuals with different amounts and types of power. It is often possible, therefore, for workers to attempt to use their power to impose their view of what the problem is and what should be done about it. However, this is an approach to assessment that is unlikely to be effective. This is because a paternalistic approach runs the risk of causing resentment and resistance. An approach based on partnership, by contrast, is more likely to produce:

○ ownership of the problem, and therefore greater commitment to solving it;
○ greater trust in the worker, and therefore a better working relationship;
○ more opportunities for co-operation and effective collaboration; and
○ a less tense atmosphere that allows the client to adopt a more relaxed attitude.

An emphasis on working together is therefore an important aspect of assessment (see Chapter 20).

Assess situations, not people

One danger to be avoided is that of adopting too narrow a focus and thereby failing to take account of important aspects of the wider context. It has to be remembered that it is not the individual that is being assessed, but rather the situation, including the person and the environment in which he or she lives. Too narrow a focus on the individual can produce a tendency to be judgemental.

It would clearly be a mistake to exclude from the assessment consideration of the people concerned. However, it can also be seen to be highly problematic to focus almost exclusively on the people themselves and, in so doing, to neglect significant issues in relation to the wider circumstances: home, family, work, class, culture, organizational context and so on.

Think–Feel–Do

This important three-dimensional framework is particularly relevant to assessment. It can be used to guide the process to ensure that all three dimensions are taken into account:

O *Think.*   What thoughts or 'cognitive' aspects of the situation are relevant? What impact do these have on the current circumstance or on what needs to change?
O *Feel.*   What emotional issues need to be considered? How do our own feelings feature in making sense of, and responding to, the situation?
O *Do.*   What significant events have happened to date that have shaped the current situation? What needs to happen to move forward constructively?

Sometimes, we can focus on one or two of these dimensions without developing a more rounded approach that addresses all three. It is therefore important to check, from time to time, that we are covering all three aspects.

Strengths

It is understandable that people workers, who concentrate primarily on problem solving, should be attuned to negative aspects of a situation, but this can lead to an imbalance in which the more positive aspects can be neglected. A balanced assessment should cover strengths as well as weaknesses, opportunities as well as threats (see the discussion of SWOT analysis in *The People Solutions Sourcebook*).

It is necessary to identify strengths, as these can often counterbalance actual or potential problems. For example, in determining the degree of risk a person faces, the strengths that apply can reduce the risk or affect the amount of importance that we attach to that risk (Brearley, 1982).

Sometimes, the circumstances people workers encounter are so fraught with difficulties that it can 'go against the grain' to think in terms of strong points. None the less, if we ignore the positive aspects, we are likely to produce a distorted and unbalanced assessment.

Significant changes

Often, the situations that are being assessed have existed for quite some time but have only recently come to our attention. This raises a very important question that we need to address: Why now? That is, what significant change has taken place that has necessitated our involvement? Or, to put it metaphorically, what was the straw that broke the camel's back?

Finding out 'Why now?' can give us some important insights into the circumstances leading up to the current problems and what needs to be done to address them. Sometimes, people will readily be able to identify key 'triggers' with little prompting. At other times, however, it may require some degree of 'detective work' to identify any key factors that brought about the present scenario.

Practice focus 23.2

Graham was a very keen and competent worker, although with relatively little experience. In one particular situation he found that he was not able to make any progress. A family had asked him for help but he was finding it very difficult to work out what the problem was or what they were hoping he could do for them. The discussion was quite chaotic and unfocused, with family members speaking over each other and contradicting one another. However, what really helped to pull it all together and allow progress to be made was Graham's key question: 'Why now?' By focusing on what had been the last straw that led the family to seek help, Graham began to get down to the key issues and begin to establish a clearer picture of the situation – to cut through the chaos that this 'last straw' had plunged the family into.

Responding to crisis

The 'trigger' that leads someone to seek help may prove to be a crisis, in the sense of a turning point or breakdown in normal coping. Where this is the case, a number of issues arise, including the following:

○ Crises generate a lot of emotional energy that can be used positively and constructively to promote change.
○ Crises tend to be resolved fairly quickly, and so a prompt response is required if the positive potential of the crisis is to be drawn upon.
○ People's behaviour in a crisis is often very different from what it would normally be. If we do not recognize that a person is in crisis, then our assessment is likely to be inaccurate and distorted.

Responding to crisis is a complex and skilled undertaking (Thompson, 2011b) that presents the worker with a number of challenges. However, the first step towards success in this endeavour is being able to recognize a crisis situation.

Respond to need, not demand

There is a subtle, but vital, distinction between need and demand. Demand refers to what people ask for, which may not be what they need. For example, someone may request a particular service (demand) but their situation may actually be better dealt with by a different service or intervention (need).

This is an important distinction because the presenting problem is often different from the underlying problem. For example, a request for residential care for an elderly person because he or she is struggling to cope may be better dealt with by arranging a package of community care services.

Note, however, that efforts should be taken to ensure that a paternalistic approach is not allowed to creep in. Negotiating with a client over what he or she needs is not the same as imposing your own definition of what is needed.

Confidentiality

Much of the information gathered through the process of assessment is confidential, in the sense that it should not be revealed to others without the permission of the client. However, as we saw in Chapter 14, there are limits to confidentiality. For example, the information given to a worker 'belongs' to his or her agency, rather than to the individual worker.

A central aspect of good practice in assessment, then, is being clear with clients about how the information they provide is likely to be recorded and used. If this is not clarified, then a subsequent legitimate use of such information may be deemed by the client to amount to a breach of confidentiality.

Separate fact from opinion

The point was also made in Chapter 14 that it is important to distinguish between fact and opinion. Assessment is likely to draw upon both established facts and more speculative opinions. We need to be clear, though, about which is which. For example, to represent an opinion as if it were a fact can be very misleading.

The overview of a situation we gain from assessment is an essential part of developing a plan of action. If, at this stage, we confuse fact and opinion, our subsequent intervention may prove ineffective if a particular opinion turns out to be wrong. If we know something is a matter of opinion, we can act accordingly by treating the information cautiously.

Avoid jargon

It is quite easy to alienate people by speaking a language they do not understand – that is, to use jargon or technical language that creates barriers between us. For example, I know of a social work client who became distressed when she rang the social services office, only to be told that her social worker was 'in an interview'. She did not understand that 'interview' was being used in a technical sense and assumed that her social worker had applied for another job.

The process of assessment therefore needs to be characterized by clarity and openness, without recourse to language that is confusing or exclusive.

Avoid vagueness

As was emphasized in Chapter 22, vagueness and a lack of clear focus are a barrier to good practice. This applies in particular to the process of assessment, as any drift that creeps in at the early stages can confuse or invalidate the plan of action decided upon – or can mean that such an action plan does not emerge.

An essential part of assessment, then, is to avoid vagueness and not to tolerate vagueness in others. This involves asking clear, specific questions, and continuing to pursue the issue if the answers given are not also clear and specific. For example, if a person states that a particular individual is 'at risk', it would be necessary to clarify: at risk of what? Such questions, tactfully and sensitively put, can dispel a great deal of vagueness and provide a much firmer basis from which to work.

Set clear objectives and timescales

Chapter 22 also stressed the importance of clear objectives as the basis of systematic practice. This needs to be reiterated within the specific context of assessment, as it is at this stage that objectives begin to be formulated.

One misunderstanding of assessment is that it is simply a process of gathering information. However, information on its own is not a sound basis for intervention – it needs to form the basis of a plan of action that includes the objectives to be worked towards.

What is also helpful, as part of this process of action planning, is to identify timescales. These need not be rigid or restrictive, but it can be of considerable benefit to have target timescales to aim for. This can provide considerable motivation and also provides a mechanism for gauging progress. Timescales can be reviewed and amended if necessary but, if they are not agreed in the first place, there is an increased possibility of drift occurring.

Conclusion

Assessment is clearly a complex and multifaceted undertaking. It requires a great deal of patience, skill, clear thinking and vision. However, the investment of time and energy required to develop the skills and knowledge base of assessment is fully repaid by the benefits of high-quality assessment work. Poor assessment can be a recipe for disaster, while good assessment work can make subsequent intervention a great deal easier, and thereby significantly increase the chances of success.

Assessment, it should be remembered, is an iterative process. That is, assessment and re-assessment should be recurring themes in our practice. The initial assessment can be seen as a hypothesis that is then tested by our intervention. We then need to check whether the hypothesis was appropriate and, if not, amend or abandon it as we see fit. Assessment and intervention, then, intertwine and support each other, thereby providing the basis for informed and sensitive practice.

Exercise 23

The Importance of Information

For this exercise you should take a piece of work that you are currently working on, or look back over a piece of work you have previously undertaken. Your task is to look at the information you have about this situation and relate it to some of the points covered in this chapter. For example, have timescales been set? Have strengths been identified? Are fact and opinion separated? This should help you to develop your skills in assessment. Use the space below to make notes.

chapter **24**

Planning

Introduction

This chapter addresses the important question of planning in people work and relates it to four particular sets of issues:

- direction and meaning in people's lives;
- meeting needs, and the effects of unmet need;
- human development and the life course; and
- contracts and agreements.

A unifying theme across these five areas is the importance of forward planning, the need to look beyond the immediate circumstances and adopt a proactive approach.

I shall discuss each of these five areas in turn, outlining some of the key issues that arise. It should be noted, though, that each of these areas could be a major topic of discussion in its own right, and so my comments are necessarily brief and selective. They are intended to be introductory, serving as a gateway to the wider literature and knowledge base, in keeping with the spirit of the book as a whole.

Direction and meaning

Many of the problems that people workers are called upon to deal with can be associated with a lack of meaning, direction and purpose in people's lives.

Practice focus 24.1

Alan was a 15-year-old boy who had lost interest in school and could not wait to leave. He had not developed any particular interests or hobbies, and had no ambitions in terms of future employment opportunities. He soon began to drift into truancy, and then into crime. He began with shoplifting but soon moved on into burglary. The irony was that he did not steal things he wanted, or things he could sell. He had just drifted aimlessly into this type of behaviour.

The theme of meaning and direction can be seen to be a much more common one than is usually recognized. For example, it is a recurring theme in situations that involve loss and/or a need for counselling (Neimeyer and Anderson, 2002). The main implication of this for people workers is a recognition of the need to help certain people in certain circumstances to find or strengthen a thread of meaning in their lives. This can be seen to apply in particular to certain groups of people, such as:

○ Children in substitute care, where plans need to be in place to ensure, as far as possible, that security and continuity are maintained.
○ People whose lives have been seriously disrupted by alcohol dependency or other forms of drug abuse.
○ People who are returning to the community after an extended period in institutional care (or custody).
○ People who experience an imposed major change of lifestyle – for example, through acquired disability or serious illness.
○ Older or disabled people who need to give up their home and enter residential care.

Loss, change and crisis are amongst the key factors that relate to the question of direction and meaning. This raises two issues in relation to planning:

1 We need to plan a careful response as and when such situations arise in order to help maintain or regain a thread of meaning and a sense of purpose and direction.
2 Many occurrences of loss, change and crisis can be predicted to a certain extent – for example, when a person is terminally ill. In such cases, planning can begin well in advance of the loss occurring. Such planning can then play a significant part in preparing for the loss and minimizing the harm caused by it.

Practice focus 24.2

Margaret's life was devastated when her son, Ian, aged 11, was killed in a road traffic accident. As a single parent, Margaret had reached the point where Ian was the centrepiece of her life. It was no exaggeration that her life revolved around him. It was no great surprise, then, that Margaret became very depressed and remained so for a considerable period of time. She had lost not only her son, but also purpose, direction and meaning.

Responding to need

Some human needs are common to all people – the need for food, water, air, for example. Other needs are not common to all, but are shared by members of certain groups or social categories. Cultural or religious needs would be examples of this. However, there are yet other needs that are unique to the individual, due to his or her background, experiences, emotional responses and so on.

As many of these needs are predictable, there is considerable scope for prior planning in order to keep potential problems to a minimum. In this way, we can respond to need in a *proactive* way, thereby reducing the need to respond in a *reactive* way at a later date. That is, planning can help to equip us for preventative work, so that scarce resources can be used with the greatest efficiency.

In order to facilitate such planning and proactivity, we need to develop an understanding of needs and some of the key issues that apply to them. A very significant point to recognize, to begin with, is that needs are interrelated or 'layered'. That is, it is not a simple matter of: 'I need x'. It is more a case of 'I need x in order to . . .'. This phrase, 'in order to', is a central one, as it illustrates that:

○ Needs are linked to one another, they are interrelated – one need has implications for others. They are 'layered' (see Figure 24.1).
○ Apart from basic survival needs, our needs are not absolute – they are linked to purposes and intentions, to what we are trying to achieve.
○ Needs will change over time. It is therefore essential to re-assess needs, as we cannot assume that they will stay the same.

Another key issue relating to the question of needs is the importance of recognizing that many problematic situations arise in response to unmet need. Such scenarios would include examples such as the following:

○ An elderly woman's need for bereavement counselling is not recognized, and so attempts to support her in the community have little success as her frame of mind does not allow her to take advantage of the services provided.
○ An unemployed person's need for self-esteem continues to go unmet, resulting in social withdrawal and depression, thereby creating a vicious circle in which the chances of gaining employment are reduced still further.
○ A child's need for clear boundaries outlining what is acceptable and what is not can, if it remains unmet, produce a situation in which behaviour difficulties are to the fore.

These examples, and the many others that could have been given, serve to illustrate the difficulties that can arise in circumstances where people's needs remain unmet. It is therefore important that people workers are able to recognize situations of unmet need so that we are able to respond appropriately. That is, there is a need to develop the skills that will give us the sensitivity to issues of unmet need that makes for good practice.

Figure 24.1   'Layers' of need (source: Thompson, 1993)

One final point to note in relation to unmet need is the question of our own unmet needs. If we have unmet needs of our own (for example, the need for recognition), then we may find it difficult to be sensitive and responsive to other people's unmet needs. This then raises the issue of supervision, as discussed in Chapter 7. The obstacles that can arise as a result of the worker's own needs not being met underline the need for effective supervision to help maximize the worker's potential for positive intervention.

A further point to be made concerning needs is that they can be linked to the stages of human development. That is, at different stages of the life course, our needs will be different. It is therefore important to take the life course into consideration.

The life course

An important and highly relevant factor with regard to planning is the ability to predict what is likely to happen. Planning is a process of developing a vision of the future so that we are in a better position to shape that future, to make it as positive as we possibly can.

Our knowledge of human development and the life course therefore has a crucial role to play in helping us plan for the future. Understanding the life course will not, of course, guarantee what will happen, but it does give us some degree of insight into likely developments, patterns and tendencies.

In what has become a classic text, Michael Rutter argued that:

children are developing organisms so that assessment needs to be made in the context of a developmental framework. This means that clinicians must have a good knowledge and understanding of child development, both normal and abnormal. Children behave differently at different ages and it is necessary to know what behaviour should be expected at each age.

(1975, p. 16)

These comments relate specifically to children but can be extended to apply to any stage of the life course. There are specific issues that apply at each stage, although we need to recognize that these are, to some extent, culturally variable. There is considerable debate about when particular life stages begin or end. However, in very broad outline, the life stages can be mapped out as follows:

○ *Infancy.* Characterized by a high level of dependence on parents or other carers – a time of considerable vulnerability.
○ *Childhood.* A time of exploration, learning and play, associated with preparing for future adult roles.
○ *Adolescence.* A period of transition from childhood to young adulthood, often characterized as rebellious and traumatic although these characteristics are often exaggerated (see my comments below on stereotyping).
○ *Young adulthood.* A time of 'finding one's feet' in the adult world, beginning to develop work and family lifestyle patterns.
○ *Early middle age.* Characterized by relatively stable patterns and expectations, often associated with career development and children growing up.
○ *Later middle age.* Broadly seen as the time between the adjustment to children having left home and retirement.
○ *Post-retirement.* Characterized by the transition from employment to leisure.
○ *Old age.* Often misrepresented in unduly negative terms (S. Thompson, 2005), but having many positive aspects.

It should be remembered that these are broad and loose headings, and should not be seen as rigid categories or fixed patterns.

Before leaving the topic of the life course, it is worth highlighting some of the potential dangers associated with it:

○ Although different problems can be associated with specific life stages (for example, adjusting to children leaving home in early middle age), these do not necessarily apply. The notion of life stage is a broad generalization and becomes oppressive if it is seen as a fixed set of expectations.

○ We need to be wary of life course stereotypes (for example, that adolescents are necessarily rebellious or older people are necessarily frail). These can be both misleading and oppressive.

○ The life course is a social phenomenon and should therefore not be seen in narrow, biological terms (Hunt, 2005). For example, there are likely to be significant cultural and gender differences that have a part to play.

In view of these, we need to use the concept of the life course cautiously and critically. It offers a framework to assist planning, but we must be wary of applying it too rigidly or allowing it to become a means of disadvantaging or oppressing certain groups or individuals.

Contracts and agreements

Written agreements or 'contracts' can be a very effective means of promoting change. The process involves worker and client coming together to agree a way forward, step by step, through a set of identified tasks. In this way a planned approach to problem solving can be implemented.

Unfortunately, however, contracts are often used inappropriately without having been thought through carefully enough. In order to avoid such problems, it is necessary to ensure that contracts or working agreements are:

○ *Negotiated.* For a contract to work, its contents must be agreed by the people concerned. There is little point trying to impose tasks and duties on reluctant people, as this is highly unlikely to produce a successful outcome. Where the actual nuts and bolts of the contract are agreed through a process of negotiation, there is a considerably higher likelihood of success, due to the commitment and sense of ownership generated by participating in the process.

○ *Clear and explicit.* The processes of change and problem solving can be seriously hampered by a lack of clarity and explicitness. Indeed, much of the power of agreements to achieve success derives from the discipline of having clear and explicit steps to follow. The benefits of a structured framework can be lost if the steps to be taken are not expressed explicitly in clear, jargon-free language.

○ *Realistic.* As with the setting of objectives as part of the assessment process, the steps identified in an agreement have to be realistic and achievable. If they are not, we are guilty of setting clients up to fail. This can have a disastrous effect on confidence and commitment, thereby seriously undermining the chances of success.

○ *Two way.* A central concept underpinning contract work is the sharing of tasks. That is, it is not simply a matter of giving the client a list of tasks to complete. It is a question of allocating tasks appropriately, and this should include the worker, where appropriate, as this encourages partnership and takes some of the pressure off the client.

○ *Time limited.* By agreeing timescales as well as tasks, we can avoid the dangers of drift, and provide clear time targets to aim for. Of course, these need to be flexible, as rigid deadlines can bring undue pressure and can also set people up to fail. It is better to set a deadline and then, if necessary, extend it, rather than set no deadline and run the risk of drift creeping in.

○ *Reviewed.* Sometimes, contracts do not go beyond being written documents. They do not become working tools to guide practice and promote change, and are therefore of little or no value. Contracts need to be consulted and reviewed regularly. If they are not, there is a danger that new circumstances may evolve and develop, thereby invalidating the agreement unless it is amended in line with the changes. You could be pressing ahead in a direction that is no longer appropriate or doing things that are no longer likely to take you in the direction you want to go. The importance of reviewing practice will be emphasized in Chapter 27.

Contracts or working agreements have excellent potential for bringing about change in problematic situations. However, as we have seen, they need to be handled carefully and sensitively. They are not short cuts to be used unthinkingly or uncritically.

Planning as an ongoing activity

Some writers present planning as a stage in the helping process, in between assessment and intervention. However, my preference is to see it as an ongoing dimension of all the stages of the helping process, rather than a distinctive stage in its own right. For me, it works best as follows:

○ *Assessment.* Planning needs to be part of assessment. That is, it is not enough simply to gather information and form a picture of the situation; we also need to identify what needs to be done and how – and that is precisely what planning is about.

○ *Intervention.* Engaging in helping activities needs to be based on reflective practice (see Chapter 30), and this involves adopting a planful approach to our efforts. Planning is therefore also part of intervention.

○ *Review.* By its very nature review involves planning, in so far as it is a process of looking back over the period under review and looking forward in terms of what needs to change. This future dimension is, in effect, planning (see Chapter 27).

○ *Ending.* Bringing our helping role to an end will often involve an element of planning in terms of helping the client to look forward to how they can build on the progress made and guard against 'backsliding'.

○ *Evaluation.* This is a process of seeing what worked and what did not and, importantly, what we can learn from this. This too includes an element of planning, in so far as it involves looking toward how the learning gained can be put to good use in future.

However, whether we conceptualize it as a dimension of other stages or a stage in its own right, the importance of planning should not be underestimated.

Conclusion

Planning is an essential part of good practice in people work, in so far as a focus on future developments allows a more proactive approach. That is, by using our knowledge, experience and skills to anticipate future developments, we are in a much stronger position to shape those future developments. In this way, we are decreasing the likelihood of problems occurring (or continuing), and we are increasing the likelihood of positive outcomes.

This makes planning a fundamental basis for our practice, and it should therefore take its place alongside the other core elements of people work as an essential part of high-quality professional practice. We therefore need to ensure that we do not allow a focus on immediate pressures and concerns to lead us into a situation where we make the false economy of neglecting the role of planning. While it is understandable that busy, pressurized practitioners may be tempted to 'press on' with their work without finding the time for proper planning, this temptation remains a potentially disastrous pitfall.

Exercise 24

Using Planning

For this exercise you are asked to consider the extent to which planning features in your work. Consider the following questions and make notes in the space provided:

1 How could you help people regain or maintain a thread of meaning in their lives?
2 Can you think of examples of how unmet need has a damaging effect on people's lives?
3 How can you make sure that planning features in all stages of the helping process?

Once again, this exercise is not a test, so do feel free to consult with colleagues and make use of the opportunities to learn together.

chapter **25**

Decision making

Introduction

Working with people is, of course, not simply a matter of following orders. It involves having to make decisions. This is because the nature of people work is so complex and subtle that it would be totally unrealistic to expect to be able to carry out our duties simply by following instructions. Each day we are faced with new situations where we have to make a judgement about how to proceed. Decision making is therefore a basic element of people work on a day-to-day basis. However, at times, we have particularly important decisions to make, decisions that can have significant, long-term consequences. This chapter explores some of the key issues relating to the complexities of decision making. We begin by setting decision making in the context of risk and uncertainty before moving on to explore one framework for decision making and a number of factors that influence us when we are making decisions.

Risk and decision making

In Chapter 26 we shall examine what is involved in managing risk, but, before we get to that point, we need to recognize that decision making in general (and not just decisions specifically and explicitly about risk) involves weighing up risks. This is because decisions involve opening up one set of possibilities (in line with the option decided upon) while closing off various others (in line with the options rejected). How do we know that we are choosing the best option? How do we know that options we are rejecting do not offer a better way forward? Of course, the short answer is that we do not know: decision making is not a scientific process based on certainty. It is more a case of carefully considering options and basing our decisions on *probabilities*: which option seems to be the most appropriate in the circumstances?

Practice focus 25.1

Ken was used to writing reports that analysed the situation in question so that the management team concerned could decide on what to do based on an informed view of the situation. However, in his new post he was called upon to write reports that not only analysed the issues involved, but also provided recommendations as to how the organization should deal with the matters under discussion. To begin with he saw this as one small step beyond what he had been doing for years, and so it did not bother him. However, once it came down to writing his first report with recommendations, he felt very anxious indeed. For a while he felt paralysed by the pressure on him, as he realized that his recommendations could have very significant consequences, positive or negative. Fortunately, he had supportive colleagues who helped him through, but it had dawned on him quite clearly that he would have to take his responsibilities very seriously.

The decision-making process

Decision making, then, involves dealing with uncertainty (recognizing that there are few certainties in working with people) and trying to reduce the amount and impact of that uncertainty by looking, in as much detail as the time available will permit, at the risks involved and weighing up what the consequences are likely to be. It is not a question of looking for 'the right answer', as if there is one definitive approach to each situation. Life in general is not that simple, and when it comes to people work, then it is certainly far more complex than that! In any situation there will be a number of possible options, some of which will be positive and productive if we pursue them, some of which will not.

The challenge of decision making, then, is that of looking at options, evaluating which we feel is the most appropriate way forward and then watching carefully to see whether we have made a wise move (Hardman, 2009). There are, then, no guarantees that what we decide to do will be 'correct' or helpful. It is up to each of us, in making decisions, to make as well informed and as well thought through a choice of course of action as we can in the circumstances, while recognizing that nothing will guarantee that we have got it right.

We cannot guarantee that any decision we take will be the *right* decision, but we can ensure that it is a *good* decision. By that, I mean that we can take all reasonable steps to make sure that the decisions we take are well informed, carefully considered and as appropriate to the circumstances as we can make them. A good decision is one that has these characteristics, and until crystal balls become standard issue for those of us employed in the people professions, it is the best we can hope for.

Sometimes people can produce what turns out, with hindsight, to have been the *right* decision (in the sense of a decision that turns out to be very highly suited to the circumstances and to the events that unfold), but because the decision was based on uneducated guesswork, prejudice, simply copying others or other such dangerous grounds for making a decision, it cannot be seen to have been a *good* decision. While it is to be hoped that our good decisions will also turn out to be right decisions, it is clearly important to focus on what is involved in good decision making, rather than rely on the vagaries of chance and hope that our poorly informed decision making none the less produces the right outcome by pure chance. Such a dangerous approach is particularly significant in relation to professional accountability. Someone who produces the 'right' decision, but by dubious means, will be in a very weak position if called upon to justify their actions. Ironically, someone who has taken their decision-making responsibilities seriously and has acted in good faith will be in a much stronger position in terms of professional accountability, even if their decision making does not produce the best outcome.

The fact that there are no guarantees, however, does not mean that there is nothing that can assist us in making decisions. There are tools and frameworks available to assist us. One such framework is that developed by Adair (1985). It consists of working through five stages, as shown in Figure 25.1.

Figure 25.1   Five stages of decision making

This is not intended as a rigid, mechanical process to follow unthinkingly, but rather as a flexible framework to assist in the process of weighing up the options.

Kourdi argues that it is the fourth stage, that of evaluation, that is most likely to be problematic:

> Evaluating the various options and deciding the best course of action is the crux of decision making – and this is the point where people can go wobbly, become anxious, procrastinate, fudge or simply break down!
>
> (1999, p. 4)

He suggests that there are several issues which need to be addressed to deal effectively with the process of evaluating options. These are:

○ What obstacles are there in relation to each option?
○ What risks are involved?
○ How can these be removed or minimized?
○ Which decisions are feasible?
○ Which of these offer a realistic chance of success?
○ How attractive are the options available to us?
○ Does one simple decision need to be made or can a combination of decisions be made?
○ What timeframe are we working to?
○ What might we need to do to keep options open for the future?
○ How well does the decision to be made fit in with existing strategies?

It is not, of course, being proposed that all these questions should be answered every time we make a decision, as that would clearly be unworkable. However, Adair's framework and Kourdi's addition to it do give us a basic framework to act as a starting point, particularly for those decisions that are likely to have major consequences for us.

Factors influencing decision making

Of course, important decisions are not generally made at random without considering a range of relevant factors. But what are those factors? What do we need to take into consideration when making a decision? The following is not an exhaustive list, but it does provide a starting point for developing a clearer picture of what is involved in decision making.

Information

Making decisions in the dark is clearly not a good idea. It is therefore important to make sure that we have the information we need to make as informed a decision as possible or, where we are unable to obtain the information we need, we are aware of what risks we are taking in forming a judgement in the absence of important aspects of the information base.

One danger to be aware of here is the effect of anxiety and the pressure to make a rapid decision. If we are not careful, we can pressurize ourselves (or allow others to pressurize us) into making hasty decisions without taking account of all the relevant information available to us. Sadly, it is not uncommon for decisions to be made despite the fact that there was information freely available which contraindicated opting for that particular course of action.

One common example of this problem is when one or more people are anxious about a situation and are pressing for a resolution. 'Something must be done', they may say quite forcefully, but we must be careful that we do not allow such pressure to force us into making a rash decision. See my comments below about urgent decisions.

Time constraints

Decisions generally have a timeframe associated with them. For example, if I need to decide whether or not to apply for a particular job that has been advertised, then I do not have limitless time in which to make up my mind, as clearly there will be a closing date by which the decision has to be made – or, indeed, much time before the closing date to allow me to complete an application if I decide to do so. Timeframes are therefore important in shaping the decision-making process.

It is often the case in people work that we have to make a decision in a fairly short space of time. Indeed, many decisions can be made more or less on the spur of the moment, such is the nature of dealing with people and their problems. However, this is not always the case. We therefore have to be able to distinguish between those situations which require a fairly quick decision and those which do not. If we are not able to do so, then we run the risk of delaying important, urgent decisions and/or rushing ones that could have been looked at more closely and carefully.

This is a point that is worth emphasizing, as getting it wrong can have very detrimental consequences. It is important to keep a clear head so that we recognize genuinely urgent situations and act accordingly, but also recognize those circumstances where there may be a lot of pressure to act quickly, but no actual justification for doing so (other people's anxiety is not a basis for rushing an important decision).

Clarity about objectives

In Chapter 22 the importance of being clear about what we are trying to achieve was emphasized. This point is worth repeating here. This is because what we are trying to achieve – our objectives – will influence the course of action we take. For example, if our objective is to boost someone's self-esteem, then we should be careful not to make decisions which may undermine his or her confidence. This may seem an obvious statement to make, but it is surprising how often this can be forgotten, as in the case of a tutor's comments on a student's essay which are so harsh and punitive as to undermine confidence, rather than empower the student by facilitating learning.

Chapter 22's message of the importance of systematic practice in avoiding drift and distorting priorities is therefore very applicable here in the context of decision making.

Hidden agendas

It is often the case that there is as much going on 'beneath the table' as there is on it. That is, hidden agendas are not uncommon. People may be ostensibly working towards particular goals, and may therefore have much in common, but may be very strongly divided by the presence of one or more hidden agendas. This may be quite transparent at times, but may also be very deep and well hidden, affecting decision making in subtle ways – often to the detriment of others involved or the stated objectives of the group of people trying to work together. This is well illustrated in Practice Focus 25.2.

Practice focus 25.2

Veronica was pleased to have the opportunity to chair the development committee, as she wanted to make sure that this venture was a big success. However, what she did not bargain for was how difficult it would be to get the committee to make decisions. Whenever the time came to make a decision there would be so much dissension and so many conflicting voices that, for a while, she did not know whether she was coming or going. What really puzzled her for quite some time was that some people seemed to be arguing for contradictory courses of action. However, what helped her make sense of it all was when she remembered what she had learned about hidden agendas – the goings on 'under the table' that could make what happens 'on the table' so complex and, sadly, so often ineffective. She realized now that her challenge was going to be to get to grips with these hidden agendas and get rid of them as far as possible.

Management style

Styles of management can be placed on a continuum from autocratic at one end, to democratic at the other. What this means is that some managers take full responsibility for their decisions and do not involve others in the process of deciding while, at the opposite extreme, some managers prefer to be more democratic and involve others in the process. These are, of course, the extremes, and many people fall at various points in between. But, the important point to recognize is that the point on which the manager concerned can be located on this continuum is likely to be a significant factor in terms of not only the way the decision is made, but also what course of action is actually chosen. And, of course, this does not only apply to managers. Anyone's approach to decision making will be affected by the extent to which they involve others in the process.

Skills

How skilful people are at making decisions is also going to have a bearing on how decisions are reached. Kourdi regards the following skills as highly relevant:

- managing knowledge and analysing information
- fostering innovation and creativity, and exploiting synergies
- analysing and appraising competing options
- delegating and empowering people
- motivating people
- leading successful teams
- focusing on customers and understanding market needs
- leading change
- resolving problems and removing obstacles effectively.

(1999, p. 6)

Of course, these are not the only skills, but the point is that skills (or the absence of skills) can be seen as major factors in shaping decision-making processes.

Political pressures

Decision making does not occur in a political vacuum. Political factors relating to the balance of power (within an organizational structure, for example) can have a significant bearing. It may be, for example, that in some circumstances, a person making a decision feels that course X is the appropriate course of action but actually chooses course Y because he or she realizes that 'the powers that be' may well object to course X, or may respond to it in such a way as to make the decision maker regret having chosen that option.

It would therefore be naive to see decision making as a purely rational process that involves carefully weighing up the options. The influence of political pressures is likely to mean that some courses of action are not possible, while others may be possible but likely to lead to undesirable consequences. Political pressures may also mean that some people try to block decision-making processes (through delaying tactics, for example). Decision making involves the exercise of power and therefore has to be understood in its political context.

Conclusion

Decision making is something we cannot avoid (refusing to make a decision is, in itself, a decision!), and so it is important that we are as well equipped as possible to make the decisions that fall to us. This chapter has shown that there can be no guarantees – it is necessarily a case of wrestling with the uncertainties and making the wisest choice possible in the circumstances. Effective decision making is more of an art than a science, and it is certainly something that can be developed with time and experience.

An important part of all this is confidence. As we have seen, making decisions necessarily involves taking risks. Sometimes our decisions will go wrong and we will face the consequences. However, we should learn from such situations, rather than let them deter us. Effective decision making requires clear thinking, and the anxiety associated with an approach based on fear and low confidence will only serve to make the process more difficult and, potentially at least, more stressful. It is therefore important to think carefully about what is involved in decision making, learning as we go along, from both our own experiences and the help and support we can enlist from more experienced and perhaps more confident colleagues.

Exercise 25

Using Adair's Five Stages

Look carefully again at Adair's five-stage framework for making decisions and use it to look at a particular decision you have to make. This may be a simple decision (such as what to have for lunch) or a more complex decision with more serious consequences. The type of decision is not what is important, as this is simply an opportunity to familiarize yourself with the five-stage process so that you can decide whether or not this is helpful for you.

chapter **26**

Managing risk

Introduction

Simply being alive involves a number of risks, and when we engage in people work, we become involved in a number of significant risk factors. We have to make sure that, in helping people, we are aware of the risks involved both to ourselves and to them. If we undertake our work without being 'tuned in' to the risk factors present, then we leave ourselves open to unnecessary dangers. An effective people worker will be somebody who is aware of the risks involved in any given situation, who is sensitive to them, but who does not become overly concerned with them to the extent that the worker encounters the possibility of being paralysed by the fear factor associated with risk.

In this chapter, we will explore some significant factors involved in risk and, from that, we will proceed to look at what needs to be taken into consideration in managing the risks associated with dealing with people and their problems. As with the other chapters in this book, it will not provide you with all you need to know about managing risk – the subject is far too complex for that – but it should provide you with a basic grasp of the issues involved and stimulate you to find out more (see the 'Guide to further learning' at the end of the book).

Understanding risk

Every day of our lives involves taking risks of some description. Even doing something as simple as entering a building involves taking the risk that the building will collapse. And, of course, using the roads, whether as a motorist or a pedestrian, involves a number of risks – some of them potentially life threatening. But this does not stop us in our tracks, of course, as we just keep going, taking it all in our stride. Risk, then, is an ever-present part of our lives, and it is not something that we should panic about.

An important point to recognize is that making a decision about risk is not simply a matter of determining whether or not to take a particular risk. It is, in fact, much more complex than this, as it involves *balancing* risks. Deciding upon one course of action instead of another involves avoiding one set of risks and accepting another. For example, if a person is invited to two meetings which are due to take place at the same time on the same day, he or she has to decide between them. Going to one meeting runs the risk of missing something very important, crucial even, at the other meeting. Whichever meeting is chosen, the same applies – the risks involved in missing the other meeting plus, of course, the risks involved in actually attending a meeting (being criticized or even ridiculed, for example). We therefore have to be careful not to fall into the trap of equating risk management with risk *avoidance* or risk *elimination*. This is a point to which we shall return below.

A key issue here is that of *consequences*. Different courses of action will have different sets of consequences but, at the time of deciding, we do not know what those consequences will be. We have to gamble that the consequences will be desirable ones. This involves making a 'risk assessment' – weighing up the possible negative outcomes against the possible positive ones, bearing in mind which are more likely to occur in the circumstances. Such risk assessments form the basis of decision making, as we noted in Chapter 25.

Practice focus 26.1

When Liam discovered that his budget would not sustain both projects until the end of the financial year, he realized that one would have to be curtailed, at least until next year's budget figures were known. Which project would have to be suspended? This was an extremely difficult decision to make, as they were both important and worthwhile projects. However, he knew there was no way round it – he would have to use funds from one to sustain the other. He had several sleepless nights over this, because he knew it was vitally important to make the right decision. Either way there would be negative consequences, but how could he keep these to a minimum? Which project would cause fewer problems if it were suspended? Liam had known for some time that his job carried a lot of responsibility, but he was really feeling the weight of it now. This was probably the most difficult situation he had ever had to deal with in his career to date, and he hoped that he would not have to make such decisions too many times in the future. Suspending either project would have significant consequences, so he knew he had to do a very good job of assessing the relative sets of risks involved.

One important issue that needs to be recognized is that informed risk-taking is the basis of person-centred work in the people professions. It involves finding the balance between, on the one hand, not wrapping people up in cotton wool, and on the other hand, leaving them vulnerable. Finding this balance is quite a skilled undertaking and quite a challenge, and so it is to this topic that we now turn.

Meeting the risk challenge

Many theoretical approaches (existentialist philosophy, for example) help us to appreciate 'the contingency of being' – that is, the nature of human existence as something that inevitably involves risk. There are few guarantees in this life and so many factors that can introduce danger into our lives. Meeting the risk challenge is therefore not a question of eliminating risk, as that would be both impossible and, to a large extent, undesirable (given the positive benefits of risk, as we shall see below). The challenge, then, is one of *managing* risk – that is, finding ways of handling the risk issues we encounter to maximize the positives and to minimize the negatives.

There is an important link here with the concept of 'ontological security' – the feeling that we are reasonably safe in terms of our identity, our place in the world and in wider society. Our sense of ontological security can be seen as not something that is fixed or given. Rather, it refers to our ability to deal with the insecurities of human existence. Life is characterized by risk and uncertainty, and so trying to establish a position of complete security (in the sense of freedom from danger) is clearly impossible. A much wiser approach is to try to establish confidence in our ability to manage the risk factors that we encounter as we go about our business, both in life in general and specifically within the context of working in the people professions. Having security in this sense, then, comes from our ability to deal with life's insecurities, rather than naively trying to establish a set of circumstances that do not involve risk or danger.

A further important point to consider is that the anxieties and insecurities associated with risk can lead to a situation in which people develop what I shall refer to as 'risk paranoia' – a phenomenon that can be oppressive and disempowering. Some people can become so concerned about the risks involved in their work that they adopt quite a heavy-handed, rigid approach to any risk factors. The technical term for this is being 'risk averse' – that is, reluctant to take risks, even though the result of taking such risks could be very positive indeed and avoiding taking the risks could, ironically, actually make the situation worse. Figure 26.1 shows the dangers involved in either extreme – naivety about risk and risk paranoia.

Risk paranoia is, in part, based on a failure to recognize the positive, life-affirming and enhancing aspects of risk. Risk factors present the potential for one or more points of growth and can be a major source of pleasure and satisfaction.

For example, I have run training courses on assessing and managing risk where I have asked participants to consider experiences in their life where taking a risk produced a positive outcome for them. I have yet to encounter a single participant who could not identify a positive part of their current situation, or even of their identity, arising from the positive use of risk as a life-affirming process. Common examples include the following:

Naivety about risk	Paranoia about risk
Fails to appreciate the dangers involved	Overemphasizes the dangers involved
Leaves vulnerable people unprotected	Can be oppressive and disempowering
Gives clients no confidence in their level of understanding or awareness	Can undermine confidence and self-esteem, possibly leading to panic
Prevents realistic plans from being developed	Prevents realistic plans from being developed

Figure 26.1   Avoiding the extremes

○ *Cookery.*   Risks in using gas and electricity in combination with water; risks of food poisoning or an allergic response; risks of disappointment and embarrassment if people do not like or enjoy what is served – these are all issues that have been raised by people who regard being a good cook as an important part of their identity and lifestyle and who see cookery as a significant source of pleasure.

○ *Sports.*   Risks of injuring oneself; risks of injuring others; risks of disappointment, embarrassment or even humiliation – these are ever-present features of being involved in sporting activities, and yet for so many people involvement in sport is an important part of their sense of self in general and their self-esteem in particular.

○ *Career choices.*   Decisions about whether or not to apply for a particular job; whether to change career direction altogether or continue on the same path; whether to go for promotion or not – these can all have important implications and therefore have a number of significant risks associated with them.

○ *Relationships.*   Sustaining existing relationships and developing new ones are both risky undertakings, and yet our relationships are a key part of who we are. They are also, potentially at least, significant sources of pleasure.

○ *Transport.*   For many people, driving, motorcycling or cycling are important elements of their sense of self. For many people also, other modes of transport – bus, train, aeroplane – are significant parts of their life. And, of course, any one of these forms of transportation involves risk of death or injury. They are far from risk-free undertakings.

Risks also have the positive benefit of bringing people together in a spirit of shared endeavour – sporting or political activities, for example. They can be a significant source of camaraderie and thus of positive feelings of support and group identity. For people experiencing difficulties in their lives, this sort of support can be invaluable.

Risk, then, is clearly a basic part of human experience and one that can bring great pain and suffering, but which can also have major positive benefits. Therefore, as noted above, simply trying to remove risk is both unrealistic and potentially oppressive, as our efforts in this regard could have the effect of denying someone a great deal of pleasure and may actually go so far as to undermine their identity and cut off important sources of self-esteem. Paranoia about risk is therefore something that we have to be very careful to avoid. What is needed, then, is an approach that aims to *manage* risk rather than seeking to eradicate it.

Practice focus 26.2

Khaled was generally a very confident person, but when it came to dealing with risky situations, he tended to feel quite anxious, as he was aware that the consequences of making a misjudgement could be very significant. As a result of this anxiety, he developed a tendency to be overcautious in matters relating to risk. It was fair to say that elements of risk paranoia had crept into his work. Fortunately, he had a very experienced and insightful manager, Ruth, who noticed what was happening. She was able to help Khaled realize what he was doing and how potentially very problematic it was. She spoke to him about her concerns and offered to help. He was reassured by having her support and this in itself made him feel less anxious, so he was already beginning to move away from risk paranoia. Together they decided that it would be a good idea for Khaled to attend a risk assessment and management course when a suitable one became available. Ruth also suggested some basic reading that Khaled could do in the hope that, by developing his understanding of risk factors, he would be more confident and therefore less anxious in dealing with them in his work.

When it comes to attempting to manage risk, it is important to begin with an assessment of the key factors involved. There are various methods available – for example, see the discussion of the Brearley model in *The People Solutions Sourcebook*. However, here I shall not repeat what appears in that book but, rather, provide an additional method that I shall entitle 'The incidence and impact approach'.

This is illustrated in Figure 26.2. (Note that there are links here with conflict management, as the same grid can be used in terms of judging whether or not to deal with a conflict.) 'Incidence' refers to how likely it is that the risk will produce a negative outcome. For example, if we are concerned about the possible occurrence of violence, then we need to be clear about how likely such an occurrence is. 'Impact' refers to what effect such violence is likely to have if it does occur – in other words, how serious is it likely to be?

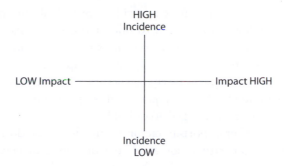

Figure 26.2 The incidence and impact approach

The incidence and impact approach can be helpful in plotting where a particular situation can be located in terms of the two axes. This can then give us some helpful insights about the level of priority of the risks involved and therefore guide us in terms of how quickly and to what extent we respond to the risks identified:

○ *High incidence, low impact (top left-hand corner).* This refers to situations where the danger feared is quite likely to happen, but the impact of it is not likely to be very serious. In such cases an assessment will need to be made of what, if anything, needs to be done to address this situation. For example, are there any steps that can be taken to reduce the likelihood of the problem occurring?
○ *High incidence, high impact (top right-hand corner).* In such situations, the likelihood of occurrence is high, as is the likelihood of significant harm. This, then, is clearly the 'high danger' zone and therefore needs to be handled very carefully. Close attention needs to be paid to what can be done to reduce both the likely incidence and the likely impact.
○ *Low incidence, low impact (bottom left-hand corner).* Here there is relatively little to worry about. The assessment will need to consider whether anything needs to be done at all – although it should not be assumed that it is automatically the case that a situation in this area needs no intervention at all.
○ *Low incidence, high impact (bottom right-hand corner).* These situations can be very difficult to deal with. They relate to circumstances in which the problem is unlikely to arise, but if it does, the consequences are likely to be quite serious. Careful monitoring may be needed so that, if circumstances change to increase the likelihood of occurrence, appropriate steps can then be taken. However, if the likelihood of occurrence is so low, it may not be cost-effective to monitor the situation. Once again, careful assessment is needed.

This approach will not do the assessing for you, but it will provide you with a useful framework for ordering your thoughts and thereby forming a picture of the risk factors involved.

It is important to note that this approach should not be seen as a static one. Assigning a situation to one of the four boxes in the grid is just a snapshot, an overview of how the situation stands at the moment. Risk factors can change very quickly, so it is important to keep the circumstances under review so that, if a change occurs, resulting in the matter in hand now being found in a different quarter of the grid, our plans for dealing with that situation can be changed accordingly.

One further important factor to consider in relation to risk is the question of mental capacity. If somebody has dementia or is psychotic or otherwise lacking in mental capacity, then we need to have an understanding of this and be ready to seek professional help in terms of an assessment of their capability to make decisions and to take risks. It is essential that we do not adopt an absolute approach to risk that fails to take account of the fact that some people, due to factors of mental capacity, are not in a position to make safe decisions about the risk factors they face.

Conclusion

Dealing with risk can be quite challenging work, but it can also be very rewarding and bring about very positive changes in people's lives. Coping with risk is a major feature of human experience, and to oversimplify what is involved would do a significant disservice not only to the important work we do in the people professions, but also to the complexity of the people's lives that we become involved with. A skilled people worker is therefore somebody who has a good knowledge of, and sensitivity to, the risk factors involved in any situation. He or she also has the confidence to deal with risk issues constructively and effectively without going to either unhelpful extreme of (i) neglecting the significance of risk, on the one hand; or (ii) becoming overly rigid or paranoid about risk factors, on the other (see Figure 26.1). If we are not careful, we could do more harm than good by leaving people in vulnerable situations when we could have helped or, at the other extreme, by stifling people's options, creativity and potential for growth by being unduly protective in terms of the risks involved.

Exercise 26

Incident and Impact

Using the incident and impact approach as shown in Figure 26.2, analyse an aspect of either your own personal life or your professional duties in terms of the grid and consider what this may tell you about the significance of these risks and how you might approach them. Repeat this exercise with other sets of risk issues until you feel comfortable in using this as a professional tool.

chapter **27**

Review and evaluation

Introduction

Review and evaluation are two important processes that have a key role to play in maintaining professional standards and helping workers to improve their practice. Both are closely linked with assessment, as they continue the process that assessment initiates. While assessment is geared towards identifying what needs to be achieved, both review and evaluation consider the extent to which it has been achieved.

Review is a process that should recur during the course of intervention. It involves stepping back from what is being done and considering its effectiveness, so that any changes that are necessary can be made. It is a process of monitoring and checking whether we are on course, and making the necessary adjustments if we are not.

Evaluation has much in common with review, except that it tends to occur at the end of intervention, or when the worker's performance is being examined (for example, as part of a process of appraisal). Evaluation involves identifying the strengths and weaknesses of the assessment and intervention stages so that lessons for future practice can be learned.

Review and evaluation are also closely linked with planning, as discussed in Chapter 24, in so far as they identify a range of issues that can have a significant bearing on future work. The lessons to be learned from review and evaluation can provide useful insights to guide the planning of further work.

Chapter 22 stressed the value of adopting a systematic approach to practice, with clear objectives and a clear focus on how they can be met. Review and evaluation are consistent with, and supportive of, systematic practice, as they both use objectives as a central focus. The points raised in this chapter therefore build on the foundations laid in that chapter.

It is worth noting that, although I argue in this chapter that review and evaluation are very important and valuable processes, we also need to recognize that there is a great deal of resistance to using them on the part of some people. This is perhaps understandable, in so far as we may not like what review and evaluation tell us – for example, that our work has not been as effective as we thought. However, although such resistance is understandable, we need to make sure that we do not allow it to stand in the way of reviewing and evaluating our work, for, unless we examine our practice in this way, we shall be missing opportunities to identify what works and what does not and thereby to learn from the process.

Review

Reviewing practice as a matter of course is a positive habit to develop due to the many benefits it offers. However, before considering some of the central issues relating to review, it is worth identifying the key times at which a process of review should apply:

○ *Significant changes.* At times when a significant change occurs, this can be an opportune moment to review what has been done to date and what remains to be done. This is because a significant change in circumstances can have a major bearing on: the problems that need to be addressed; the ways of addressing them; and people's attitudes towards them. For example, if a member of a family leaves the family home, this may alter the situation quite considerably, perhaps to the point where a reassessment is necessary – especially if that person plays a key role in the situation.

○ *Statutory requirements.* In certain circumstances, there is a legal requirement to review a particular situation. For example, children who are in the care of the local authority are subject to a review procedure that involves periodic meetings to monitor progress and ensure that needs are being met as far as possible. It is therefore important that we are aware of our statutory duties with regard to review requirements.

○ *Predefined review points.* In many cases, when a plan of action is agreed, one element of that agreement is the point at which the arrangements will be reviewed. For example, in planning a particular programme of work with a client, we may wish to decide how long we continue the work before reviewing whether it is appropriate or effective. A common time frame is three months, but we have to be careful not to allow this to become a rigid routine. Each situation needs to be judged on its merits and a review period determined accordingly.

○ *When feeling stuck.* It may sometimes be the case that we reach the point where we are not sure what to do. We may be dealing with a complex, 'messy' situation and a suitable way forward may be very difficult to plot. It is often at such times that reviewing what we are trying to achieve, and how we are trying to achieve it, can give us a clearer overview and a fresh set of insights. Review can therefore help to get us out of a situation in which we feel bogged down.

○ *Before a period of absence.* It pays dividends to review particularly difficult, demanding or complex pieces of work prior to a period of leave or other planned period of absence. This helps to develop a clear, up-to-date picture of the situation. This can be extremely helpful in two ways:

1 It provides a good basis for any work that needs to be done by a colleague during our absence.
2 Having reviewed the situation prior to the absence, we are then in a stronger position to continue intervention upon our return.

○ *Prior to transfer.* If there is a need for another worker to take over a piece of work for whatever reason, then it is helpful to review the situation at that point, partly to assist the new worker, and partly because the change of worker constitutes a change in circumstances that may, in itself, prompt the need for review.

○ *When ending intervention is being considered.* If the worker is wondering whether the time has come to end intervention, then a process of review can help us decide how close we are to closure, and what needs to be done to get there. This is a point to which I shall return in Chapter 28.

Being able to recognize the appropriate times to begin a process of review is an important people skill in its own right. If a review is not undertaken when it should be, valuable insights and opportunities may be lost, and the result may be a period of drift.

Key issues in review

An important point to recognize is that review is an 'iterative' process. That is, it is a recurring process, rather than a one-off event. In this way, review provides the stimulus, and basis, for reassessment. As such, it is an important aspect of systematic practice, in so far as it revisits the three key questions:

○ What are you trying to achieve?
○ How are you going to achieve it?
○ How will you know when you have achieved it?

The process of review builds on these three questions by posing a further four questions that can help us to retain a clear focus on what we are doing and why we are doing it:

1 *Were the original objectives appropriate?* With the benefit of hindsight, we can sometimes see that we were mistaken in deciding upon certain

objectives. This could be because: additional information has come to our attention; we see previous information in a new light; it emerges that previous information was inaccurate or not entirely honest; or people have changed their mind, or their perspective on a particular issue. We may very well find that the original objectives identified are not, in fact, realistic. It may be necessary to change one or more objectives in order to make them achievable. If there is a need to change objectives at the point of review, then this should not be seen as a sign of weakness or failure. Assessment is an inexact science and we should be careful not to blame ourselves unduly, as this can be a significant source of stress (see Chapter 3).

2 *Are there obstacles to achieving the objectives?* Reviewing a situation can sometimes reveal that there are factors that stand in the way of progress that were not apparent when the initial assessment (or previous review) was undertaken. For example, in working with a particular family, there may be a family member who subtly blocks progress because he or she has something to lose by the family solving their problems. Sometimes, this may be deliberate sabotage, but at other times the person concerned may not even realize what he or she is doing. There may be other obstacles, such as the negative influence of a third party or the absence of a resource that was expected to be available. Obstacles to progress can be many and varied, and we need to be wary of naively failing to take them into account.

3 *Have the circumstances changed?* The process of review can bring to our attention subtle and gradual changes that have taken place over a period of time. This is parallel with the situation where parents do not notice growth or changes in their children until someone who has not seen the children for some time comments: 'Haven't they grown?' We tend to notice sudden or drastic changes but we are much less likely to notice subtle and gradual changes. We may therefore find that a set of circumstances have changed a great deal but we have failed to realize this because we have been very close to the situation as it has evolved and developed. Indeed, this is one of the major benefits of review, it allows us to take a step back and get more of an overview of the overall situation.

4 *Is the plan appropriate?* We may have decided that the original objectives were appropriate but still not be on course for meeting them. That is, we may have got it right in terms of what we are trying to achieve, but got it wrong in terms of how we should go about trying to achieve it. It is therefore important to review not only the objectives, but also the strategy being used in an attempt to meet them. This involves identifying the degree of success to date, along with any problems or obstacles encountered, and considering whether the chosen route forward is actually the best one. Once again, review gives us the benefit of hindsight and can enable us to see flaws or oversights that were not apparent to us earlier.

> **Practice focus 27.1**
>
> Nathan had a lot of experience of working with groups on a short-term basis but this group was the first one he had worked with over an extended period of time. At the suggestion of one of his colleagues, he decided to review progress within the group – to revisit their original objectives and the steps they had taken towards meeting them. When Nathan met with the group to undertake this review, he was amazed to realize just how much had changed. New concerns had arisen and old ones had faded into the background. Nathan was now firmly convinced that the reviewing of groups, and indeed all aspects of his work, was to be a must from now on.

These four questions provide a basic structure and framework for review as a process of revisiting objectives and strategies, with a view to building on strengths and rectifying or guarding against weaknesses. The framework can be used as part of a formal review process, within a statutory review meeting, for example. Equally, though, it can form the basis of a more informal process of review, with less official overtones, as part of one's own attempts to achieve and maintain high-quality practice.

However formal or informal the review process is, one thing that needs to be remembered is that review is not a solitary activity – it needs to be undertaken in a spirit of partnership and participation. The views of others involved have an important part to play and, if changes are to be made to objectives or strategies, then a renewed commitment and sense of ownership needs to be generated. This cannot be achieved by working in isolation from the key people involved. Review can not only benefit from partnership, but also actually reinforce such partnerships.

Evaluation

As I mentioned earlier, evaluation has much in common with review. However, there are also some issues relating specifically to evaluation that are worth commenting on. First of all, it is important to note that evaluation focuses on three particular aspects of practice.

Effectiveness

Evaluation seeks to measure how effective the intervention has been. This involves establishing:

○ the extent to which objectives were met;
○ reasons for the relative success or failure of the intervention; and
○ the appropriateness of the objectives, and the strategies chosen to meet them.

Of course, the evaluation of effectiveness is very difficult, if not impossible, unless clear objectives were set in the first place. That is, if we were not clear about what we were trying to achieve, how can we judge how successful we have been?

Efficiency

Evaluation also seeks to make a judgement about how efficient intervention has been. This is because we work in a context of scarce resources. The nature of people work is such that demand is always likely to outstrip supply, in so far as human needs are not of a finite nature. Evaluation therefore needs to address important questions of efficiency such as:

○ Were appropriate priorities set?
○ Were these priorities observed, or reviewed, as appropriate?
○ Were resources used to best effect, with minimal waste or duplication?
○ Were alternative approaches considered?

A focus on efficiency has an important part to play in order to guard against waste and ensure that the limited resources available are used to best effect. However, we should note that there can often be a conflict between efficiency and effectiveness. This is because the most efficient approach may not be the most effective. A solution that uses fewer resources in the short term may turn out to be less effective, and may therefore involve a higher level of resourcing in the long run. We therefore need to balance efficiency and effectiveness in order to get the best results.

The lessons to be learned

Evaluating intervention allows us to draw out any lessons that are to be learned from examining how situations were dealt with. It is well known that, by looking back over what was done, we can learn from our mistakes – we can see where we went wrong and try to make sure that we do not make the same mistake again. This is an important part of learning, as it helps us to improve our practice.

However, what is not appreciated quite so fully is the lessons that can be learned from our successes, from what we did well. We are often very sensitive to mistakes, as there can be a high price for making them. However, we can take our strengths for granted, or perhaps not even notice that they are there. In this case, we need to put our modesty to one side and empower ourselves to learn from our successes by identifying what works, and why. This links in with the discussion of self-awareness in Chapter 1. We should not be complacent about what we do well, but neither should we fail to learn from it.

Practice focus 27.2

June was dreading her appraisal meeting. She felt sure that the meeting would focus on all the mistakes she had made in the past year. She knew that learning from her mistakes was a positive step, but she was not looking forward to being reminded of the errors she had made. However, June was very pleasantly surprised at the meeting to find that much of the time was spent looking at her strengths and how she could develop these even further. She came out of the meeting keen to learn not only from her mistakes but also from her successes.

Similarly, we can learn from the strengths and successes of others involved in the intervention. This is one of the benefits of working in partnership – it continually offers opportunities to benefit from the experiences of others.

Key issues in evaluation

In evaluating practice there are a number of issues that have a bearing on the outcome. These include:

○ *The perceptions of others*. As with review, evaluation should not be a solitary activity. It is important to take into account the feelings and perceptions of others. The views of other people can offer insights that our own personal perspective cannot capture. That is, we can gain a much broader perspective by taking on board the perceptions of others. This can be particularly beneficial when other people's views differ from our own. This is because a divergence of opinion forces us to rethink our own view of the situation, and this can be a very constructive stimulus to learning, involving a broadening of our horizons.
○ *The law*. In evaluating practice, we should consider the legal dimension. We should check that statutory duties were carried out. We should also consider what legal powers were applicable in the situation and whether they were used appropriately – or were not used when they could have been put to good use. The law provides the framework for practice, it determines what can be done (powers) and what must be done (duties). It is therefore helpful to evaluate intervention by reference to the legal context.
○ *Organizational requirements*. The policies and procedures of our employers also provide a framework that shapes practice. It therefore makes sense to evaluate our practice by reference to these requirements. This is not only a process of 'checking up' that procedures were followed. It is also a means of assessing to what extent those procedures helped or hindered the intervention. If they proved to be a hindrance, we may have the opportunity of feeding this back through whatever channels are available to influence policy.

○ *Moral and professional requirements.* These form a third framework to shape and guide practice. We need to be clear that our actions were consistent with professional values and other moral principles. If they were not, we need to identify what needs to be different in future to make sure that we do not encounter the same problems again. Also, such issues are often the subject of debate and conflicting opinions – they are rarely clear cut. In this way, evaluation can help us to develop our understanding of, and sensitivity to, ethical issues.

○ *Principles of good practice.* Each intervention should be evaluated in its own right by reference to the identified aims. However, there is also much to be gained by relating the work done to principles of good practice. To what extent did the intervention reflect these principles? With hindsight, can the work done be seen to be consistent with expectations of good practice? Was the work consistent with relevant Codes of Practice or official guidelines? These are important questions that help us to evaluate our work at a broader level, and provide good opportunities for learning.

Evaluation is a positive process whereby we can identify our strengths in order to build on them, and identify areas for development so that we can seek to turn weaknesses into strengths.

Common themes

It should be clear from this chapter that there are a number of common themes across review and evaluation. It is worth emphasizing some of these in particular. Both review and evaluation involve:

○ *Improving standards of practice.* Reconsidering work that has been undertaken enables us to view future practice in the light of past experience. If we do not review or evaluate our practice, we miss significant opportunities to identify means of enhancing quality standards.

○ *Helping to identify mistakes.* We will always be prone to making mistakes, however skilled, experienced or knowledgeable we may be. The least we can do, then, is to make sure that we learn from our mistakes so that negatives can become positives.

○ *Enhancing professional credibility.* Success in people work often depends on winning the trust and respect of clients and other professionals. Review and evaluation make a positive contribution to this by demonstrating that we work in a professional manner that enhances our credibility.

○ *Providing opportunities for learning.* Review and evaluation can make a major contribution to continuous professional development. This is partly through providing opportunities for improving standards of practice, as mentioned above. It is also partly through a process of identifying training needs or other developmental issues. That is, review and evaluation help us to note what direction our future learning can or should take.

These two processes are therefore potentially very helpful and constructive aspects of people work, and we should be receptive to the benefits that can be gained if we are prepared to make the necessary commitment.

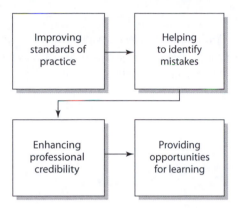

Figure 27.1   The benefits of evaluation

Conclusion

It is ironic that review and evaluation often fall by the wayside when the worker's workload pressures increase, and yet this is precisely the time when they can be of most value in terms of:

○ clarifying priorities;
○ identifying what is effective and what is not;
○ increasing the worker's sense of control and confidence;
○ assisting in the development of partnership; and
○ preventing vagueness and drift.

It is therefore important that we do not allow pressures of work to stand in the way of reviewing and evaluating our practice. These are essential elements of good practice and so we need to use our time management and assertiveness skills to ensure that they are not 'squeezed out' by other pressures.

Exercise 27

Reviewing Our Work

This exercise is designed to help you develop your familiarity with the process of reviewing work. Imagine that you have been asked to review a piece of work that you are involved in. Consider the following questions and use the space provided to make some notes:

1 In order to review a particular piece of work, who would you consult (in order to work in partnership)? List the range of people who may be involved.
2 What difficulties do you think might arise in reviewing?
3 How might you deal with these?

chapter **28**

Ending

Introduction

The process of bringing intervention to a close is an important aspect of people work, and yet it is one that is often neglected. The termination of our involvement with a particular person or persons is part of the helping process and therefore needs to be handled carefully and sensitively. If it is mishandled, then much of the good work that has previously been done may be undone.

However, it is more than a simple matter of tying up loose ends. Effective ending of intervention is a skilled process that helps to reduce the likelihood of further problems arising. This is because a well-handled ending can be a positive part of the change process, rather than simply an end to it.

A central feature of appropriate ending of intervention is the retention of a clear focus, a continuation of systematic practice. If we have lost sight of what we are trying to achieve or how we are intending to achieve it, then we are also going to be unclear when and whether to end our intervention. Therefore, the discussions of endings in this chapter need to be seen in the context of systematic practice.

I shall address three sets of issues in this chapter: why endings are important; reasons for ending intervention; and obstacles that can stand in the way of intervention being brought to an appropriate close.

Why endings are important

There are a number of reasons why endings are not only important but also an essential part of good practice. This can be seen to apply in the following ways.

Empowerment

A basic feature of empowerment is the need to avoid creating dependency. If people become dependent upon us, the degree of control over their own lives is decreased, rather than increased. By working towards specific objectives with a view to ending our intervention in due course, this has the effect of lowering the likelihood of dependency developing, and is therefore a contributory factor to the process of empowerment. Where there is no clear focus on working towards ending, intervention becomes open ended and can therefore become characterized by drift and a risk of dependency developing.

Even in situations where intervention needs to be over an extended period of time, open-ended work is still not the only option. This is for two reasons:

1 It is a mistake to assume that focused, systematic practice applies only to short-term work. Long-term work has a purpose and so, by definition, objectives can be set, even if they may take years to achieve (for example, in working with a child in foster care).
2 In some cases, intervention is likely to last for the person's lifetime (such as, in working with a severely disabled person). However, endings are still an important issue, in so far as intervention can be broken down into stages or discrete elements. For example, a person's life is not static, and there will be new developments that need to be addressed systematically, with clearly identified goals to work towards, and a focus on the eventual termination of that particular piece of intervention.

It should be clear, then, that an unfocused, open-ended approach that loses track of ending can have the effect of undermining empowerment by increasing the possibilities for dependency developing.

Workload management

If work continues longer than is necessary, this can cause problems in terms of workload management. People work is generally characterized by a demand for services in excess of supply. Consequently, there is a need to set priorities, to determine which calls upon our time are the most important. Such priorities are likely to be distorted and undermined if we continue to be involved in situations where our active intervention is no longer necessary or is of a low priority. Effective, appropriate and timely ending of intervention can therefore be a significant factor in the successful management of a heavy workload.

Labelling

At times there may be a degree of stigma associated with being the user of a service. For example, users of mental health services are often subjected to prejudice as a result of their status as the users of such services. Similarly, families who have cause for social work services may be seen as 'problem families', rather than families with problems. That is, the potential benefits of intervention do not come without a price.

Extended intervention without purpose or focus can therefore be counterproductive, in so far as it can bring about the negatives of intervention without bringing any of the positives. That is, an important benefit of retaining a clear focus on working towards ending is that it reduces the likelihood of clients being labelled or stigmatized.

Job satisfaction

Open-ended, unfocused work can produce a great deal of psychological pressure. Being involved with a number of people, but without a clear plan for moving forward, can leave us feeling confused, demotivated and unstimulated. Working towards endings – and achieving them – can, by contrast, act as a considerable source of motivation and job satisfaction.

This is of benefit to all concerned, as it means that people are more likely to receive a good service from a worker who is keen, committed, creative and responsive, rather than tired and worn down.

Transfer

The notion of 'ending' applies not only to the end of a process or stage of intervention, but also when one worker takes over from another (as discussed below). That is, one worker's role may end, but the work may continue in the hands of another worker. The skills of ending one's involvement effectively and appropriately are therefore important in order to transfer work when necessary.

There are, then, various ways in which endings play an important role in contributing to good practice in people work. In view of this, it is necessary to be able to recognize the times when endings should occur so that we can be as well equipped as possible to deal with them constructively. To help develop this understanding, it is worth considering the main reasons for drawing our intervention to a close.

Reasons for ending intervention

Ending one's intervention with a particular individual, group or family can arise in response to a variety of factors. I shall comment on a number of these, outlining briefly some of the important issues. Coulshed (1991) identifies 11 reasons for ending intervention, which are summarized in Figure 28.1 and discussed below.

○ *Agreed goals being achieved within a pre-set time limit.*   If clear goals are established through systematic practice, achieving those goals can be the trigger for ending intervention.
○ *Clients deciding they have been helped enough.*   There are various reasons why someone may wish not to proceed, the most positive being that they now feel confident enough to continue unaided.

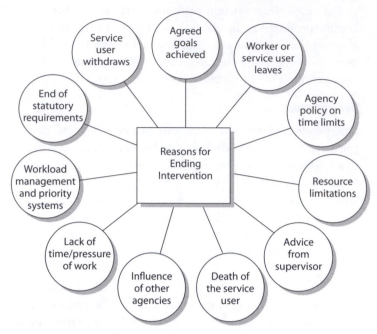

Figure 28.1   Reasons for ending intervention

○ *Workers leaving or clients moving from the district.*   Of course, an ending becomes necessary if either party moves away. In these circumstances it is important that effective communication ensures continuity if someone else is going to be continuing the work (for example, through a clear and explicit transfer summary).

○ *The end of statutory requirements.*   Sometimes intervention is for legal reasons (as a result of a court order, for example) and may therefore end when the order expires – although it may continue on a voluntary basis if that is appropriate.

○ *Agency policy on time limits.*   An example of this would be a hospital-based service which ends when the patient is discharged (or within a fixed time limit thereafter).

○ *Workload management and priority systems.*   At times relatively low priority work may have to be brought to an end because of the demands of higher priority work requiring greater attention.

○ *Resource limitations.*   The lack of a particular resource may make it difficult if not impossible to continue, although a creative response may be a useful way forward in such circumstances (see Chapter 8).

○ *Lack of time and pressure of work.*   Unfortunately, work can sometimes be ended 'by default'. That is, unlike the planned ending of work on the basis of clear priorities, some pieces of work may simply 'fizzle out' if they are not given time and attention. This is a very unsatisfactory way of ending.

○ *Advice from supervisor.* Sometimes one's line manager, being that little bit removed from the situation, may be able to see reasons for ending the work that you perhaps cannot see for yourself (see Chapter 7 on the value of supervision).

○ *Influence of other agencies.* It may be, for example, that a worker from one organization 'pulls out' to avoid duplication with another organization whose responsibilities overlap to a certain extent.

○ *Death of the client.* Ironically, the death of the client does not automatically lead to the end of intervention, as there may be issues related to grieving that need to be attended to (Thompson, 2012b).

Obstacles to ending intervention

Very often, ending of intervention does not take place when it should, thereby distorting priorities and allowing drift to undermine systematic practice. For each piece of work that continues longer than is needed, there is a new piece of work that has to wait. Consequently, there is much to be gained in identifying some of the key factors that stand in the way of ending.

Dependency

If we allow people to become dependent on us, then a great deal of difficulty can be encountered when attempts are made to move towards bringing intervention to a close. If dependency is allowed to develop, ending can undo the work that has been done and leave the person or persons concerned in a very weakened or distressed state.

Dependency therefore puts the worker in a very difficult position when it comes to endings. He or she faces a difficult decision that involves either bringing our work to a close (while recognizing that this will cause the client some difficulty) or continuing to be involved unnecessarily. Clearly, then, it is vitally important that people work should be geared towards empowerment, with a clear aim of not allowing dependency to develop.

Practice focus 28.1

Siobhan was very committed to being part of the helping professions. She was an extremely caring person who took her tasks and duties very seriously. She worked hard and never complained about working conditions or other problems – she was just glad to be able to help people in need. However, what Siobhan did not realize was that, in her enthusiasm to be helpful, she was actually hindering some individuals. When people had reached the stage where they could do a lot of things for themselves, Siobhan was reluctant to end her involvement with them. She had not learned to let go and so, in this way, she was actually creating dependency, and thereby undoing a lot of the good work she had done.

Resistance to change on the part of the client

It is understandable that people may feel uncomfortable about the changes brought about by our ending our involvement, particularly where the relationship has existed over a considerable period of time. In such circumstances, resistance to change can make it difficult for us to achieve effective closure. This is particularly the case where someone lacks confidence and is anxious about being able to cope without our support. In such cases, we will need to:

○ boost confidence by focusing on strengths and potential;
○ identify other sources of support available – family, other organizations and so on; and
○ make it clear that it may be possible to resume the working relationship if circumstances change and make this necessary.

Resistance to change on the part of the worker

Clients are not the only ones who may be prone to feeling uncomfortable about change. This can again be a matter of confidence. We may worry about: 'What if I end my involvement and things go wrong?' or 'What if it's too soon?' These types of worry and hesitancy can be constructive if kept in perspective. However, where they are allowed to grow out of all proportion, they can be very problematic as they can lead to intervention continuing for a lot longer than is necessary or helpful.

The solution to this is, of course, supervision. The supervisor can help to clarify whether or not ending is appropriate, and, if the worker is being unduly hesitant, this can be explored and a positive way forward agreed.

Worker satisfaction

We can gain a great deal of satisfaction from working with certain people and, in such cases, we can be reluctant to end our involvement. We may therefore be tempted to continue our work for our own benefit, to meet our own needs, rather than to provide a service.

While this is understandable to a certain extent, it can also be very problematic in terms of distortion of priorities and blurring of the professional relationship. Once again, supervision has a role to play in helping the worker keep a clear focus and gain satisfaction from the job itself.

Pressure from others

Relatives, neighbours, friends and other workers can all, at times, put us under pressure to continue working with a particular individual, group or family. This may be due to their anxieties about people not being able to manage without our support. Or, it may be due to their own agendas. That is, if we cease to be involved, this withdrawal may put pressure on others or cause them difficulties in some way. For example, if a community psychiatric nurse discontinues visits to a person with mental health problems, relatives may then feel that more responsibility falls on their shoulders.

While it is important to take account of the views and feelings of others, it is also important not to allow our professional judgement to be unduly influenced by the pressures that are brought to bear.

Unresolved feelings

Certain work situations can trigger off significant emotional responses because aspects of the situation 'echo' aspects of our own personal experience. For example, in working with children, we may recognize in a child's circumstances a painful situation that reminds us of our own childhood. Where such 'triggers' occur, we may be reluctant to end our intervention when the time comes, due to the unresolved feelings that have been resurrected.

We may need to remember that the 'feel' element of Think–Feel–Do applies to us as well as to the people we are seeking to help. We have to take account of how our own feelings affect the situations we deal with.

Lack of clarity about objectives

Of course, if we are not clear about what we are trying to achieve, we will not be able to recognize that we have achieved it. Ending may therefore be thwarted by an unfocused approach that allows drift and vagueness to cloud the issues.

Failure to review objectives

An important aspect of review is to consider whether previously identified objectives are still appropriate. However, if we fail to review objectives, we may find ourselves trying to achieve the impossible, and therefore obstructing the process of ending intervention. For example, a review might have brought to light new information that was not available at the time of the initial assessment. This new information may indicate that the original plan was not appropriate, but, if the plan is not reviewed, the worker may continue to pursue the plan regardless.

Practice focus 28.2

Sandy had known the Stevensons over a long period of time, particularly in relation to their disabled son, Paul. She had worked with them to address a number of issues, some very serious, some less so. She was fond of Paul and enjoyed working with the family. However, despite the fact that she had achieved a lot in her work with this family, what Sandy had not done was to review the objectives initially agreed. In this way, she had allowed her work to drift. She had begun to lose her professional role and was beginning to be seen by the family as more of a friend than a professional worker. She had created a situation in which it was going to prove difficult to bring her involvement to an end without hurting their feelings.

Disorganization

Poor time management and a disorganized approach to one's workload can mean that pieces of work are not brought to a satisfactory conclusion. A disorganized worker may have a number of pieces of work that become 'dormant' because they are not receiving the attention they require. Eventually, such work may, as discussed earlier, come to an end 'by default'. However, where this occurs, the benefits of effective ending of intervention can be lost for all parties.

Conclusion

This chapter has raised a number of important issues in relation to bringing intervention to a close and, in so doing, has no doubt conveyed how complex and skilled a process it is when it is given the attention it deserves.

It is very sad indeed when high-quality, painstaking work is spoiled or undermined by a failure to bring it to a close in a sensitive and appropriate way. The tendency to neglect endings as a fundamental part of the process of intervention is therefore a costly one, as it can lead to many of the problems outlined in this chapter.

Exercise 28

Pitfalls and Pointers

For this exercise you will need to reread this chapter and note down:

• the pitfalls to avoid, and the common errors to be wary of; and
• the pointers to follow, and the steps towards better practice.

In this way, you will be able to construct your own guide to good practice in relation to ending intervention. Use the space below to make notes.

chapter **29**

Responding to trauma: promoting healing and recovery

Introduction

When people experience a trauma, the consequences can be quite major. When a situation arises that involves a traumatic reaction, the results can be quite devastating, mainly for the people directly involved but also for a broader group of people as a result of the wider ripple effect. This chapter explores the significance of trauma, beginning with a discussion of its definition. From this we move on to look at how we make sense of trauma, and 'making sense' is an important term because that is precisely what we have to do when trauma strikes. It has the effect of turning our systems of meaning on their head and leaving people bewildered and confused. Finally, we discuss some of the ways in which we can help people to deal with the traumas they face in life.

Defining trauma

The word 'trauma' comes from the Greek word for wound. It is used within the medical profession to refer to a physical wound, but is also used more broadly in the helping professions to refer to a psychological wound brought about as a result of a significant crisis or key turning point in a person's life that has the effect of bringing about a profound change. Many people use the term 'trauma' very loosely to refer to any difficult or distressing situation. It is important to differentiate between this loose usage of the term, as in comments like: 'I've been on the phone an awful lot lately, so it's going to be quite traumatic when I get the bill', and the more precise usage here. In its more scientific sense it refers to a psychosocial entity. That is, it is something that has both psychological and social dimensions to it – although much of the literature focus is narrowly on only the psychological elements (see Bracken, 2002, for a critique of this).

A central feature of trauma is loss, in so far as trauma both creates a strong sense of loss (trauma as cause) and arises from losses (trauma as effect). There is therefore a close link between trauma and grief. In fact, trauma can be seen as a particular type of grief reaction, where it is so intense that it has the effect of leaving us feeling psychologically wounded by the circumstances. Not all loss is traumatic, as we manage to respond to the majority of losses without in any way being 'wounded', even though the experience may be extremely painful. A traumatic loss is one that goes far beyond the everyday experiences of loss in people's lives.

Grief *challenges* our coping resources

Crisis *overwhelms* our coping resources

Trauma *devastates* our coping resources

Figure 29.1   Grief, crisis and trauma (from Thompson, 2012b)

Making sense of trauma

Trauma can be caused by a wide range of factors, such as bereavement or other major loss, especially where that loss is unexpected or where there are cumulative losses (several losses over a relatively short period of time) involved or, indeed, multiple losses (several losses at the same time – for example, as a result of a house fire). In addition to losses related to the death of one or more people, trauma can arise because of the loss of a sense of security we experience as a result of being the victim of a crime, for example. Experiencing violence, or even simply the threat of violence, can also be sufficient to generate a traumatic response to the situation.

Trauma is also connected with major disasters – for example, large-scale fires, floods and other natural catastrophes or human-made disasters, such as mass shootings, terrorist incidents or other such horrifying events. However, we should not make the mistake of assuming that trauma is a rare or exceptional thing that only affects a small minority of people. Brewin makes it clear that traumatic experiences are not uncommon:

> Who are the victims of trauma? The answer is 'most of us.' Surveys have been carried out in the United States to document the likelihood of a person experiencing or witnessing physical assaults, accidents, disasters, or other incidents involving the risk of death or serious injury. Generally, between 70 and 80 percent of people will experience one of these events over the course of a lifetime.
>
> (2003, p. 8)

These figures relate to the USA but it would be reasonable to assume that they can be generalized to other industrialized nations to a certain extent at least.

Trauma is often associated with PTSD (or post-traumatic stress disorder, to give it its full name). However, there are two dangers involved in the use of this term. On the one hand, it is important to distinguish between PTSD and post-traumatic stress. PTSD is regarded as a significant psychological condition that arises in a minority of cases of trauma, whereas most, if not all, people experiencing a trauma will encounter some degree of post-traumatic stress. That is, experiencing a trauma is inherently stressful, but in only a small minority of cases does this reach the level where it can be regarded as a psychological disorder. It is important not to confuse the two and thereby develop a misleading or inaccurate assessment of the situation when we try and help someone deal with a trauma in their life.

The second problem associated with PTSD is that it is often presented uncritically as a medical condition. As I have argued elsewhere (Thompson, 2011c), there are dangers in presenting psychosocial conditions as biomedical illnesses. This is particularly the case with trauma, as popular literature, television and film have created a strong cultural image of the trauma 'victim' who needs 'treatment' for his or her psychiatric 'illness'. This type of conceptualization reinforces passivity and a sense of helplessness – often features of trauma in their own right.

Whether medicalized or not, trauma can have a huge impact on people's lives. It can undermine a person's sense of identity, for example. Sometimes there is such an overwhelming sense of powerlessness and such a breakdown of normality that people experiencing a trauma often have a sense of not knowing who they are any more. What has happened is that their ontological security – their sense of feeling relatively safe in terms of how they fit into the wider world (see Chapter 20) – has broken down. In this respect, the impact of trauma includes a very strong grief reaction and so, in order to understand trauma, we have to have a good understanding of grief.

What makes a situation even more complicated is that trauma often goes unrecognized, especially when the trauma has not arisen in dramatic circumstances. So, in many cases, people will have experienced a trauma that has not been recognized or acknowledged as such because there was no sense of drama that is often associated with a trauma (as in the case of disasters, for example). If someone is the victim of violence, especially extreme violence, then it is likely that any traumatic reaction will be recognized as such. However, in many cases, even the threat of violence can be enough to trigger a traumatic reaction but, because no actual violence took place, the genuinely traumatic nature of the incident may not be understood. This can apply to both children and adults. For children, trauma is often the result of some form of abuse, and this may well be the case for many adults.

> ### Practice focus 29.1
>
> Anthony was walking through the car park, intending to drive to a meeting a few miles away when he was shoved from behind and had his briefcase snatched from him. He turned to see a young man, clutching his briefcase, disappearing round the corner. He felt he should run after him, but it was as if he was paralysed – he just stood there in shock. When he got back to his office and told his colleagues what had happened, they were quite supportive to begin with, and reassured him that at least there was nothing of value in the briefcase and he was not injured in the incident. However, very soon they had put the incident behind them and got on with their lives without attaching too much significance to what came to be seen as a minor incident with no real harm done. For Anthony, though, it was not quite so simple. He kept going over the incident again and again in his mind. He kept remembering being shoved from behind and feeling powerless to do anything about the situation. It was as if he was just waiting for the situation to arise again. He found the whole thing quite distressing, and the fact that other people were not tuned in to his distress made him feel even worse, even more powerless. He wondered whether he would be able to continue to work there, as being in the same building, with the same people, using the same car park was constantly triggering off painful memories and 'flashbacks'. The company's failure to recognize the significance of trauma meant that they were likely to lose a highly valued employee who would be very difficult to replace.

Dealing with trauma

Trauma has been described as an assault on our sense of self (Harvey, 2002). It therefore has significant spiritual connotations, in so far as it is concerned with such important issues as meaning, direction, connectedness and hope. Supporting people in dealing with trauma therefore involves helping them find order and meaning in their lives after their taken-for-granted reality (the 'assumptive world') has been shattered.

Schiraldi (1999) divides the human response to trauma into two steps. The first is one of 'healing'. This refers to the short-term coping that lays the foundations for rising to the challenges involved. Literally, healing means becoming whole again and should be interpreted in a spiritual rather than a medical sense (becoming a whole person, not simply a whole body). This first step of healing is about supporting people in dealing with the immediate aftermath of a traumatic situation. For many people, this is all that is required. They quickly re-establish their sense of equilibrium and move on with their life. However, for very many people, a longer period of adjustment and change is needed. For a proportion of people, what is needed is what can be referred to as 'recovery'. This involves finding ways of integrating the traumatic experience into their overall sense of self, so that they no longer feel harmed or 'damaged' by the events. They are able to continue as whole people, equipped to deal with life's challenges without having the wound of the traumatic experience holding them back in some way.

There are certain elements of risk associated with a trauma. The traumatic experience is a form of crisis, a turning point in somebody's life. As a result of experiencing a trauma the person concerned may be left weaker, less able to cope with life's challenges, or they may grow and strengthen as a result of the experience. For example, there is research to show that many people experience what has come to be known as post-traumatic growth (Calhoun and Tedeschi, 2014). This refers to the way in which people can be stronger, better equipped to cope with life's pressures – for example, by finding greater closeness and intimacy in their relationships with others and by having a greater sense of purpose and direction in their lives. Helping people to deal with their trauma can therefore be seen as a form of crisis intervention, based on the principle of trying to maximize the positive potential of the situation. It is not, therefore, simply a matter of helping people 'get over' the trauma, but of actually going a step further by helping them to find, and capitalize on, opportunities for post-traumatic growth.

Practice focus 29.2

Larry was a quiet, withdrawn and fairly unconfident individual with few friends and no real interests to speak of. He worked as a porter in a local hospital. He was reasonably happy with his lot for the most part, but was prone to depression from time to time. However, all this changed one day when, while Larry was working with two colleagues removing some boxes that had been dumped in the hospital parking lot, two youths in a stolen car raced through at high speed. Larry managed to jump out of the way but his two colleagues did not – they were killed instantly right in front of his eyes. He was quite shocked by this and found the intense feelings the incident generated extremely hard to deal with in the coming weeks and months. There were times when he wondered whether he might 'crack up' as he could not get the incident out of his mind.

Over time, though, he managed to recover from the trauma with the help of a social worker. He was able to start to get things into proportion. However, he was also able to go beyond this. Seeing two young men killed instantly had made him review his life and consider carefully what he wanted out of it and where he wanted it to take him. As a result of this he decided to attend night classes to gain the entry qualifications that would allow him to commence nurse training. After realizing how fragile life can be, he now had a clear sense of wanting to do something positive with his life rather than just let it drift past. The trauma had turned out to be a point of growth for him – an intensely painful experience, but one that ultimately brought important positive benefits.

(Source: Reproduced with permission from Thompson, 2009b)

However, balanced against these potentially very positive outcomes are the dangers of:

1 *Retraumatization.* This refers to situations where talking about the traumatic experience can lead to further distress. Helping people in a post-trauma situation therefore needs to be handled carefully and sensitively. It is not something that we should rush into without assessing the situation very carefully.

2 *Secondary traumatization.* There is also the danger of secondary or vicarious traumatization. This refers to situations in which other people, not directly involved in the original trauma, can experience a trauma reaction. This applies to people closely associated with the individual(s) directly involved in the incident: friends, relatives and so on. It can also apply to professional staff and volunteers involved in trying to provide help, either directly in the aftermath of a disaster, or over the medium to longer term. This is a significant danger, and so anyone working with people who have experienced trauma needs to have access to adequate support mechanisms, both formal and informal.

To sum up, in dealing with trauma, it is important that we take account of the following:

1 *Tuning in to meaning.* The meanings people associate with their experience are of central importance – the use of narrative or storytelling is a fundamental part of this.

2 *Working together.* Trauma tends to bring about an immense and overwhelming sense of powerlessness, and this can easily become infectious, metaphorically speaking. It is therefore vitally important that people support one another, partly for their own safety and well-being, and partly to ensure that they provide the best possible support in these very difficult circumstances (see Chapter 20).

3 *Not getting out of our depth.* In entering the world of trauma, we are stepping towards huge challenges that can be very profound in the impact they can have, both on us as helpers and on the people we are trying to help. We should not do so lightly or be ill-prepared for what we are likely to face. We should ensure that we take the opportunity to learn as much as we can about trauma before we encounter such challenging situations (see the 'Guide to further learning' at the end of the book) and, where possible, we should take advantage of attending relevant courses. Also, with this in mind, we should not forget my earlier comment about the importance of working together. Nobody should be on their own in tackling the immense challenges of trauma.

Conclusion

The unrecognized nature of trauma in so many of the situations people workers encounter means that the tasks we are charged with in the people professions will often have an unacknowledged link with experiences of trauma. Such trauma can be the primary reason for the problems people are experiencing (stress and tension, for example) or may serve to exacerbate other problem areas (adding extra strain on relationship difficulties, for example). Having an awareness of, and sensitivity to, trauma issues is therefore an important part of our professional knowledge repertoire – we ignore it or brush it under the carpet at our peril. We can do people a considerable disservice if we do not recognize trauma and its implications, and we can actually make the situation much worse.

We can therefore see that there are two sides to responding to trauma: one open and one hidden. On the one hand, there is the challenge of working directly with those situations where trauma is clearly and openly a key factor while, on the other hand, there is a much wider range of situations – for example, in dealing with children or adults who have been abused – where the impact of trauma is less visible, but none the less very significant, despite being more hidden.

Exercise 29

Learning about Trauma

Think of a novel, play or film where someone has been traumatized (for example, as a result of loss, being a victim of crime or being involved in a disaster) and consider the following questions:

- What led to the trauma being experienced?
- How does the trauma manifest itself?
- What impact does it have on the person's life?
- What impact does it have on the lives of people close to that person?
- Are there any lessons about helping people through trauma that this teaches us?

If you cannot think of a suitable novel, play or film, discuss this with family, friends or colleagues and see what examples they come up with. If you have time, repeat the exercise with other examples. The more you do it, the greater the learning potential.

chapter **30**

Reflective practice

Introduction

The concept of reflective practice is one that is closely associated with the work of Donald Schön (Schön, 1983, 1987, 1992). It is an approach to professional practice that emphasizes the need for practitioners to avoid standardized, formula responses to the situations they encounter. Reflective practice involves coming to terms with the complexity, variability and uncertainty associated with human services work.

This chapter therefore explores the implications of developing reflective practice. It begins by addressing the basic question: 'What is reflective practice?' From this we move on to consider the process of applying theory to practice. This involves clearing up some misunderstandings about the relationship between theory and practice, and establishing why it is important for practice to be based on theory. Finally, I shall explore the role of creativity in facilitating both systematic and anti-discriminatory practice.

What is reflective practice?

Reflective practice begins from the premise that human problems cannot be solved by the simple application of technical solutions. People's problems are far too complex and 'messy' to be resolved in this way. Schön draws a distinction between the 'high ground' of theory and research and the 'swampy lowlands' of practice. He describes this as follows:

> In the varied topography of professional practice, there is a high, hard ground which overlooks a swamp. On the high ground, manageable problems lend themselves to solution through the use of research-based theory and technique. In the swampy lowlands, problems are messy and confusing and incapable of technical solution. The irony of the situation is that the problems of the high ground tend to be relatively unimportant to individuals or to society at large, however great their technical interest may be, while in the swamp lie the problems of greatest human concern.
>
> (Schön, 1983, p. 54)

One significant implication of this is that practitioners cannot sit back and wait for 'experts' to provide them with solutions on a plate. Workers have to engage with the complexities of practice and navigate a way through them. That is, reflective practice is an active process of constructing solutions, rather than a passive process of following procedures or guidelines.

In order to do this, we must first undertake what Schön (1983) calls 'problem setting'. The messy situations workers encounter do not come with clearly defined problems ready made for the practitioner to start working on. Consequently, the first task the worker faces is to make sense of the situation, to develop a picture of the problem(s) to be tackled. This, then, is the process of 'problem setting'. As Schön puts it: 'Problem setting is a process in which, interactively, we *name* the things to which we shall attend and *frame* the context in which we will attend to them' (1983, p. 40). Problem setting is part of the process of assessment and illustrates the point that assessment should not be seen as routine or mechanical – it is an active process of forming a picture, identifying problems and mapping out a way forward.

In this way, we can see that the 'high ground' of theory is not going to provide 'off the peg' solutions. Rather, what needs to happen is for the overview we gain from the high ground to be combined and integrated with the specific insights we gain by being 'close to the action' within the actual situations we are dealing with. That is, workers need to use their experience and expertise in such a way that it comes to be 'tailor made' for the specific situation they are working with at any particular time.

A reflective practitioner, then, is a worker who is able to use experience, knowledge and theoretical perspectives to guide and inform practice. However, this does not mean applying ideas in a blanket form, unthinkingly and uncritically, regardless of the circumstances. Reflective practice involves cutting the cloth to suit the specific circumstances, rather than looking for ready-made solutions.

To inexperienced workers, this may sound very difficult and daunting. However, it is based on a set of skills that can be developed with experience, and offers a sound basis for high-quality practice and high levels of job satisfaction.

Relating theory to practice

Reflective practice involves being able to relate theory to practice, drawing on existing frameworks of ideas and knowledge so that we do not have to 'reinvent the wheel' for each new situation that arises. I shall therefore address some of the key issues relating to the integration of theory and practice. I shall begin by outlining two common misunderstandings concerning the relationship between theory and practice.

First, we need to recognize that the relationship is not a simple or straightforward one. Theory influences practice in a number of subtle and intricate ways, but practice can also influence theory (Thompson and Thompson, 2008). These are important points to recognize, as they help to dispel the myth that theory and practice are separate, unconnected domains. I shall discuss below the dangers of driving a wedge between theory and practice. Second, it is also important to realize that theory does not provide hard and fast answers or clear, simple solutions to problems. To see it otherwise is to misconceive the part that theory plays in guiding practice.

These two sets of issues represent the two extremes of a continuum. At one extreme, the tendency to separate theory from practice is problematic in terms of cutting off an important resource for understanding practice situations. At the other extreme, it is unhelpful to have unrealistic expectations of what theory can or should offer, as this too can have the effect of driving a wedge between theory and practice.

The middle ground between these two extremes is where reflective practice operates. It involves recognizing the ways in which the general principles offered by theory can be adopted and 'tailored' to fit the specific circumstances of each situation dealt with. The tendency to divorce theory from practice is a dangerous one in so far as it leaves us open to a number of possible difficulties. These should become clear when we consider why we should integrate theory and practice as effectively as possible.

Figure 30.1   Reflective practice

In a previous text (Thompson, 2000), I identified the following six reasons for relating theory to practice. I shall comment briefly on each of the six.

Anti-discriminatory practice

As we have noted in earlier chapters, discrimination and oppression are inherent in the way society is organized. We therefore need to pay attention to theories of discrimination and oppression if we are to challenge their destructive effects. A reliance on 'common sense' is likely to reflect, rather than challenge, dominant discriminatory attitudes. It is for this reason that reflective practice needs to be *critically* reflective practice – that is, to take account of the wider social and political circumstances that shape the situations we deal with (Thompson and Thompson, 2008).

The fallacy of theoryless practice

Even if a framework of ideas is not used deliberately or explicitly, it is inevitable that our actions will be guided by sets of ideas and assumptions. The idea that we can have practice without theory is therefore a fallacy. A theory does not have to be a formal or 'official' theory as found in books or academic journals. Theory can refer to any ideas or frameworks of understanding that are used to make sense of our everyday experience and practice situations.

Theory is therefore inevitably applied to practice, but, if we do not apply such theory explicitly or deliberately, we are relying on untested assumptions and therefore leaving a lot to chance.

Evaluation

Evaluating our practice gives us useful opportunities to learn from our experience by identifying what worked well and what was problematic (see Chapter 27). In order to do this we have to draw on a theory base. For example, in evaluating a particular approach that was adopted, we need to have at least a basic understanding of the ideas on which that approach is based.

Continuous professional development

In Chapter 9 the case was made for making a commitment to continuous professional development, an attitude of lifelong learning. This, too, depends on a theory base. The process involves avoiding 'getting into a rut' of unthinking, uncritical routines. Continuous professional development rests on our ability and willingness to adopt a reflective approach, to think creatively and critically about our work.

Practice focus 30.1

Dennis had learned a great deal from his professional training but was anxious about getting into a rut and not being able to continue learning and developing as he gained the experience he needed. During his course he had found it very helpful to keep a learning diary or reflective log – brief details of the issues that had arisen each day, his thoughts on the subject and what he had learned from the day's work. He decided that he would continue to do this as his career progressed. He recognized that he might not have the time to do this on a daily basis but he was determined to make sure it happened at least weekly.

Professional accountability

As professionals, people workers are accountable for their actions. Consequently, we need to be able to explain and justify the decisions we make and the steps we take. It is difficult, if not impossible, to do this without reference to a theory base. Professional accountability demands reasoned arguments to justify our actions, and this, of course, involves drawing on a set of concepts that guide and inform our practice.

Inappropriate responses

If we rely on 'common sense' responses to the problems we encounter, there is a serious danger that our actions may not only prove ineffective but actually make the situation worse:

> A failure to draw on theoretical knowledge may lead to an inappropriate response on the part of the worker. We may misinterpret what is happening and react in a way which is not helpful or which even makes the situation worse. For example, a person experiencing a bereavement may express considerable anger towards the worker. If the worker does not recognise such anger as a common part of the grieving process, he or she could easily misread the situation and interpret the anger as a rejection of the worker's help.
>
> (Thompson, 2000, p. 35)

Reflective practice, as these six examples illustrate, owes much to a purposeful integration of theory and practice. This goes far beyond an implicit, uncritical use of theory, and involves a proactive approach to using theoretical ideas and knowledge as a framework for maximizing effectiveness.

This brings us to the question of how we can integrate theory and practice – what needs to be done to draw on the benefits that theory can offer? This is a vast topic and so, in the space available, I shall limit myself to outlining the following six steps that can be taken to promote reflective practice:

○ *Read.* For theory to be used to best effect it is important that we break down the barriers by challenging the assumption that reading is for students or staff in training and not for fully-fledged practitioners. Unfortunately, it is commonly assumed by many people that reflecting on theory is a task for students but not for practitioners. For example, an experienced social worker once told me that he missed being a student as he had enjoyed reading widely on the subject of social work and related topics. When I asked him what was stopping him from continuing to do so, he struggled for an answer. In the end, he replied that it was because it was 'not the done thing'. It is important, then, that such a 'reading is for students only' culture is broken down. Some may argue that they do not have enough time to read. However, there are two points that need to be made in response to this. First, time spent reading is an *investment* of time and can, by enhancing our practice, save time in the long run. Second, reading can increase our levels of job satisfaction by giving us a broader perspective and greater insights into people work. In view of this, I feel it is worth devoting some of our own time, outside of working hours, to read about subjects related to our work.

○ *Ask.* Asking' can apply in two ways. First, in relation to reading, much of the people work literature base is written in a jargonistic academic style that makes it difficult to understand. It can be helpful, then, to ask other people about such issues so that you can get past this barrier. The danger is that some people may give up on reading because they feel uncomfortable with the style of writing being used. Second, we can learn a great deal from other people's practice. Students often learn a great deal by asking questions like: 'Why do you do it that way?' or 'Have you any ideas how I might tackle this situation?' There is much to be gained from creating an open, inquiring, mutually supportive atmosphere in which all staff, not just students, can learn from each other.

○ *Watch.* There is much to be learned from developing an enhanced level of awareness in terms of observational skills. Much of the time we may miss significant issues because we treat situations as routine and commonplace. We need to remember that every situation is unique in some ways, and so we need to be attuned to what is happening and not make blanket assumptions. Practising in a routine, uncritical way can mean that we are, in effect, going around with our eyes closed, oblivious to significant factors that could be very important in terms of how we deal with the situation. Theoretical knowledge can help us understand and explain our experience, but if our experience is closed off by a failure to be sensitive to what is happening, then we will not notice that there is anything to be explained. Reflective practice relies on developing a sensitivity to what is happening around us.

○ *Feel.* The emotional dimension of people work is, as we have seen, a very important one. Our emotional responses can, at times, be painful and difficult to deal with. At the other extreme, using theory can sometimes be seen as cold and technical. However, this does not mean that the two – thinking and feeling – cannot be reconciled. Thought can help us understand (and therefore deal with) feeling, and feelings can help bring theory to life, turn concepts into working tools, and thereby develop a reflective approach.

○ *Talk.* Sharing views about work situations and how these can be dealt with encourages a broad perspective. It provides opportunities for people to learn from each other's experience, to find common ground and identify differences of approach. Constructive dialogue about methods of work, reasons for taking particular courses of action and so on can be an excellent way of broadening horizons, deepening understanding and enhancing skills. Such dialogue also helps to create an open and supportive working environment, and this, in itself, can be an important springboard for reflective practice.

○ *Think.* There are two main barriers to a thoughtful approach to practice. These are routines and pressure. A routinized approach amounts to working 'on automatic pilot' and is clearly a dangerous way of dealing with sensitive issues. As I mentioned earlier, dealing with situations in a routine, unthinking way leaves us very vulnerable to mistakes. Pressure can also stand in the way of thinking about our practice. If we are very busy we have to be wary of allowing ourselves to be pressurized into not thinking about what we are doing. We need to remain in control of our workload (see Chapter 2) so that we are able to think about our actions. Thinking time should be seen as an essential part of good practice, rather than a luxury that has to be dispensed with when the pressure is on.

These steps are not the only ones that can be taken to develop reflective practice but they should provide a good 'launch pad' for working out patterns of practice that can draw on the benefits of a reflective approach. One further important step towards reflective practice is the development of creative approaches, and so the discussions in Chapter 8 should be seen as closely linked with the development of reflective practice.

Practice focus 30.2

Lee was becoming increasingly interested in reflective practice after attending a training course on it and subsequently reading up on the subject. However, it was only after a new colleague joined his team that he started to appreciate the significant role of creativity as a basis for reflective practice. Jenny had always enjoyed working in very imaginative ways and brought this way of working to her new post. When Lee started to understand how innovative Jenny was in terms of the breadth of ideas she drew on in tackling her work tasks, he came to realize just how routinized and narrow his own approach had become over the years. He now wanted to learn from Jenny's example and make a reality of reflective practice by being more open to new ideas and more imaginative in his approach to his work. Jenny's arrival had proved to be a breath of fresh air for him.

Conclusion

Reflective practice involves drawing on theory, in so far as this represents the accumulated experience and expertise of others. In this way, we can use the theory base to avoid the need to 'reinvent the wheel'. However, theory does not come tailor made for practice – the cloth has to be cut to fit the circumstances. The reflective practitioner therefore has to *engage* with theory, to use it and shape it creatively in a constructive and positive way, rather than simply wait passively for theory to provide ready-made solutions.

Reflective practice is, then, a creative and proactive practice, one that casts the practitioner in an active role. This is an approach to practice that is entirely consistent with people work, a form of work where the situations we deal with have many common themes, but are also, in some ways, special and unique. Reflective practice offers the use of a theory base to help us understand the common themes, and a focus on creativity to help us deal with the unique aspects of each situation we encounter.

Exercise 30

Reflecting on Practice

A point made in this chapter is that we often underestimate the extent to which theory informs practice. This exercise illustrates this point by asking you to consider a piece of work you have been involved in. Consider what theoretical knowledge you drew upon in deciding what to do. Use the space below to make some notes. The headings may help you to think of ways in which theory influences practice.

The law/policy requirements about individuals and groups

Human psychology

Sociology – class, gender, race and so on

Problem-solving methods

Specialist knowledge

Conclusion

People work in its various forms is a complex and demanding activity. It is rooted in an extensive knowledge base, a wide range of skills and a challenging set of values. The work is characterized by problems, pain, distress and uncertainty, and is therefore by no means a simple or straightforward undertaking.

There is much to be learned and many mistakes to be made, and so the process of becoming a skilled and experienced people worker is not without its difficulties and disappointments. No book can guarantee any degree of success, but it is to be hoped that this book has been able to contribute to the firm foundations needed to develop good practice.

The ideas presented here are not intended as simple formulae to be followed unthinkingly. They are intended as a framework to stimulate further thought, discussion and guidelines for effective practice. They represent a set of tools that can be used to guide practice and inform professional development. However, such ideas inevitably apply at a general level and have to be adapted to the specific setting and circumstances that each worker encounters. Indeed, being able to apply general principles to specific situations is a key part of reflective practice, as discussed in Chapter 30. As we noted in that chapter, the nature of people work is such that simple, technical solutions are not appropriate. The worker needs to 'craft' a constructive way forward, rather than look for a ready-made solution.

In order to help develop these skills in crafting solutions to complex problems, the book was divided into three parts: personal effectiveness, interaction skills and intervention skills. By way of conclusion, I shall revisit and summarize some of the key themes and issues to arise in each of the three parts.

First, under the heading of 'personal effectiveness' came a number of issues relating to the question of self-management. The basic principle here is: if we are not able to manage ourselves effectively, then we will be seriously weakened in our attempts to manage the various processes that go to make up people work. This was covered under the following headings:

○ *Self-awareness.* People work involves 'engaging' with other people person-to-person. We therefore have to have a good understanding of ourselves in terms of how we are perceived by other people, our characteristic responses and reactions and our own needs.

○ *Time management.* People workers are subjected to a range of demands on their time and energy. There are, then, important lessons to be learned in terms of organizing one's time, maximizing energy levels, setting priorities and so on.

○ *Stress management.* Many pressures impinge on people workers and so the dangers of experiencing stress are never very far away. It is therefore important to be able to recognize what causes us stress, what strategies are available to counter it and what support we can draw upon.

○ *Managing information.* We face a constant flow of new information. If we are not well organized enough to manage that flow effectively, then it is likely that we will be overwhelmed by it sooner or later, and that will have the effect of seriously undermining our personal effectiveness.

○ *Assertiveness.* In dealing with people, we need to be able to strike a constructive balance between submissiveness and aggression. This is so that the rights of each partner can be respected and an appropriate basis for partnership established.

○ *Beating the bully.* Sadly, we have yet to eradicate the problem of bullying and harassment in the workplace and, until we do, it will be necessary for people workers to guard against the negative effects of bullying.

○ *Using supervision.* Supervision can play an important role in ensuring accountability, facilitating staff development and providing staff care. It is therefore in workers' interests to take whatever steps they can to ensure they receive appropriate supervision.

○ *Being creative.* 'Thinking outside the box', as the current jargon has it, is an important part of our work. Getting stuck in tramlines and acting in routinized, unimaginative ways is not likely to be very effective, nor is it likely to create a great deal of job satisfaction, motivation or morale.

○ *Continuous professional development.* People work continually brings new demands and new challenges. It is therefore important that we continue to learn and develop, partly to keep up to date with changes, and as a source of stimulation, motivation and job satisfaction.

○ *Being realistic.* Finding the helpful balance between naive optimism and cynical defeatism is a significant challenge, but the dangers of going to one unhelpful extreme or the other make it a very worthwhile one to rise to.

In Part II of the book, the focus shifted from personal effectiveness to interaction skills. Here, a basic principle is that we need to be well informed about, and skilled in handling, the complex interactions between people that are such an important, indeed fundamental, part of the work. This was addressed in terms of the following sets of issues:

○ *Dealing with diversity.* The people who become clients are very diverse in terms of their background – class, culture, gender and so on. We therefore need to be sensitive to differences and avoid stereotypical assumptions that act as a barrier to effective interactions.

○ *Verbal communication.* The use of speech as a form of interpersonal communication is a central part of interactions with clients and other professionals. A clear and appropriate use of language is a basic requirement of good practice in promoting effective communication.

○ *Nonverbal communication.* In addition to speech, the use of nonverbal signals such as gesture, posture and touch can also be a very significant dimension of interpersonal interactions. This makes the ability to 'read' and use nonverbal communication an important set of skills to develop.

○ *Written communication.* Written records, reports and so on are also important forms of communication. Much good work can be undermined by a failure to make appropriate records or communicate effectively in writing. Clarity and a focused approach are important elements to develop here.

○ *Interviewing.* Interviewing is a basic tool of people work. A poorly handled interview can spoil any possibility of positive interactions, whereas a skilfully managed interview can provide a firm basis for further work. The basic skills of interviewing are therefore important abilities to develop.

○ *Influencing skills.* Having a positive and constructive influence over other people is a fundamental part of people work, and so the skills involved are important ones to develop as far as we possibly can.

○ *Leadership.* Leadership is not restricted to managers – anyone who works in the people professions can (and should) be a leader, in the sense of someone who positively influences the culture in which work is taking place. The skills involved are important people skills and are therefore well worth developing.

○ *Handling feelings.* The emotional dimension of people work is often a difficult one to deal with. However, we need to be wary of falling into the trap of ignoring the feelings element, as this can often be a crucial factor. We need to be able to deal sensitively and constructively with both our own feelings and those of clients.

○ *Handling aggression.* An aggressive encounter is an ever-present possibility in people work. However, there are steps that can be taken to minimize the risk of violence occurring and, where it does occur, to minimize the harm that can be done. Managing aggression and violence involves using negotiation skills in an attempt to keep the situation under control.

○ *Multidisciplinary working.* People professionals rarely work in isolation. Much of the time we are working as part of a broader network of people. This brings with it a number of challenges. A key to this aspect of people work is being able to appreciate other people's perspectives and not simply pursue our own agenda without reference to the needs, interests and perspectives of others.

Interaction skills are important for developing effective working relationships, and relationships are potentially a powerful vehicle for promoting change. However, there is a danger, a very significant danger, that too much reliance will be placed on the use of relationships to get the job done. That is, we also need intervention skills as well as interaction skills. Or, to put it technically, interaction skills are a necessary condition for success, but not a sufficient one.

Part III therefore addressed the process of intervention, the skills and methods used to deal with the problems identified. A range of important issues were covered, structured under the following headings:

○ *Anti-discriminatory practice.* Very many of the people who require the help of a people worker are discriminated against or oppressed in some way. Workers therefore have to ensure that their practice not only avoids reinforcing such discrimination, but also actively challenges and undermines it.

○ *Being systematic.* Effective practice can be undermined by a tendency towards vagueness and drift. A systematic approach is one that involves agreeing clear goals to aim for and identifying appropriate strategies for working towards them. This requires the ability to be clear and focused without being rigid and unresponsive.

○ *Assessment.* A basic feature of systematic practice is the significance of assessment – the process of gathering information, making sense of it, identifying appropriate objectives to pursue, and agreeing an action plan for attempting to achieve them. Once again, a clear, focused approach pays dividends.

○ *Planning.* People workers are not expected to be clairvoyants, but there are clear benefits to planning for the future, particularly in terms of anticipating problems, hazards and obstacles to progress. Planning can boost confidence for both worker and client, and is therefore an aspect of practice to be encouraged.

○ *Decision making.* Intervening positively in people's lives necessarily involves making decisions. It is therefore important that we are as fully aware of the issues as we can be so that we are well equipped to handle the pressures of decision making as effectively as we can.

○ *Managing risk.* In the people professions risk is never far away. It is therefore important that we are able to find the balance between being complacent about risk on the one hand and becoming paranoid about it on the other. This is not always easy, but there are steps that we can take to ensure that we develop our knowledge and skills over time.

○ *Review and evaluation.* Progress towards achieving our aims needs to be reviewed from time to time to take account of changing circumstances and reconsider the initial assessment. Similarly, there is much to be gained by evaluating practice when our intervention comes to an end. The process of revisiting and reconsidering practice to date is an important basis for learning and practice development.

○ *Ending.* Drawing our intervention to a close is a skilled task that, unfortunately, is often not given the attention it deserves. A neglect of the process of ending intervention can undo good work previously done, cause resentment and distort priorities. The skills involved in appropriate endings are therefore well worth developing.

○ *Responding to trauma.* Trauma is a very powerful influence on people's lives, the effects of which are often unrecognized, even by experienced professionals. Trauma is also far more common than most people realize. It is therefore very important indeed that people workers are tuned in to the significance of trauma as a key factor in so many people's problems.

○ *Reflective practice.* There are no simple, formula answers in people work. One of the worker's tasks is to 'craft' a response appropriate to the circumstances. This involves understanding the general principles contained within the theoretical knowledge base but also having the skills and confidence to tailor these to the specific situation being dealt with. Developing reflective practice can be seen as quite a demanding challenge, but one where the benefits more than justify the investment of time and effort involved.

One further key theme that emerges in various chapters is that of partnership. Chapter 20 looks specifically at *multidisciplinary* partnerships (worker–worker partnerships), but there is also the need to give full attention to partnership with the people we are trying to help (worker–client partnerships). At its simplest level, partnership means working in ways that involve doing things *with* people, rather than *to* them.

People work involves working alongside people to meet needs, solve problems and improve quality of life. Trying to achieve these aims without involving the client in the process, without gaining his or her commitment to change, is far less likely to succeed than an intervention premised on partnership. Even where the worker is in a position of authority (and needs to draw on that authority) there is still scope for working in partnership to as great an extent as possible – it is not a case of authority *or* partnership. Working in partnership, then, is not so much an option to consider, as a fundamental ingredient of good practice.

People work will continue to be challenging and demanding and, at times, painful. We shall continue to make mistakes and we shall continue to find that many problems cannot be solved. However, we should also continue to be committed to making a positive difference wherever we can. The discussions of the knowledge and skills base underpinning practice in this book will not guarantee success, but can at least make a constructive contribution to equipping workers for the challenges that present themselves to us.

Guide to further learning

The point was made in the Introduction that a little knowledge is a dangerous thing. This book is a 'gateway' text, in the sense that it provides introductory information about a wide range of people skills, rather than a more in-depth treatment of particular issues. The intention is that each chapter should provide you with an appetite for finding out more about the topics covered. This section of the book is therefore designed to provide guidance on developing your understanding further by reading widely on the specific topics. The suggestions given are by no means comprehensive, but should be sufficient to help you get started in broadening and deepening your knowledge of these important topics.

Please note that the suggested readings range from quite straightforward practical guidebooks to some quite in-depth highly theoretical works. Each reading will offer something different to our understanding. Please also note that the inclusion of a particular source in this section does not mean that I necessarily agree with what it says or accept the premises on which it is based. My aim is to provide a broad-based overview of the literature, rather than simply offer my own personal recommendations.

The works chosen represent a broad range of academic disciplines and professional groups. I strongly believe that it is important to explore the breadth of insights that can be gained from across the board. For example, nurses who will not read anything unless it has 'nursing' in the title, social workers not interested in anything unless it is specifically for social workers or managers thinking they have nothing to learn from sources that are not focused specifically on management issues are missing out on a great deal of cross-disciplinary learning and a wide range of potentially helpful insights. You are therefore encouraged to explore a wide range of sources and not restrict yourself to the confines of your own particular discipline.

It is important for me to stress that a major feature of my work over the years has been an emphasis on the need to integrate theory and practice. I have long been of the view that theory that has little to offer practice is largely self-indulgent, but – perhaps more importantly – that practice that divorces itself from theory (from the professional knowledge base) is actually quite dangerous, as it can lead to ill-informed decisions and actions and a distorted and oversimplified view of the situations we encounter. The major focus of this book has been on practice, but I want to make it crystal clear that the ideas presented here are rooted in important theoretical perspectives, traditions and insights. The practical focus should therefore not be interpreted as in any way a rejection of theory or an attempt to suggest that practice does not need theoretical underpinning. In fact, I have argued explicitly on a number of occasions that such an approach would be very unwise indeed (see, for example, Thompson, 2000; 2010). This guide to further learning should therefore not be seen as tokenistic, but rather as an important gateway to taking your learning further by reading more widely about the topics covered.

And, finally, I would want to remind you of the 'companion volumes' of *The People Solutions Sourcebook* (Thompson, 2012a) and *People Management* (Thompson, 2013), which should serve you well in extending and deepening your understanding of 'people issues'.

Self-awareness

To be as effective as possible in making use of, and developing, our people skills, we need to be tuned in to what is going on around us, how it is affecting us and what part our presence is playing in shaping the situation.

Key text

Butler, G. and Hope, T. *Managing Your Mind: The Mental Fitness Guide*, 2nd edn, Oxford University Press, 2007.

An interesting and well-written book that offers a great deal of food for thought as well as practical guidance around a number of key areas of people skills, including self-awareness.

Other sources

Rungapadiachy, D. M. *Self-Awareness in Healthcare: Engaging in Helping Relationships*, Palgrave Macmillan, 2007.

Zahavi, D. *Self-Awareness and Alterity: A Phenomenological Investigation*, Northwestern Universities Press, 2000.

Time management

We all have limited resources of time and energy, and so the more effective we are at managing these resources, the more of an impact we can have.

Key text

Allen, D. *Getting Things Done: The Art of Stress-free Productivity*, 2nd edn, Penguin, 2015.

This book offers a very useful overview of positive steps that can be taken to manage the range of tasks we face without becoming overwhelmed.

Other sources

Adair, J. *Effective Time Management*, 2nd edn, Pan, 2009.

Clayton, M. *Brilliant Time Management: What the Most Productive People Know, Do and Say*, Pearson Business, 2011.

Forster, M. *Do It Tomorrow and Other Secrets of Time Management*, Hodder & Stoughton, 2006.

Gleeson, K. *The Personal Efficiency Program: How to Get Organized to Do More Work in Less Time*, John Wiley, 3rd edn, 2003.

Stress management

Keeping stress at bay can be a major challenge, but it is important that we manage to do this, as the negative effects of stress can be of major proportions.

Key text

Thompson, N. *Stress Matters*, an e-book published by Avenue Media Solutions: www.avenuemediasolutions.com, 2015.

This is a short introduction and overview that I developed to help busy people prevent their pressures from overspilling into stress.

Other sources

Cooper, C. L. (ed.) *From Stress to Wellbeing, Volume 1: The Theory and Research on Occupational Stress and Wellbeing*, Palgrave Macmillan, 2013.

Cranwell-Ward, J. and Abbey, A. *Organizational Stress*, Palgrave Macmillan, 2005.

Haworth, J. and Hart, G. (eds) *Well-being: Individual, Community and Social Perspectives*, Palgrave Macmillan, 2012.

Palmer, S. and Cooper, C. L. *How to Deal with Stress*, Kogan Page, 2007.

Robertson, I. and Cooper, C. L. *Well-being: Productivity and Happiness at Work*, Palgrave Macmillan, 2011.

Weinberg, A., Sutherland, V. J. and Cooper, C. L. *Organizational Stress Management: A Strategic Approach*, 2nd edn, Palgrave Macmillan, 2010.

E-learning

I have developed two e-learning courses on stress, one called *Dealing with Stress*, which is for everyone, and *Managing Stress*, which is specifically for managers: www.avenuelearningcentre.co.uk.

Information management

In today's world of information overload it is essential that we have a clear plan for keeping on top of things.

Key text

Floridi, L. *Information – A Very Short Introduction*, Oxford University Press, 2010.

Although not directly about information *management*, this short book offers a good introduction to the concept of information, which should then be useful in guiding how to manage the information that comes our way.

Other sources

Cartwright, R. I. *Key Concepts in Information and Communication Technology*, Palgrave Macmillan, 2005.

Hinton, M. *Introducing Information Management: The Business Approach*, Butterworth-Heinemann, 2005.

Jones, W. and Teevan, J. (eds) *Personal Information Management*, University of Washington Press, 2007.

Ling, R. and Donner, J. *Mobile Communication*, Polity, 2009.

Marchand, D. and Davenport, T. H. (eds) *Mastering Information Management*, Prentice Hall, 1999.

Rosen, L. *iDisorder: Understanding Our Obsession with Technology and Overcoming its Hold on Us*, Palgrave Macmillan, 2012.

Whiteley, D. *Introduction to Information Systems: Organisations, Applications, Technology, and Design*, Palgrave Macmillan, 2004.

Assertiveness

Being assertive draws on a number of the skills discussed in this course as it is an important basis for interacting with other people, not pushing them into a corner, but not allowing them to push us into a corner either.

Key text

Back, K. and Back, K. *Assertiveness at Work: A Practical Guide to Handling Awkward Situations*, 3rd edn, McGraw-Hill, 2005.

This is a highly respected text on an important subject, with lots of useful guidance.

Other sources

Blair, M. and Wilson, L. *C is for Confidence*, Russell House Publishing, 2004.
Carr, D. L. *Brilliant Assertiveness*, Prentice Hall, 2012.
Dryden, W. and Constantinou, D. *Assertiveness Step by Step (Overcoming Common Problems)*, Sheldon Press, 2004.
Paterson, A. J. *The Assertiveness Workbook: How to Express Your Ideas and Stand Up for Yourself at Work and in Relationships*, New Harbinger Publications, 2001.

Bullying and harassment

It is sadly the case that bullying and harassment are alive and well in a wide range of organizations. It is therefore important that we have a good understanding of the issues involved.

Key text

Fevre, A., Lewis, D., Robinson, A. and Jones, T. *Trouble at Work*, Bloomsbury Academic, 2014.

An important feature of this book is that it emphasizes the importance of organizational culture and highlights the dangers of individualizing bullying and related problems.

Other sources

Peyton, P. R. *Dignity at Work: Eliminate Bullying and Create a Positive Working Environment*, Brunner-Routledge, 2003.
Stephens, T. and Hallas, J. *Bullying and Sexual Harassment*, Chandos, 2006.
Tehrani, N. *Workplace Bullying: Symptoms and Solutions*, Routledge, 2012.
Thompson, N. Tackling Bullying and Harassment in the Workplace, an e-book published by Avenue Media Solutions: www.avenuemediasolutions.com, 2015.

Supervision

The subtitle of Mosley, Mosley and Pietri's book sums up supervision for me: the art of inspiring, empowering and developing people. It really is that important.

Key text

Morrison, T. *Staff Supervision in Social Care*, 3rd edn, Pavilion, 2006.

Although written specifically for a social care readership it has important messages about supervision that apply across all sectors and disciplines.

Other sources

Hawkins, P. and Shohet, R. *Supervision in the Helping Professions*, 3rd edn, Open University Press, 2007.

Morrison, T. *Staff Supervision in Social Care*, 3rd edn, Pavilion, 2006.

Mosley, D. C. Jr, Mosley, D. C. Sr and Pietri, P. *Supervisory Management: The Art of Inspiring, Empowering and Developing People*, 9th edn, Cengage, 2015.

Shohet, R. (ed.) *Passionate Supervision*, Jessica Kingsley, 2007.

Thompson, N. *Promoting Workplace Learning*, Policy Press, 2006.

Thompson, N. and Gilbert, P. *Supervision Skills: A Learning and Development Manual*, Russell House Publishing, 2011.

Being creative

Avoiding getting stuck in tramlines will help to maximize the effectiveness of our people skills.

Key text

Isaksen, S. G., Dorval, K. B. and Treffinger, D. J. *Creative Approaches to Problem Solving: A Framework for Innovation and Change*, 3rd edn, Sage, 2011.

Other sources

Adair, J. *The Art of Creative Thinking: How to Be Innovative and Develop Great Ideas*, 3rd edn, Kogan Page, 2007.

Bono, E. de *Lateral Thinking: A Textbook of Creativity*, Penguin, 1990.

Bono, E. de *How to Have Creative Ideas: 62 Exercises to Develop the Mind*, Vermilion, 2007.

Hamer, M. *The Barefoot Helper*, Russell House Publishing, 2006.

Pope, R. *Creativity: Theory, History, Practice*, Routledge, 2005.

Robinson, K. *Out of Our Minds: Learning to be Creative*, 2nd edn, Capstone, 2011.

Continuous professional development

Continuing to learn throughout our careers is an important part of building up our people skills over time.

Key text

Thompson, N. *Promoting Workplace Learning*, Policy Press, 2006.

Provides an overview of various aspects of learning.

Other sources

Clutterbuck, D. *Everyone Needs a Mentor: Fostering Talent at Work*, 3rd edn, Chartered Institute of Personnel and Development, 2001.

Honey, P. *How to Become an Effective Learner*, Peter Honey Publications, 2003.

Honey, P. *Continuing Personal Development*, Peter Honey Publications, 2007.

Thompson, S. and Thompson, N. *The Critically Reflective Practitioner*, Palgrave Macmillan, 2008.

Waldman, J. *Help Yourself to Learning at Work*, Russell House Publishing, 1999.

E-learning

I have developed a free *Learning to Learn* online course that is the equivalent of a full day's continuous professional development. Details are available from www.avenuemediasolutions.com.

I have also developed an innovative online learning community based on principles of reflective practice and self-directed learning. Unlike conventional courses, which are tutor led, this programme is about creating a supportive online learning community in which individuals can determine, and pursue, their own learning pathway, with tutor support and guidance. Details are available from www.apdp.org.uk.

Being realistic and resilient

Finding the balance between the extremes of optimism and pessimism is what being realistic is all about. Being resilient is about being able to 'bounce back' from adversity. Being realistic helps us to be resilient.

Key text

Kent, M., Davis, M. C. and Reich, J. W. *The Resilience Handbook: Approaches to Stress and Trauma*, Routledge, 2014.

A thorough and detailed textbook with a strong psychological focus.

Other sources

Camus, A. *The Myth of Sisyphus*, Penguin, 2005.

Chang, E. C. (ed.) *Optimism and Pessimism: Implications for Theory, Research and Practice*, American Psychological Association, 2000.

Dienstag, J. F. *Pessimism: Philosophy, Ethic, Spirit*, Princeton University Press, 2006.

Ehrenreich, B. *Smile or Die: How Positive Thinking Fooled America and the World*, Granta, 2009.

Norem, J. K. *The Positive Power of Negative Thinking: Using Defensive Pessimism to Harness Anxiety and Perform at Your Peak*, Basic Books, 2002.

Segerstrom, S. C. *Breaking Murphy's Law: How Optimists Get What They Want from Life – and Pessimists Can Too*, Guilford Press, 2006.

Seligman, M. E. P. *Learned Helplessness: On Depression, Development, and Death*, W. H. Freeman, 1975.

Seligman, M. E. P. *Learned Optimism: How to Change Your Mind and Your Life*, Vintage Books, 2006.

Diversity/anti-discriminatory practice

Inequality creates a wide range of problems and difficulties and prevents people from fulfilling their potential.

Key text

Thompson, N. *Promoting Equality: Working with Diversity and Difference*, 3rd edn, Palgrave Macmillan, 2011.

This book provides a theoretical analysis of equality and diversity while also offering a strong practical focus.

General

Baker, J., Lynch, K., Cantillon, S. and Walsh, J. *Equality: From Theory to Action*, Palgrave Macmillan, 2004.

Baxter, C. (ed.) *Managing Diversity and Inequality in Health Care*, Bailliere Tindall, 2001.

Moss, B. *Values*, Russell House Publishing, 2006.

Mullaly, B. *Challenging Oppression and Confronting Privilege*, 2nd edn, Oxford University Press, 2010.

Thompson, N. *Power and Empowerment*, Russell House Publishing, 2007.

Thompson, N. *Anti-Discriminatory Practice*, 5th edn, Palgrave Macmillan, 2012.

Ageism

Bernard, M. and Scharf, T. (eds) *Critical Perspectives on Ageing Societies*, Policy Press, 2007.

Daatland, S. O. and Biggs, S. (eds) *Ageing and Diversity: Multiple Pathways and Cultural Migrations*, 2nd edn, Policy Press, 2006.

Levenson, R. *Auditing Age Discrimination: A Practical Approach to Promoting Age Equality in Health and Social Care*, King's Fund, 2003.

Macnicol, J. *Age Discrimination: An Historical and Contemporary Analysis*, Cambridge University Press, 2006.

O'Dempsey, D., Jolly, S. and Harrop, A. *Age Discrimination Handbook*, Legal Action Group, 2006.

Disablism

Borsay, A. *Disability and Social Policy in Britain since 1750: A History of Exclusion*, Palgrave Macmillan, 2004.

Oliver, M. *The New Politics of Disablement*, 2nd edn, Palgrave Macmillan, 2011.

Oliver, M., Sapey, B. and Thomas, P. *Social Work with Disabled People*, 4th edn, Palgrave Macmillan, 2012.

Shakespeare, T. *Disability Rights and Wrongs Revisited*, Routledge, 2013.

Swain, J., French. S., Barnes, C. and Thomas, C. (eds) *Disabling Barriers – Enabling Environments*, 3rd edn, Sage, 2013.

Thomas, C. *Sociologies of Disability and Illness: Contested Ideas in Disability Studies and Medical Sociology*, 2nd edn, Palgrave Macmillan, 2007.

Racism

Back, L. and Solomos, J. (eds) *Theories of Race and Racism: A Reader*, Routledge, 2009.

Okitikpi, O. (ed.) *Working with Children of Mixed Parentage*, Russell House Publishing, 2005.

Rattansi, A. *Racism: A Short Introduction*, Oxford University Press, 2007.

Sallah, M. and Howson, C. (eds) *Working with Black Young People*, Russell House Publishing, 2007.

Sexism

Bates, L. *Everyday Sexism*, Simon & Schuster, 2014.

Bird, C. E. *Gender and Health: The Effects of Constrained Choices and Social Policies*, Cambridge University Press, 2008.

Connell, R. *Gender*, 2nd edn, Polity, 2009.

Freedman, E. B. (ed.) *The Essential Feminist Reader*, The Modern Library, 2008.

Other forms of oppression

Graham, J. *Autism, Discrimination and the Law: A Quick Guide for Parents, Educators and Employers*, Jessica Kingsley, 2008.

Morland, I. (ed.) *Queer Theory*, Palgrave Macmillan, 2005.

Richardson, D. and Monro, S. *Sexuality, Equality and Diversity*, Palgrave Macmillan, 2012.

Rogers, A. and Pilgrim, D. *A Sociology of Mental Health and Illness*, 5th edn, Palgrave Macmillan, 2014.

Thompson, N. *Effective Communication*, 2nd edn, Palgrave Macmillan, 2011.

User participation

Nolan, M., Hanson, E., Grant, G. and Keady, J. *User Participation in Health and Social Care Research*, Open University Press, 2007.

Shaping Our Lives National User Network *Shaping Our Lives: What People*

Think of the Social Care Services They Use, Joseph Rowntree Foundation, 2003.

Thompson, N. *Power and Empowerment*, Russell House Publishing, 2007.

Warren, J. *Service User and Carer Participation in Social Work*, Learning Matters, 2007.

Communication

Communication is at the heart of human interaction and is therefore a central part of people skills.

Key text

Thompson, N. *Effective Communication*, 2nd edn, Palgrave Macmillan.

This book provides an overview of important theoretical issues relating to communication, while also offering practical guidance,

Other sources

Christopher, E. (ed.) *Communication Across Cultures*, Palgrave Macmillan, 2012.

Marsen, S. *Communication Studies*, Palgrave Macmillan, 2006.

Moss, B. *Communication Skills in Health and Social Care*, 2nd edn, Sage, 2012.

O'Rourke, L. *For the Record*, Russell House Publishing, 2002.

O'Rourke, L. and Grant, L. *It's All in the Record*, Russell House, 2005.

Stanton, N. *Mastering Communication*, 5th edn, Palgrave Macmillan, 2009.

Interviewing

Interacting with someone in a focused and effective way is what interviewing is all about.

Key text

Moss, B. *Communication Skills in Health and Social Care*, 2nd edn, Sage, 2012.

Although the title refers specifically to health and social care, this excellent book will be of value to anyone working in the people professions.

Other sources

Hargie, O. *Skilled Interpersonal Communication: Research, Theory and Practice*, 5th edn, Routledge, 2010.

Stanton, N. *Mastering Communication*, 5th edn, Palgrave Macmillan, 2009.

Thompson, N. *Effective Communication*, 2nd edn, Palgrave Macmillan, 2011.

Trevithick, P. *Social Work Skills and Knowledge: A Practice Handbook*, 3rd edn, Open University Press, 2012.

Leadership

Having a clear sense of direction and helping people move in that direction is what leadership is all about.

Key text

Gilbert, P. *Leadership: Being Effective and Remaining Human*, Russell House Publishing, 2005.

The subtitle captures very well a key aspect of leadership.

Other sources

Gill, R. *Theory and Practice of Leadership*, 2nd edn, Sage, 2011.
Grint, K. *Leadership: Limits and Possibilities*, Palgrave Macmillan, 2005.
Hames, R. D. *The Five Literacies of Global Leadership*, Jossey-Bass, 2007.
Northouse, P. G. *Leadership: Theory and Practice*, 6th edn, Sage, 2012.

Influencing skills

Bringing about constructive change involves being able to influence people in a positive direction.

Key text

Cialdini, R. *Influence: The Science and Practice*, 5th edn, Allyn & Bacon, 2009.

A classic work that offers a good basis of understanding.

Other sources

Borg, J. *Persuasion: The Art of Influencing People*, 4th edn, Prentice Hall, 2013.
Dalley, D. and Burton, L. *Developing Your Influencing Skills: How to Influence People by Increasing Your Credibility, Trustworthiness and Communication Skills*, Universe of Learning, 2010.
Huczynski, A. *Influencing within Organizations*, 2nd edn, Routledge, 2004.
Pink, D. H. *To Sell is Human: The Surprising Truth about Persuading, Convincing, and Influencing   Others*, Canongate Books, 2014.

Handling feelings

Effective work in the people professions owes much to being able to handle feelings effectively.

Key text

Howe, D. *The Emotional Intelligent Social Worker*, Palgrave Macmillan, 2008.

Although focused specifically on social work, this important book has much to offer anyone engaged in the people professions.

Other sources

Bolton, S. C. *Emotion Management in the Workplace*, Palgrave Macmillan, 2005.

Burkitt, I. *Emotions and Social Relations*, Sage, 2014.

Goleman, D. *Destructive Emotions and How We Can Overcome Them: A Dialogue with the Dalai Lama*, Bloomsbury Publishing, 2004.

Jordan, B. *Social Work and Well-Being*, Russell House Publishing, 2007.

Mervelede, P. E., Bridoux, D. and Vandamme, R. *7 Steps to Emotional Intelligence*, Crown House Publishing, 2001.

Parkinson, B., Fischer, A. H. and Manstead, A. S. R. *Emotion in Social Relations: Cultural, Group and Interpersonal Processes*, Psychology Press, 2005.

Thompson, N. *Grief and its Challenges*, Palgrave Macmillan, 2012.

E-learning

I have developed an e-learning course entitled *Emotional Competence: Developing Emotional Intelligence and Resilience*. See www.avenuemedia solutions.com for details.

Handling conflict

Conflict is often seen as a breakdown of normality, whereas in reality it is part of normality. We learn basic conflict management skills as part of our upbringing, but we can take them to a more advanced level if we learn more about what is involved. Handling conflict well in the early stages can prevent aggression from arising.

Key text

Lewis, C. *Workplace Mediation and Managing Conflict at Work*, RoperPenberthy Publishing, 2009.

This text provides a useful introduction to the significance of conflict.

Other sources

Booker, O. *Averting Aggression*, 2nd edn, Russell House Publishing, 2004.

Clark, J. and Linsley, P. *Violence and Aggression in the Workplace: A Practical Guide for All Healthcare Staff*, Radcliffe Publishing, 2006.

Cloke, K. and Goldsmith, J. *Resolving Conflicts at Work: Ten Strategies for Everyone on the Job*, 3rd edn, John Wiley & Sons, 2011.

Deutsch, M., Coleman, P. T. and Marcus, E. C. (eds) *The Handbook of Conflict Resolution: Theory and Practice*, 3rd edn, John Wiley & Sons, 2014.

Moore, C. W. *The Mediation Process: Practical Strategies for Resolving Conflict*, 4th edn, John Wiley & Sons, 2014.

Murphy, T. and Oberlin, L. H. *Overcoming Passive-Aggression: How to Stop Hidden Anger from Spoiling Your Relationships, Career and Happiness*, Da Capo Press, 2005.

Webster, C. D. and Hucker, S. J. *Violence Risk: Assessment and Management*, 2nd edn, Wiley Blackwell, 2013.

E-learning

I have developed an e-learning course on *Handling Aggression*. Details are available from www.avenueonlinelearning.co.uk.

Multidisciplinary working

It is often necessary for professionals from different disciplines to work together to get the best results.

Key text

Thomas, J., Pollard, K. and Sellman, D. (eds) *Interprofessional Working in Health and Social Care: Professional Perspectives*, 2nd edn, Palgrave Macmillan, 2014.

A fairly comprehensive overview of some important issues.

Other sources

Glasby, J. and Dickinson, H. *Partnership Working in Health and Social Care: What is Integrated Care and How Can We Deliver It?* Policy Press, 2014.

Leathard, A. (ed.) *Interprofessional Collaboration: From Policy to Practice in Health and Social Care*, Brunner-Routledge, 2003.

Murphy, M. *Developing Collaborative Relationships in Interagency Child Protection Work*, 2nd edn, Russell House Publishing, 2005.

Payne, M. *Teamwork in Multiprofessional Care*, Palgrave Macmillan, 2000.

Sullivan, H. and Skelcher, C. *Working across Boundaries: Collaboration in Social Services*, Palgrave Macmillan, 2002.

Weinstein, J., Whittington, C. and Leiba, T. (eds) *Collaboration in Social Work Practice*, Jessica Kingsley, 2003.

Systematic practice

Key text

Thompson, N. *Understanding Social Work: Preparing for Practice*, 4th edn, Palgrave Macmillan, 2015.

Although developed specifically for a social work readership, the section on systematic practice is applicable across the people professions.

Other sources

Compton, B. R., Galaway, B. and Cournoyer, B. R. *Social Work Processes*, 7th edn, Wadsworth, 2004.

Egan, G. *The Skilled Helper*, 10th edn, Cengage Learning, 2013.

Marsh, P. and Doel, M. *The Task Centred Book*, Routledge, 2005.

Thompson, N. *Practising Social Work*, Palgrave Macmillan, 2009.

Thompson, N. and Thompson, S. *The Social Work Companion*, Palgrave Macmillan, 2008.

Assessment

High-quality assessment is essential for good practice as it lays down the foundations for all subsequent work.

Key text

Parker, J. and Bradley, G. *Social Work Practice: Assessment, Planning, Intervention and Review*, 4th edn, Learning Matters, 2014.

A new edition of a well-established text. It focuses specifically on social work but has much to offer to other professions.

Other sources

Compton, B. R., Galaway, B. and Cournoyer, B. R. *Social Work Processes*, 7th edn, Wadsworth, 2004.

Holland, S. *Child and Family Assessment in Social Work Practice*, 2nd edn, Sage, 2010.

Milner, J. and O'Byrne, P. *Assessment in Social Work*, 3rd edn, Palgrave Macmillan, 2009.

Stuart, C. C. *Assessment, Supervision and Support in Clinical Practice: A Guide for Nurses, Midwives and Other Health Professionals*, 2nd edn, Churchill Livingstone, 2006.

Planning

It is important to keep a clear focus in our work, and so planning has a central role to play.

Key text

Parker, J. and Bradley, G. *Social Work Practice: Assessment, Planning, Intervention and Review*, 4th edn, Learning Matters, 2014.

This book is also helpful in relation to planning.

Other sources

Cambridge, P. and Carnaby, S. *Person Centred Planning and Care Management with People with Learning Disabilities*, Jessica Kingsley, 2005.

Hall, A., Wren, M. and Kirby, S. (eds) *Care Planning in Mental Health: Promoting Recovery*, 2nd edn, WileyBlackwell, 2013.

Hunt, S. *The Life Course: A Sociological Introduction*, Palgrave Macmillan, 2005.

Rogoff, B. *The Cultural Nature of Human Development*, Oxford University Press, 2003.

Decision making

Formal and informal decision making are both important elements of people work.

Key text

Adair, J. *Decision Making and Problem Solving Strategies*, 2nd edn, Kogan Page, 2013.

Adair's work is normally a good blend of theory and practice and this book is no exception.

Other sources

Baron, J. *Thinking and Deciding*, 4th edn, Cambridge University Press, 2007.

Bazerman, M. H. and Moore, D. A. *Judgment in Managerial Decision Making*, 8th edn, John Wiley, 2013.

Carson, D. and Bain, A. *Professional Risk and Working with People: Decision-Making in Health, Social Care and Criminal Justice*, Jessica Kingsley, 2008.

Kourdi, J. *Business Strategy: A Guide to Effective Decision-making*, 2nd edn, Economist Books, 2009.

O'Sullivan, T. *Decision Making in Social Work*, 2nd edn, Palgrave Macmillan, 2010.

Tschäppeler, R. and Krogerus, M. *The Decision Book: Fifty Models for Strategic Thinking*, Profile Books, 2011.

Managing risk

It is essential to get the balance right with risk – not being complacent, but not over-reacting and being 'risk averse' either.

Key text

Carson, D. and Bain, A. *Professional Risk and Working with People: Decision-Making in Health, Social Care and Criminal Justice*, Jessica Kingsley, 2008.

A helpful exploration of some key issues relating to risk assessment and risk management.

Other sources

Denney, D. *Risk and Society*, Sage, 2005.

Harding, T. *Rights and Risk: Older People and Human Rights*, Help the Aged, 2005.

Langan, J. and Lindow, V. *Living with Risk: Mental Health Service User Involvement in Risk Assessment and Management*, Policy Press/Joseph Rowntree Foundation, 2004.

Martin, J. *Safeguarding Adults*, Russell House Publishing, 2007.

Webb, S. *Social Work in a Risk Society: Social and Political Perspectives*, Palgrave Macmillan, 2006.

Review and evaluation

Making sure plans are on track, amending them as necessary and drawing out the lessons from the work carried out are all important processes.

Key text

Squirrell, G. *Evaluation in Action: Theory and Practice for Effective Evaluation*, Russell House Publishing, 2012.

This book provides a thorough overview of evaluation and its importance.

Other sources

Dickinson, H. *Evaluating Outcomes in Health and Social Care*, Policy Press, 2008.

Parker, J. and Bradley, G. *Social Work Practice: Assessment, Planning, Intervention and Review*, 4th edn, Learning Matters, 2014.

Shaw, I. F. *Evaluating in Practice*, 2nd edn, Ashgate, 2011.

Thompson, N. and Thompson, S. *The Social Work Companion*, Palgrave Macmillan, 2008.

Thompson, S. and Thompson, N. *The Critically Reflective Practitioner*, Palgrave Macmillan, 2008.

Ending

Bringing our involvement with an individual or group of people is an important element of people skills, but one that is often paid scant attention.

Key text

Thompson, N. and Thompson, S. *The Social Work Companion*, Palgrave Macmillan, 2008.

Another book that focuses specifically on social work but which also offers insights that are relevant to all people workers. It places the ending process in its wider context.

Other sources

Compton, B. R., Galaway, B. and Cournoyer, B. R. *Social Work Processes*, 7th edn, Wadsworth, 2004.
Marsh, P. and Doel, M. *The Task Centred Book*, Routledge, 2005.
Murdin, L. *How Much Is Enough? Endings in Psychotherapy and Counselling*, Routledge, 1999.

Trauma

The effects of one or more traumatic experiences can be profound and far reaching. Working with people and their problems, whether as practitioners or managers, will often bring us into contact with the destructive effects of trauma.

Key text

Thompson, N. *Grief and its Challenges*, Palgrave Macmillan, 2012.

This book explains how trauma can be understood as a form of grief.

Other sources

Bracken, P. *Trauma: Culture, Meaning and Philosophy*, Whurr, 2002.
Brewin, C. R. *Posttraumatic Stress Disorder: Malady or Myth*, Yale University Press, 2007.
Calhoun, L. G. and Tedeschi, R. G. *Facilitating Posttraumatic Growth: A Clinician's Guide*, Routledge, 2014.
Joseph, S. and Linley, P. A. *Trauma, Recovery, and Growth: Positive Psychological Perspectives on Posttraumatic Stress*, John Wiley, 2008.
Rosen, G. M. (ed.) *Posttraumatic Stress Disorder: Issues and Controversies*, John Wiley & Sons, 2004.
Tomlinson, P. *Therapeutic Approaches in Work with Traumatized Children and Young People: Theory and Practice*, Jessica Kingsley, 2004.
Warren, M. P. *From Trauma to Transformation*, Crown House, 2006.

Reflective practice

The notion of 'reflective practice' is widely misunderstood and oversimplified, but remains an essential foundation of good practice.

Key text

Thompson, S. and Thompson, N. *The Critically Reflective Practitioner*, Palgrave Macmillan, 2008.

This book explores both theory and practice relating to reflective practice and explains why practice needs to be *critically* reflective.

Other sources

Jasper, M. *Beginning Reflective Practice*, 2nd edn, Cengage, 2013.

Schön, D. A. *The Reflective Practitioner*, Ashgate, 1983.

Taylor, B. J. *Reflective Practice: A Guide for Nurses and Midwives*, 2nd edn, Open University Press/McGraw-Hill Education, 2006.

Thompson, N. *Theorizing Social Work Practice*, Palgrave Macmillan, 2010.

References

Adair, J. (1985) *Effective Decision Making*, Basingstoke, Macmillan Press – later Palgrave Macmillan.

Adams, R. (1994) *Skilled Work with People*, London, Collins.

Alinsky, S. (1989) *Rules for Radicals*, New York, Vintage Books.

Arroba, T. and James, K. (1992) *Pressure at Work: A Survival Guide for Managers*, 2nd edn, London, McGraw-Hill.

Beardwell, I. and Claydon, T. (2011) *Human Resource Management: A Contemporary Approach*, 6th edn, London, Prentice Hall.

Berne, E. (1968) *Games People Play*, Harmondsworth, Penguin.

Bono, E. de (1983) *Atlas of Management Thinking*, Harmondsworth, Penguin.

Bono, E. de (1986) *Conflicts*, Harmondsworth, Penguin.

Bracken, P. (2002) *Trauma: Culture, Meaning and Philosophy*, London, Whurr.

Breakwell, G. (1989) *Facing Physical Violence*, London, Routledge.

Brearley, P. (1982) *Risk and Social Work*, London, Routledge.

Brewin, C. R. (2003) *Posttraumatic Stress Disorder: Malady or Myth?* New Haven, CT, Yale University Press.

Brown, G. W. and Harris, T. (1978) *The Social Origins of Depression*, London, Tavistock.

Burnard, P. (1992) *Communicate!* London, Edward Arnold.

Calhoun, L. G. and Tedeschi, R. G. (2014) *Facilitating Posttraumatic Growth: A Clinician's Guide*, London, Routledge.

CD Project Steering Group (eds) (1991) *Setting the Context for Change*, London, CCETSW.

Cialdini, R. B. (2009) *Influence: Science and Practice*, 5th edn, Boston, MA, Allyn & Bacon.

Compton, B. R. and Galaway, B. (1989) *Social Work Processes*, 4th edn, Pacific Grove, CA, Brooks/Cole.

Coulshed, V. (1991) *Social Work Practice: An Introduction*, 2nd edn, London, Macmillan Press – later Palgrave Macmillan.

Cranwell-Ward, J. and Abbey, A. (2005) *Organizational Stress*, Basingstoke, Palgrave Macmillan.

DoH (Department of Health) (1991) *Child Abuse: A Study of Inquiry Reports 1980–1989*, London, HMSO.

Egan, G. (1977) *You and Me*, Monterey, CA, Brooks/Cole.

Ehrenreich, B. (2009) *Smile or Die: How Positive Thinking Fooled America and the World*, London, Granta.

Family Rights Group (1991) *The Children Act 1989: Working in Partnership with Families*, London, HMSO.

Field, T. (1996) *Bully in Sight*, Wantage, Success Unlimited.

Fontana, D. (1990) *Social Skills at Work*, London, Routledge.

Giddens, A. (2006) *Sociology*, 5th edn, Cambridge, Polity.

Gilbert, P. (2005) *Leadership: Being Effective and Remaining Human*, Lyme Regis, Russell House Publishing.

Gomm, R. (1993) 'Issues of Power in Health and Welfare', in Walmsley et al. (1993).

Hardman, D. (2009) *Judgment and Decision Making: Psychological Perspectives*, Chichester, John Wiley & Sons.

Hartley, P. (1993) *Interpersonal Communication*, London, Routledge.

Harvey, J. H. (2002) *Perspectives on Loss and Trauma: Assaults on the Self*, London, Sage.

Howe, D. (2008) *The Emotionally Intelligent Social Worker*, Basingstoke, Palgrave Macmillan.

Hunt, S. J. (2005) *The Life Course: A Sociological Approach*, Basingstoke, Palgrave Macmillan.

Isaac, B. (1991) 'Negotiation in Partnership Work', in Family Rights Group (1991).

Isaksen, S. G., Dorval, K. B. and Treffinger, D. J. (2011) *Creative Approaches to Problem Solving: A Framework for Innovation and Change*, 3rd edn, London, Sage.

Ishmael, A. (1999) *Harassment, Bullying and Violence at Work*, London, The Industrial Society.

Jakubowski, P. (1977) 'Self-Assertion Training Procedures for Women', in Rowlings and Carter (1977).

James, O. (2007) *Affluenza*, London, Vermilion.

James, O. (2008) *The Selfish Capitalist: Origins of Affluenza*, London, Vermilion.

Johannsen, H. and Page, G. T. (1990) *International Dictionary of Management*, 4th edn, London, Guild Publishing.

Johnson, D. W. (1993) *Reaching Out*, 5th edn, London, Allyn & Bacon.

Kadushin, A. (1976) *Supervision in Social Work*, New York, Columbia University Press.

Kaufmann, W. (2013) *Nietzsche: Philosopher, Psychologist, Antichrist*, 4th edn, Princeton, NJ, Princeton University Press.

Knapp, M. L. (1978) *Non-Verbal Communication in Human Interaction*, New York, Rinehart & Winston.

Kolb, D. A. (1984) *Experiential Learning*, Englewood Cliffs, NJ, Prentice Hall.

Kourdi, J. (1999) *Decision Making*, London, Orion Business Books.

Lambert, T. (1996) *The Power of Influence: Intensive Influencing Skills at Work*, London, Nicholas Brealey.

Lawler, S. (2008) *Identity: Sociological Perspectives*, Cambridge, Polity Press.

Leighton, P. (2004) *Discrimination and the Law*, London, Chartered Institute of Personnel and Development.

Leiter, M. P., Bakker, A. B. and Maslach, C. (eds) (2014) *Burnout at Work: A Psychological Perspective*, Hove, Psychology Press.

Marsh, P. and Doel, M. (2005) *The Task-Centred Book*, London, Routledge.

More, W. S. (1990) *Aggression and Violence*, 2nd edn, Birmingham, Pepar.

More, W. S. (1997) *The New ABC of Handling Aggression*, Birmingham, Pepar.

Morrison, T. (1990) 'The Emotional Effects of Child Protection Work on the Worker', *Practice*, 4(4).

Morrison, T. (2013) *Staff Supervision in Social Care*, 3rd edn, Brighton, Pavilion.

Moss, B. (2007) *Values*, Lyme Regis, Russell House Publishing.

Moss, B. (2012) *Communication Skills in Health and Social Care*, 2nd edn, London, Sage.

Murphy, T and Oberlin, L. H. (2005) *Overcoming Passive-Aggression: How to Stop Hidden Anger from Spoiling Your Relationships, Career and Happiness*, Cambridge, MA, Da Capo Press.

Neimeyer, R. and Anderson, A. (2002) 'Meaning Reconstruction Theory', in Thompson (2002).

Northouse, P. G. (2010) *Leadership: Theory and Practice*, 5th edn, London, Sage.

Oliver, M. and Barnes, C. (2012) *The New Politics of Disablement*, 2nd edn, Basingstoke, Palgrave Macmillan.

Pickering, M. (2001) *Stereotyping: The Politics of Representation*, Basingstoke, Palgrave Macmillan.

Pink, D. (2011) *Drive: The Surprising Truth about What Motivates Us*, London, Canongate Books.

Pink, D. (2013) *To Sell is Human: The Surprising Truth about Persuading, Convincing, and Influencing Others*, London, Canongate Books.

Pruitt, D. G. and Carnevale, P. J. (1993) *Negotiation in Social Conflict*, Buckingham, Open University Press.

Richards, M. and Payne, C. (1991) *Staff Supervision in Child Protection Work*, London, National Institute for Social Work.

Riches, G. (2002) 'Gender', in Thompson (2002).

Rogers, C. (1961) *On Becoming a Person*, London, Constable.

Rowlings, E. and Carter, D. (eds) (1977) *Psychotherapy for Women*, Springfield, IL, Charles C. Thomas.

Rutter, M. (1975) *Helping Troubled Children*, Harmondsworth, Penguin.

Schiraldi, G. R. (1999) *The Post-Traumatic Stress Disorder Sourcebook: A Guide to Healing, Recovery and Growth*, New York, McGraw-Hill.

Schön, D. A. (1983) *The Reflective Practitioner*, New York, Basic Books.

Schön, D. A. (1987) *Educating the Reflective Practitioner*, San Francisco, CA, Jossey Bass.

Schön, D. A. (1992) 'The Crisis of Professional Knowledge and the Pursuit of an Epistemology of Practice', *Journal of Interprofessional Care*, 6(1).

Segerstrom, S. C. (2006) *Breaking Murphy's Law: How Optimists Get What They Want from Life – and Pessimists Can Too*, New York, Guilford Press.

Seligman, M. E. P. (1975) *Learned Helplessness: A Theory for the Age of Personal Control*, New York, Oxford University Press.

Seligman, M. E. P. (2006) *Learned Optimism: How to Change Your Mind and Your Life*, New York, Vintage Books.

Sivanandan, A. (1991) 'Black Struggles Against Racism', in CD Project Steering Group (1991).

Slovic, P. (1999) 'Trust, Emotion, Sex, Politics and Science: Surveying the Risk-Assessment Battlefield', *Risk Analysis*, 19(4).

Stephens, T. and Hallas, J. (2006) *Bullying and Sexual Harassment*, Oxford, Chandos.

Tannen, D. (1992) *You Just Don't Understand*, London, Virago.

Taylor, B. J. (2006) *Reflective Practice: A Guide for Nurses and Midwives*, 2nd edn, Maidenhead, Open University Press/McGraw-Hill Education.

Thompson, N. (1993) *Group Care with Children and Young People*, Mold, Clwyd County Council.

Thompson, N. (1995) *Age and Dignity*, Aldershot, Ashgate.

Thompson, N. (2000) *Theory and Practice in Human Services*, Buckingham, Open University Press.

Thompson, N. (ed.) (2002) *Loss and Grief: A Guide for Human Services Practitioners*, Basingstoke, Palgrave Macmillan.

Thompson, N. (2006) *Promoting Workplace Learning*, Bristol, Policy Press.

Thompson, N. (2007) *Power and Empowerment*, Lyme Regis, Russell House Publishing.

Thompson, N. (2009a) *Practising Social Work: Meeting the Professional Challenge*, Basingstoke, Palgrave Macmillan.

Thompson, N. (2009b) *Loss, Grief, and Trauma in the Workplace*, Amityville, NY, Baywood.

Thompson, N. (2010) *Theorizing Social Work Practice*, Basingstoke, Palgrave Macmillan.

Thompson, N. (2011a) *Effective Communication*, 2nd edn, Basingstoke, Palgrave Macmillan.

Thompson, N. (2011b) *Crisis Intervention*, 2nd edn, Lyme Regis, Russell House Publishing.

Thompson, N. (2011c) *Promoting Equality: Working with Diversity and Difference*, 3rd edn, Basingstoke, Palgrave Macmillan.

Thompson, N. (2012a) *The People Solutions Sourcebook*, 2nd edn, Basingstoke, Palgrave Macmillan.

Thompson, N. (2012b) *Grief and its Challenges*, Basingstoke, Palgrave Macmillan.

Thompson, N. (2012c) *Anti-Discriminatory Practice*, 5th edn, Basingstoke, Palgrave Macmillan.

Thompson, N. (2013) *People Management*, Basingstoke, Palgrave Macmillan.

Thompson, N. (2015a) *Stress Matters*, an e-book published by Avenue Media Solutions: www.avenuemediasolutions.com.

Thompson, N. (2015b) *Tackling Bullying and Harassment in the Workplace*, an e-book published by Avenue Media Solutions: www.avenuemediasolutions.com.

Thompson, N. and Gilbert, P. (2011) *Supervision Skills: A Learning and Development Manual*, Lyme Regis, Russell House Publishing.

Thompson, N., Murphy, M. and Stradling, S. (1994) *Dealing with Stress*, Basingstoke, Macmillan – later Palgrave Macmillan.

Thompson, N., Osada, M. and Anderson, B. (1994) *Practice Teaching in Social Work*, 2nd edn, Birmingham, Pepar.

Thompson, N., Murphy, M. and Stradling, S. (1996a) *Meeting the Stress Challenge*, Lyme Regis, Russell House Publishing.

Thompson, N., Stradling, S., Murphy, M. and O'Neill, P. (1996b) 'Stress and Organizational Culture', *British Journal of Social Work*, 26(5).

Thompson, S. (2005) *Age Discrimination*, Lyme Regis, Russell House Publishing.

Thompson, S. and Thompson, N. (2008) *The Critically Reflective Practitioner*, Basingstoke, Palgrave Macmillan.

Townend, A. (1991) *Developing Assertiveness*, London, Routledge.

Walmsley, J., Reynolds, J., Shakespeare, P. and Woolfe, R. (eds) (1993) *Health, Welfare and Practice: Reflecting on Roles and Relationships*, London, Sage.

Webb, S. A (2006) *Social Work in a Risk Society: Social and Political Perspectives*, Basingstoke, Palgrave Macmillan.

Woolfe, S. and Malahleka, B. (1990) 'The Obstacle Race: The Findings of the BASW Report on an Action Research Project into Ethnically Sensitive Social Work', Birmingham, BASW.

Index